1998 SUPP

HART AND WECHSLER'S

THE FEDERAL COURTS

AND

THE FEDERAL SYSTEM

FOURTH EDITION

by

RICHARD H. FALLON, JR.
Professor of Law
Harvard Law School

DANIEL J. MELTZER
Story Professor of Law
Harvard Law School

DAVID L. SHAPIRO
William Nelson Cromwell Professor of Law,
Harvard Law School

NEW YORK, NEW YORK
FOUNDATION PRESS

1998

TEXT IS PRINTED ON 10% POST
CONSUMER RECYCLED PAPER

PREFACE

This 1998 Supplement updates the Fourth Edition, which was published in April, 1996. We have sought to provide complete coverage of recent developments that we believe will be of interest to students and teachers. But since most users find if awkward and distracting to refer back and forth repeatedly between the casebook and its supplement, we have tried to avoid excessive detail.

All of the important federal jurisdiction decisions from the 1996 and 1997 Supreme Court Terms are discussed in the Supplement, including:

- City of Chicago v. International College of Surgeons, the first Supreme Court decision interpreting the supplemental jurisdiction statute, 28 U.S.C. § 1367.

- Several significant standing decisions, including FEC v. Akins and National Credit Union Administration v. First National Bank & Trust Co.

- Wisconsin Dep't of Corrections v. Schacht, in which the Court dealt with the question of the removability of a case that included some claims subject to an Eleventh Amendment defense, and also raised important questions concerning the possible waiver of that defense.

- Several important decisions interpreting the scope of substantive and procedural protections afforded to public officials in actions under 42 U.S.C. § 1983, including Kalina v. Fletcher, Bogan v. Scott-Harris, and Crawford-El v. Britton.

- Steel Co. v. Citizens for a Better Environment, in which the Court rejected the doctrine of "hypothetical jurisdiction."

- Bousley v. United States, dealing with the availability of collateral relief when a guilty plea was based on a misunderstanding of the elements of the criminal offense.

The 1998 Supplement also surveys significant lower court decisions and secondary literature, and incorporates, and updates, materials included in the 1997 Supplement, covering such important matters as:

- Supreme Court and lower court decisions interpreting the key provisions of the 1996 amendments to the federal habeas corpus jurisdiction.

- The implications of the Supreme Court's decision in Seminole Tribe v. Florida, sharply limiting Congress' power to abrogate state immunity from suit in federal courts.

We are grateful to Scott Angstreich, Grant Dixton, Marc Isserles, and Joe Liu for their very able research assistance.

R.H.F.
D.J.M.
D.L.S.

July 1998

TABLE OF CONTENTS

PREFACE--- iii

TABLE OF CASES --- ix

CHAPTER I   The Development and Structure of the Federal Judicial System --- 1

CHAPTER II   The Nature of the Federal Judicial Function: Cases and Controversies ------------------------------------- 4

Sec.
1. General Considerations--- 4
2. Issues of Parties, the Requirement of Finality, and the Prohibition Against Feigned and Collusive Suits -------------------------------- 7
3. Some Problems of Standing to Sue --------------------------------------- 10
    A: Plaintiffs' Standing--- 10
    B: Defendants' Standing--- 18
4. Mootness --- 20
5. Ripeness -- 21
6. Political Questions --- 22

CHAPTER III   The Original Jurisdiction of the Supreme Court-- 23

CHAPTER IV   Congressional Control of the Distribution of Judicial Power Among Federal and State Courts ----------- 24

Sec.
1. Congressional Regulation of Federal Jurisdiction --------------------- 24
2. Authority to Allocate Judicial Power to Non–Article III Federal Tribunals--- 28
3. Federal Authority and State Court Jurisdiction----------------------- 29

CHAPTER V   Review of State Court Decisions by the Supreme Court --- 32

Sec.
1. The Establishment of the Jurisdiction --------------------------------- 32
2. The Relation Between State and Federal Law --------------------------- 32
    A: Substantive Law-- 32
    C: Application of Law to Fact -------------------------------------- 33
3. Final Judgments and the Highest State Court ------------------------- 34

CHAPTER VI   The Law Applied in Civil Actions in the District Courts --- 36

Sec.
1. Procedure 36
2. The Powers of the Federal Courts in Defining Primary Legal Obligations That Fall Within the Legislative Competence of the States 38
3. Enforcing State–Created Obligations—Equitable Remedies and Procedure 38
4. The Effect of State Law (and of Private Agreement) On the Exercise of Federal Jurisdiction 41

CHAPTER VII Federal Common Law 43

Sec.
1. Defining Primary Obligations 43
2. Enforcing Primary Obligations 47
   A: Civil Actions by the Federal Government 47
   B: Private Civil Actions 48
   C: Remedies for Constitutional Violations 50

CHAPTER VIII The Federal Question Jurisdiction of the District Courts 52

Sec.
1. Introduction 52
2. The Scope of the Constitutional Grant of Federal Question Jurisdiction 52
3. The Scope of the Statutory Grant of Federal Question Jurisdiction 53
4. Federal Question Removal 54
5. Supplemental (Pendent) Jurisdiction 54
6. Related Heads of Jurisdiction 56

CHAPTER IX Suits Challenging Official Action 57

Sec.
1. Suits Challenging Federal Official Action 57
   B: The Sovereign Immunity of the United States and Associated Remedial Problems 57
2. Suits Challenging State Official Action 59
   A: The Eleventh Amendment and State Sovereign Immunity 59
     Seminole Tribe of Florida v. Florida 62
   C: Federal Statutory Protection Against State Official Action: Herein of 42 U.S.C. § 1983 98
3. Official Immunity 101

CHAPTER X Judicial Federalism: Limitations on District Court Jurisdiction or Its Exercise 105

Sec.
1. Statutory Limitations on Federal Court Jurisdiction 105
   B: Other Statutory Restrictions on Federal Court Jurisdiction 105
2. Doctrines of Equity, Comity, and Federalism 106
   A: Exhaustion of State Nonjudicial Remedies 106

Sec.
2. Doctrines of Equity, Comity, and Federalism—Continued
   B: Abstention: Pullman and Related Doctrines 106
   D: Parallel Proceedings... 111
   E: Matters of Domestic Relations and Probate 113

C H A P T E R XI Federal Habeas Corpus 114

Sec.
1. Introduction.. 114
2. Collateral Attack on State Judgments of Conviction....................... 115
3. Collateral Attack on Federal Judgments of Conviction 135

C H A P T E R XII Advanced Problems in Judicial Federalism 138

Sec.
1. Problems of Res Judicata 138
2. Other Aspects of Concurrent or Successive Jurisdiction................... 140

C H A P T E R XIII The Diversity Jurisdiction of the Federal District Courts 144

Sec.
1. Introduction.. 144
2. Elements of Diversity Jurisdiction.. 144
3. Jurisdictional Amount 144
4. Supplemental (Ancillary) Jurisdiction 145

C H A P T E R XIV Additional Problems of District Court Jurisdiction 147

Sec.
1. Challenges to Hurisdiction 147
2. Process and Venue in Original Actions..................................... 148
3. Removal Jurisdiction and Procedure.. 149

C H A P T E R XV Appellate Review of Federal Decisions and the Certiorari Policy 150

Sec.
2. Jurisdiction of the Courts of Appeals 150
3. Review of Federal Decisions by the Supreme Court.......................... 152
4. The Certiorari Policy.. 153

*

TABLE OF CASES

Principal cases are in bold type. Non-principal cases
are in roman type. References are to Pages.

Aaron v. State of Kan., 91
Aetna Cas. & Sur. Co. v. Ind–Com Elec. Co., 112
Alaska, United States v., 138
Allen v. R & H Oil & Gas Co., 145
Allen v. State Bd. of Elections, 49
Amchem Products, Inc. v. Windsor, 9, 12
Arizonans for Official English v. Arizona, 20, 108, 109
Arkansas v. Farm Credit Services of Cent. Arkansas, 105
Atascadero State Hosp. v. Scanlon, 89
Atherton v. F.D.I.C., 43
Auguste v. Attorney General, 27

Barefoot v. Estelle, 120
Behrens v. Pelletier, 30, 150
Benjamin v. Jacobson, 8
Bennett v. Spear, 10, 15
Blessing v. Freestone, 100
Board of County Com'rs of Bryan County, Okl. v. Brown, 99
Boerne, City of v. Flores, 91
Bogan v. Scott–Harris, 101
Boggs v. Boggs, 44, 45
Borough of (see name of borough)
Bounds v. Smith, 118
Bousley v. United States, 125, 130, 135, 137
Bowers v. Hardwick, 20
Bowersox v. Williams, 121
Boyle v. United Technologies Corp., 103
Bracy v. Gramley, 118
Breard v. Greene, 128
Brockett v. Spokane Arcades, Inc., 109
Burford v. Sun Oil Co., 107

Cagle v. Qualified Electors of Winston County, 22
Calderon v. Ashmus, 6, 122, 143
California v. Deep Sea Research, 60
Campbell v. Lousiana, 17
Caterpillar Inc. v. Lewis, 149
Charan v. Schiltgen, 28
Chavez v. Arte Publico Press, 91
Chicago, City of v. International College of Surgeons, 41, 54, 55, 111, 145
Chicago & N.W.R. Co. v. Whitton, 96
City of (see name of city)
Clark v. Barnard, 95, 98
Clark v. State of Cal., 91
Clinton v. Jones, 29, 102
Clinton v. New York, 12

Coleman v. Miller, 16
College Sav. Bank v. Florida Prepaid Postsecondary Educ. Expense Bd., 91
Connecticut Bd. of Pardons v. Dumschat, 33
Coolbaugh v. State of La. on Behalf of Louisiana Dept. of Public Safety & Corr. on Behalf of Louisiana Dept. of Motor Vehicles, 91
Cooper v. Aaron, 5
County of (see name of county)
Craig v. Boren, 18
Crawford–El v. Britton, 103
Creative Goldsmiths of Washington, D.C., Inc., In re, 91

De Buono v. NYSA–ILA Medical and Clinical Services Fund, 105
Dellmuth v. Muth, 89
Delo v. Blair, 121
Department of Interior v. South Dakota, 155
Diaz–Gandia v. Dapena–Thompson, 90
Doctor's Associates, Inc. v. Casarotto, 38
Dooley v. Korean Air Lines Co., Ltd., 45
Dorsainvil, In re, 137
Dougan v. Singletary, 8
Drinkard v. Johnson, 126

Eastern Enterprises v. Apfel, 59
Eastus v. Blue Bell Creameries, L.P., 149
Edelman v. Jordan, 95, 96, 98, 99
Edwards v. Balisok, 142
Employees of Dept. of Public Health and Welfare, Missouri v. Department of Public Health and Welfare, Missouri, 96
Estate of (see name of party)
Evitts v. Lucey, 33
Ex parte (see name of party)

Fair Assessment in Real Estate Ass'n, Inc. v. McNary, 107
Federal Election Com'n v. Akins, 11, 14
Felker v. Turpin, 25, 28, 114, 123, 133
Fernandez, Matter of Estate of, 90
Fernandez v. I.N.S., 27
Fitzpatrick v. Bitzer, 87
Florida Dept. of State v. Treasure Salvors, Inc., 60
Ford Motor Co., In re, 151
44 Liquormart, Inc. v. Rhode Island, 88

Garcia v. United States, 53
Garry v. Geils, 141
Gasperini v. Center for Humanities, Inc., 39, 41
Gavin v. Branstad, 8
Gebser v. Lago Vista Independent School Dist., 49
General Oil Co. v. Crain, 51
Goncalves v. Reno, 28
Gordon v. Willis, 120
Goshtasby v. Board of Trustees of the University of Illinois, 91
Government Employees Ins. Co. v. Dizol, 111
Gray v. Netherland, 125
Greene v. Georgia, 34
Gregory v. Ashcroft, 89, 94

Hadix v. Johnson, 8
Hans v. Louisiana, 97
Hansberry v. Lee, 140
Harlow v. Fitzgerald, 103
Heck v. Humphrey, 111, 141, 142
Henderson v. United States, 37, 59
Hilton v. South Carolina Public Railways Com'n, 97
Hohn v. United States, 152
Holman v. Page, 125
Hope v. United States, 137
Hottle v. Beech Aircraft Corp., 41
Hutto v. Finney, 89
Huynh v. King, 125

Idaho v. Coeur d'Alene Tribe of Idaho, 51, 57, 58, 60, 62, 94
Initiative Petition No. 348, State Question No. 640, In re, 22
Inmates of Suffolk County Jail v. Rouse, 8
In re (see name of party)

Janklow v. Planned Parenthood, Sioux Falls Clinic, 19
Jefferson v. City of Tarrant, Ala., 34
Johnson v. Avery, 117
Johnson v. Fankell, 30, 34, 48, 150
Johnson v. Jones, 150
Jones v. Johnson, 29

Kalina v. Fletcher, 101
Kamilewicz v. Bank of Boston Corp., 141
Keeney v. Tamayo–Reyes, 130
Kimel v. Florida Bd. of Regents, 91
Kiowa Tribe of Oklahoma v. Manufacturing Technologies, Inc., 57
Klaxon Co. v. Stentor Electric Mfg. Co., 44
Kolster v. I.N.S., 27

Lambrix v. Singletary, 125, 132
Lane v. Pena, 59
Lanier, United States v., 103
Leavitt v. Jane L., 18, 154

Lee, United States v., 61, 62
Legal Aid Society of Hawaii v. Legal Services, Corp., 5
Lewis v. Casey, 10, 13, 118
Lexecon Inc. v. Milberg Weiss Bershad Hynes & Lerach, 148
Lindh v. Murphy, 114
Lobue v. Christopher, 7
Lo Duca v. United States, 7
Lonchar v. Thomas, 120, 143
Lopez, United States v., 94
Louisiana Power & Light Co. v. City of Thibodaux, 107

Mackall v. Angelone, 129
Marbury v. Madison, 32
Marrese v. American Academy of Orthopaedic Surgeons, 139
Matsushita Elec. Indus. Co., Ltd. v. Epstein, 139
Matter of (see name of party)
Mazurek v. Armstrong, 155
Mbiya v. I.N.S., 27
McCleskey v. Zant, 132
McFarland v. Scott, 118, 121
McMillian v. Monroe County, Ala., 99
Mellon Bank (East) PSFS, N.A. v. DiVeronica Bros., Inc., 148
Miller v. Albright, 17
Milliken v. Bradley, 62, 93
Mitchell v. Forsyth, 150
Mobile, In re City of, 55
Mobil Oil Corp. v. Higginbotham, 45
Mojica v. Reno, 27, 28
Monroe v. Pape, 104
Moragne v. States Marine Lines, Inc., 48
Morse v. Republican Party of Virginia, 48
Moses H. Cone Memorial Hosp. v. Mercury Const. Corp., 108
Murphy v. F.D.I.C., 43
Murray v. Giarratano, 118

National Credit Union Admin. v. First Nat. Bank & Trust Co., 15
National Endowment for the Arts v. Finley, 20
Nevada v. Hall, 91
New Hampshire, State of v. State of Louisiana, 96
Newman–Green, Inc. v. Alfonzo–Larrain, 149
Newsweek, Inc. v. Florida Dept. of Revenue, 51
New York v. United States, 29, 94
Nixon v. Fitzgerald, 153
N. L. R. B. v. Nash–Finch Co., 106

O'Brien v. Dubois, 126, 127
O'Dell v. Netherland, 125
Ohio Adult Parole Authority v. Woodard, 33
Ohio Forestry Ass'n, Inc. v. Sierra Club, 21
O'Melveny & Myers v. F.D.I.C., 43
Ormet Corp. v. Ohio Power Co., 53
Ornelas v. United States, 33
Osborn v. Bank of United States, 59

Ozoanya v. Reno, 28

Parden v. Terminal Ry. of Alabama State Docks Dept., 96
Patsy v. Board of Regents of State of Fla., 95
Pembaur v. City of Cincinnati, 99
Pennsylvania v. Finley, 117, 118
Pennsylvania v. Labron, 32
Pennsylvania v. Union Gas Co., 89
Pennsylvania Dept. of Corrections v. Yeskey, 30
Perez v. Marshall, 126
Petty v. Tennessee–Missouri Bridge Commission, 95
Phillips Petroleum Co. v. Shutts, 140
Pierpoint v. Barnes, 152
Plyler v. Moore, 8, 25
Polido v. State Farm Mut. Auto. Ins. Co., 112
Port Authority Trans–Hudson Corp. v. Feeney, 97
Printz v. United States, 29
Procunier v. Navarette, 102
Pulliam v. Allen, 99

Quackenbush v. Allstate Ins. Co., 106, 110, 112, 113, 151
Quern v. Jordan, 89

Raddatz, United States v., 119
Raines v. Byrd, 14, 16
Reagan v. Farmers' Loan & Trust Co., 95
Regents of the University of California v. Doe, 62
Reich v. Collins, 51
Reno v. American Civil Liberties Union, 19
Richardson v. McKnight, 102
Richardson, United States v., 11
Riley, United States ex rel. v. St. Luke's Episcopal Hosp., 56
Rivet v. Regions Bank of Louisiana, 54
Robinson v. Ariyoshi, 141
Romer v. Evans, 19
Rufo v. Inmates of Suffolk County Jail, 8

Saadeh v. Farouki, 144
Sacramento, County of v. Lewis, 101, 104
Safarian v. Reno, 28
Salerno, United States v., 19
Schlup v. Delo, 125
Seminole Tribe of Florida v. Florida, 7, 8, 50, 60, 62
Shaw v. Hunt, 15
Siebold, Ex parte, 127
Smith v. Reeves, 95
South Dakota v. Dole, 97
Spencer v. Kemna, 21, 111, 142

Spokane Tribe of Indians, United States v., 90
State of (see name of state)
Steel Co. v. Citizens for a Better Environment, 5, 12, 13, 147
Stewart v. Martinez–Villareal, 134
St. Luke's Episcopal Hosp., United States ex rel. Riley v., 56
Stromberg Metal Works, Inc. v. Press Mechanical, Inc., 145
Stutson v. United States, 130, 135
Suitum v. Tahoe Regional Planning Agency, 21

Taylor v. United States, 8
Teague v. Lane, 104, 136
Texas v. Hopwood, 154
Texas v. United States, 21
Textron Lycoming Reciprocating Engine Div., Avco Corp. v. UAW, 53
Thomas v. American Home Products, Inc., 155
Tiedeman v. Benson, 120
Trest v. Cain, 131
Triestman v. United States, 137

United Food and Commercial Workers Union Local 751 v. Brown Group, Inc., 17
United States v. ____(see opposing party)
United States ex rel. v. ____(see opposing party and relator)

Vasquez v. Hillery, 117

Wallis v. Pan Am. Petroleum Corp., 43
Washington v. Glucksberg, 20
Welch v. Texas Dept. of Highways and Public Transp., 96
West Mifflin, Borough of v. Lancaster, 55
Williams v. I.N.S., 27
Wisconsin Dept. of Corrections v. Schacht, 92, 95, 98, 149
Wooley v. Maynard, 141
Wyatt v. Cole, 102

Yamaha Motor Corp., U.S.A. v. Calhoun, 45, 151
Yang v. I.N.S., 28
Yerger, Ex parte, 133
Young, Ex parte, 57, 60, 62, 93, 95, 100
Young v. F.D.I.C., 43

Zicherman v. Korean Air Lines Co., Ltd., 45

*

1998 SUPPLEMENT

THE FEDERAL COURTS
AND
THE FEDERAL SYSTEM

*

CHAPTER I

THE DEVELOPMENT AND STRUCTURE OF THE FEDERAL JUDICIAL SYSTEM

Page 1. Add to footnote 1:

A recent, important addition to the literature is Rakove, Original Meanings: Politics and Ideas in the Making of the Constitution (1996).

Page 11. Add to footnote 62:

Did the limitation of judicial authority to cases of a judiciary nature clearly preclude advisory opinions? For a negative answer, based on historical practice of both English and colonial courts as well as evidence from the Constitutional Convention, see Jay, Most Humble Servants: The Advisory Role of Early Judges 10–76 (1997).

Page 40. Add to footnote 87:

For discussion of both the long-and short-run significance of President Roosevelt's Court-packing efforts, see Leuchtenburg, The Supreme Court Reborn: The Constitutional Revolution in the Age of Roosevelt (1995); see also Cushman, *Rethinking the New Deal Court,* 80 Va.L.Rev. 201 (1994); Moglen, *Toward a New Deal Legal History,* 80 Va.L.Rev. 263 (1994); Purcell, *Rethinking Constitutional Change,* 80 Va.L.Rev. 277 (1994).

Page 41. Add to the first full paragraph:

The jurisdictional amount in diversity cases was further increased, to $75,000, by the Federal Courts Improvement Act of 1996, 110 Stat. 3847.

Page 47. Add after the second full paragraph a new footnote 131a:

131a. Provision for appeal of a magistrate judge's decision to the district court was eliminated by the Federal Courts Improvement Act of 1996, 110 Stat. 3847. Aggrieved parties now may appeal only to the court of appeals. 28 U.S.C. § 636(c)(3).

Page 54. Add to footnote 161:

For the argument that mechanisms permitting decisions without full briefing and argument inevitably yield significant inequalities in the quality of justice dispensed by the courts of appeals, see Richman & Reynolds, *Elitism, Expediency, and the New Certiorari: Requiem for the Learned Hand Tradition,* 81 Corn.L.Rev. 273 (1996). (As a solution to the problem, the authors recommend increasing the size of the federal judiciary. For discussion of the wisdom of this course, see Fourth Edition pp. 65–66.)

Page 60. Add to footnote 198:

The District of Columbia Circuit received its commissioned study of "the ways in which race and ethnicity make a difference in the work of the courts" in 1995. Special Committee on Race and Ethnicity, *Report on Race and Ethnicity,* 64 Geo.Wash.L.Rev. 189, 195 (1996). Among other topics, the report examined the circuit's employment practices and personnel

relationships, the impact of race and ethnicity within the courtroom, and the effect of race and ethnicity in the criminal justice system outside the courts. With respect to virtually all of the issues studied, the Special Committee concluded, significant numbers of minority group members tended to perceive race-based disparities that worked to the disadvantage of minorities, whereas most whites either saw no disparity or thought that racial minorities were advantaged. For example, in bench trials before a predominantly white judiciary, "whites overwhelmingly believe that attorneys are treated the same, while a significant number of minority attorneys believe that minority attorneys are at a disadvantage" (p. 275). By contrast, "[a] significant number of white lawyers believe African American lawyers have an advantage in jury trials [because most District of Columbia jurors are black], an opinion not shared by African American lawyers" (*id.*). The study offered seventeen recommendations "to enhance both the perception and reality of the fairness and effectiveness of the courts" (p. 328).

Even prior to its publication, the Special Committee's report engendered controversy. At least three of the ten judges then serving on the D.C. Circuit expressed sharply critical reactions in internal memoranda before the final report was published. See Torry, *Study of Bias in Courts Splits Judges,* Washington Post, Feb. 28, 1994, at A1. Upon the study's publication, seven of the then eleven circuit judges issued a "Statement of Disassociation". See Peterson, *Studying the Impact of Race and Ethnicity in the Federal Courts,* 64 George Wash.L.Rev. 173, 175 (1996). Among the judges' stated grounds for objection were that the study relied on perception instead of reality, ranged impermissibly into an examination of the practices of executive agencies, and fostered dangerous misperceptions concerning the role of law clerks and the bases on which law clerks should be hired. See *Showdown over Bias Task Force,* Legal Times, Apr. 10, 1995, at 12.

The Report of the Third Circuit Task Force on Equal Treatment in the Courts, 42 Vill.L.Rev. 1355 (1997), also found significant "differences in perception between whites, minorities, men and women" concerning the presence or absence of preference, bias, and differential treatment in the judicial system. Nonetheless, the Report concluded that "the overall record of the courts and administrative units of the Third Circuit is a positive one" (p. 1381).

Page 62.   Add to the second paragraph of footnote 205:

A summary of a second portion of the Federal Judicial Center's 1990 study is presented by Hellman, *By Precedent Unbound: The Nature and Extent of Unresolved Intercircuit Conflicts,* 56 U.Pitt.L.Rev. 693 (1995). Hellman concludes that "unresolved intercircuit conflicts do not constitute a problem of serious magnitude" (p. 797). Although the Supreme Court may have declined review in 200 or more cases presenting intercircuit conflicts during the 1989 Term (pp. 720–24), most of the conflicts were "tolerable." "Of 142 unresolved conflicts [that were identified] in the Court's 1984 and 1985 Terms, there remain fewer than 40 that (a) have not been put to rest, (b) have continued to generate litigation, and (c) have controlled outcomes in one or more reported cases" (p. 797 n. 408).

Page 63.   Add a new footnote 208a at the end of the second sentence of the third full paragraph:

208a. The Long Range Plan for the Federal Courts, as approved by the Judicial Conference of the United States, appears at 166 F.R.D. 49 (1996).

Page 65.   Add a new footnote 214a at the end of the first (carryover) paragraph:

214a. Many of the issues involving the structure and administration of the federal appellate system have arisen in a continuing controversy over proposals (some introduced in Congress) to split the Ninth Circuit Court of Appeals into two smaller circuits. See *Symposium: The Proposal to Split the Ninth Circuit Court of Appeals,* 57 Mont.L.Rev. 241 (1996). The Ninth Circuit is the largest of the circuits, with 28 authorized circuit judgeships, compared with 17 in the next largest circuit (the Sixth). Proponents of division argue that the Ninth Circuit's size diminishes judicial collegiality and thereby spawns delay in disposing of argued cases. An additional concern is that the circuit's en banc procedure, which involves an eleven-judge panel consisting of the chief judge and ten randomly selected judges, allows as few as six judges to determine the outcome of closely contested cases. Opponents have responded, *inter alia*, that division would not necessarily improve judicial efficiency and would only defer fundamental questions about whether the current circuit system can cope with an expanding case load. See Baker, *An Assessment of Past Extramural Reforms of the U.S. Courts of Appeals*, 28 Ga.L.Rev. 863 (1994); Tobias, *The Impoverished Idea of Circuit–Splitting*, 44 Emory L.J. 1357 (1995).

At the end of 1997, Congress established a Commission on Structural Alternatives for the Federal Courts of Appeals, charged to "study the present division of the United States into the several judicial circuits; study the structure and alignment of the Federal Courts of Appeals system, with particular reference to the Ninth Circuit; and * * * report to the President and the Congress its recommendations for such changes in circuit boundaries or structure as may be appropriate * * * ". Pub.L. 105–119, § 305(a), 111 Stat. 2440, 2491. The Commission, composed of five members appointed by the Chief Justice of the United States, is to report its recommendations within a year. *Id.*

CHAPTER II

THE NATURE OF THE FEDERAL JUDICIAL FUNCTION: CASES AND CONTROVERSIES

SECTION 1. GENERAL CONSIDERATIONS

Page 77. Add to footnote 7:

See also Harrison, *The Constitutional Origins and Implications of Judicial Review*, 84 Va.L.Rev. 333 (1998) (attempting to "provide a clear and persuasive derivation of *Marbury*'s conclusion from the constitutional text").

Page 81. Add at the end of the first paragraph of footnote 5:

Cf. Bone, *Lon Fuller's Theory of Adjudication and the False Dichotomy Between Dispute Resolution and Public Law Models of Litigation*, 75 B.U.L.Rev. 1273 (1995)(arguing that, contrary to common understanding, Fuller's theory did not categorically reject judicial resolution of polycentric disputes or institutional reform suits, and commending Fuller's nuanced approach).

Page 81. Add to footnote 5:

For the argument that federal courts lack constitutional authority to impose equitable remedies on state institutions and that, following judicial declaration of a constitutional violation, remedial responsibility should frequently fall upon Congress and the President, see Yoo, *Who Measures the Chancellor's Foot? The Inherent Remedial Authority of the Federal Courts*, 84 Cal.L.Rev. 1121 (1996).

Consider also the significance of recent steps taken by Congress to restrict or discourage certain forms of institutional reform litigation. One example, the Illegal Immigration Reform and Immigrant Responsibility Act of 1996, 110 Stat. 3009, eliminated certain kinds of class-action suits against the Immigration and Naturalization Service. Another, the Prison Litigation Reform Act of 1995 (PLRA), 110 Stat. 1321 (1996), provides that consent decrees in civil actions challenging prison conditions terminate after two years upon motion of the defendant. 18 U.S.C. § 3626(b)(1). The PLRA also dramatically eases the substantive standard under which defendants may seek termination of consent decrees, *id.* § 3626(b)(2), and specifies that attorneys' fees will not be awarded for cases that settle. 42 U.S.C. § 1997e(d). (For discussion of constitutional challenges to the PLRA, see p. 8, *infra.*) As a final example, Congress in 1996 restricted the activities that agencies receiving funding from the Legal Services Corporation (LSC) can conduct. Under 110 Stat. 1321 (1996), any person or entity receiving any funding from the LSC is forbidden, *inter alia*, to bring class action lawsuits, to participate in any suit seeking "to reform a Federal or State welfare system", and to engage in litigation challenging electoral districting. See *id.* § 504. According to Greenhouse, *How Congress Curtailed the Courts' Jurisdiction*, N.Y. Times, Oct. 27, 1996, at E5, these curbs were "the culmination of years of Congressional hostility toward the Legal Services Corporation, fueled by the view that it had become, through creative litigation, an illegitimate agent of social change instead of a dispenser of retail advice to poor people with legal problems". (At least one lower court has held that Congress overstepped constitutional bounds by forbidding agencies that receive LSC funds to use independent funds to pursue restricted activities. See Varshavsky v. Geller, No. 40767/91, slip. op. at 14–16 (N.Y.Sup.Ct. Dec. 24, 1996), reprinted in N.Y.L.J., Dec. 30, 1996, at 22; see also Note, 110 Harv.L.Rev. 1346 (1997); *but see* Legal Aid Society of Hawaii v. Legal Services Corp., ___ F.3d ___ (9th Cir.1998)(rejecting facial challenge to restrictions on agencies that receive LSC funds).)

Page 84.   Add to footnote 8:

Once it is recognized that judicial decisions can establish what are experienced as new rights and obligations, questions also arise about the permissibility of retroactive lawmaking by courts, especially in criminal cases. For illuminating discussions, see Krent, *Should Bouie Be Buoyed?: Judicial Retroactive Lawmaking and the Ex Post Facto Clause*, 3 Roger Williams U.L.Rev. 35 (1997)(discussing similarities and dissimilarities between retroactive lawmaking by courts and by legislatures); Kahan, *Some Realism About Retroactive Criminal Lawmaking*, 3 Roger Williams U.L.Rev. 95 (1997)(arguing that the judicial branch is the branch most likely to use retroactive lawmaking power wisely).

Page 91.   Add a footnote 11a at the end of subparagraph (d):

11a.   For an unqualified defense of Cooper v. Aaron, see Alexander & Schauer, *On Extrajudicial Constitutional Interpretation*, 110 Harv.L.Rev. 1359 (1997). The authors argue that a general aspiration of constitutionalism is to provide authoritative settlement of contested issues, and that "[i]f we can expect * * * lower court judges to subjugate their best professional judgment about constitutional interpretation to the judgments of those who happen to sit above them, then expecting the same of nonjudicial officials is an affront neither to morality nor to constitutionalism" (p. 1387). But see Devins & Fisher, *Judicial Exclusivity and Political Instability*, 84 Va.L.Rev. 83 (1998)(disputing the thesis of Alexander & Schauer by arguing that both political realities and constitutional values require a sharing of interpretive authority).

Page 92.   Add to footnote 1:

It remains unknown whether the questions were actually delivered to the Justices along with Jefferson's letter. See Jay, Most Humble Servants: The Advisory Role of Early Judges 136–37 (1997). In any case, the Justices were almost surely aware of the questions' general content. *Id.*

Page 94.   Add to footnote 2:

See also Jay, Most Humble Servants: The Advisory Role of Early Judges (1997). According to Professor Jay, 18th century English judges possessed a well established power to render advisory opinions (pp. 10–50); neither the constitutional text nor the discussions at the Constitutional Convention reflected any clear prohibition against advisory opinions (pp. 57–76); and Chief Justice Jay himself regularly gave informal legal advice to the Washington Administration (pp. 91–101). Against this background, Professor Jay argues that the explanation of the Correspondence of the Justices lies in a peculiar set of historical considerations, including (i) a sense that answers to some of the questions would shortly emerge in ordinary lawsuits, whereas answers to others might be inefficacious in affecting governmental action; (ii) the belief of the Chief Justice and other leading Federalists that the Executive, not Congress or the courts, should render controlling interpretations of treaties and of international law; and (iii) the desire of the Justices, who wished to be relieved of circuit riding responsibilities, to avoid entanglement in a potentially divisive political controversy (pp. 149–70).

Page 95.   Add to Paragraph (3):

In Steel Co. v. Citizens for a Better Environment, 118 S.Ct. 1003 (1998), also discussed pp. 13, 147 *infra*, Justice Scalia, in an opinion styled as that of "the Court", invoked the specter of an "advisory opinion" in holding that federal courts must resolve questions of subject matter jurisdiction—in this case standing—at the threshold. Under the rubric of "hypothetical jurisdiction", several courts of appeals had found "it proper to proceed immediately to the merits question, despite jurisdictional objections, at least where (1) the merits question is more readily resolved, and (2) the prevailing party on the merits would be the same as the prevailing party were jurisdiction denied" (p. 1012). "Hypothetical jurisdiction produces nothing more than a hypothetical judgment—which comes to the same thing as an advisory opinion", Justice Scalia reasoned (p. 1016). He acknowledged that "some of the * * * cases" cited to support the exercise of hypothetical jurisdiction "must be acknowledged to have diluted the absolute purity of the rule that Article III jurisdiction is always an antecedent question" (*id.*). He was satisfied, however, that those cases were all fairly treated as exceptional or aberrational.

When the decision of a question conclusively resolves a lawsuit, in what sense could a judicial opinion deciding that question count as "advisory"?

For an exploration of the obligations (if any) of Article III courts to avoid unnecessary decision of constitutional issues and to frame their constitutional holdings narrowly, see Kloppenberg, *Measured Constitutional Steps,* 71 Ind.L.J. 297 (1996); Kloppenberg, *Avoiding Constitutional Questions,* 35 B.C.L.Rev. 1003 (1994). Professor Kloppenberg argues that traditional views concerning avoidance and narrow framing rest mostly on policy grounds, rather than reflecting a constitutional mandate, and therefore should be subject to override to protect important constitutional interests.

Page 95.   Add to footnote 6:

See also Jay, *supra,* at 91–101 (asserting that John Jay, while serving as Chief Justice, regularly provided informal legal advice to President Washington and his administration).

Page 98.   Add to Paragraph (5):

In Calderon v. Ashmus, 118 S.Ct. 1694 (1998), a California inmate under sentence of death filed a declaratory judgment suit (as a class action) to establish whether the limitations period for filing a federal habeas corpus petition was one year or 180 days, a question that depended on whether the state had satisfied standards established under the Antiterrorism and Effective Death Penalty Act of 1996, discussed p. 27 *infra.* In a unanimous opinion by Chief Justice Rehnquist, the Court found that the suit presented no case or controversy under Article III. The "underlying" and clearly justiciable "controversy", the Court reasoned, was whether the respondent was entitled to habeas corpus relief (p. 1698). But rather than present the whole controversy for resolution, the plaintiff had attempted to "carve[] out" the issue of the applicable limitations period. And this, the Court found, was impermissible under Article III; for a declaratory judgment action to be justiciable, it must seek a ruling capable of resolving the entire, underlying case, rather than ask a court "merely" to "determine a collateral legal issue governing certain aspects of * * * pending or future suits" (p. 1699).

How tenable is the Court's distinction between declaratory judgment actions that seek resolution of an entire, underlying case and those that merely "carve[] out" certain issues for decision? Consider a suit for a declaratory judgment presenting either or both of the questions (a) whether a valid contract exists and (b) whether a dispute under the contract is subject to arbitration. Would a decision of (a), (b), or the conjunction of (a) and (b) resolve the entire, underlying controversy concerning the precise obligations of the parties and the enforceable penalties (if any) for breach?[a] If not, should the action be nonjusticiable under Article III?

SECTION 2. ISSUES OF PARTIES, THE REQUIREMENT OF FINALITY, AND THE PROHIBITION AGAINST FEIGNED AND COLLUSIVE SUITS

Page 106. Add new Paragraphs (6)(c) and (d):

(c) To effect an extradition under 18 U.S.C. § 3184, the government must file a complaint with "any justice or judge of the United States, or any magistrate", or with any judge of a state court of general jurisdiction, who then conducts a hearing. Upon a finding of probable cause that the accused has committed an extraditable crime, the presiding judge certifies this finding to the Secretary of State, who then determines whether to deliver the accused to the country seeking extradition. Does this procedure give the Secretary an unconstitutional power to revise judicial judgments? Compare Lobue v. Christopher, 893 F.Supp. 65 (D.D.C.1995)(so holding), *vacated on other grounds*, 82 F.3d 1081 (D.C.Cir.1996), with Lo Duca v. United States, 93 F.3d 1100 (2d Cir.1996)(finding that judges participating in extradition proceedings do not exercise Article III judicial power, but instead act in their individual rather than their judicial capacities as extradition officers).

Is it relevant that § 3184, although permitting the Secretary of State to exercise an analogue to clemency in cases found to satisfy the statutory requirements, does not allow the Secretary to "revise" a finding that the statutory requirements of extradition have not been satisfied? See Note, 109 Harv.L.Rev. 2020 (1996), which argues that the core of the non-revision doctrine involves judicial power to define and enforce individual rights in properly justiciable cases. Where no judicially identified right is implicated, the Note concludes, "benign" exercises of executive discretion should be upheld, based on analogies to cases in which the government waives·judgments in its favor and to the President's pardon power (pp. 2021–22).

(d) In a partial parallel to their role in extradition cases, federal courts are drawn into a possibly problematic role in a category of deportation matters by legislation enacted in 1994. Under the statute, courts convicting aliens of crimes that would provide grounds for deportation are also given jurisdiction to enter deportation orders at the time of sentencing, rather than leaving deportability to be determined in a separate administrative proceeding. See 8 U.S.C. § 1228(c). In its current version, the statute gives courts discretion whether to rule on deportability, but it also provides that "[d]enial of a request for a judicial order of removal [i.e., deportability]" does not preclude the Attorney General from initiating administrative removal proceedings. See 8 U.S.C. § 1228(c)(4). If read to authorize authorize administrative removal proceedings following a judicial decision on the merits to deny a request for a removal order,

---

a. For the suggestion that statutorily authorized suits for judicial orders compelling parties to negotiate in good faith and to mediate their disputes fall outside the judicial power under Article III, see Justice Stevens' dissent in Seminole Tribe of Florida v. Florida, 116 S.Ct. 1114 (1996), discussed p. 62, *infra*.

would the statute deprive judicial decisions of the finality required by Article III and, as a result, compel district courts to decline to exercise jurisdiction over requests for deportation orders? See Neuman, *Admissions and Denials: A Dialogic Introduction to the Immigration Law Symposium*, 29 Conn.L.Rev. 1395, 1407–10 (1997)(so arguing).

Page 107.   Add to Paragraph (7):

The Prison Litigation Reform Act of 1995, Pub. L. No. 104–131, 110 Stat. 1321 (1996), provides in part that "in any civil action with respect to prison conditions, a defendant * * * shall be entitled to the immediate termination of any prospective relief if the relief was approved or granted in the absence of a finding by the court that the relief is narrowly drawn, extends no further than necessary to correct the violation of the Federal right, and is the least intrusive means necessary to correct the violation of the Federal right." 18 U.S.C. § 3626(b)(2). Does this provision require courts to reopen final judgments in contravention of *Plaut*?

Until recently, the courts of appeals had unanimously concluded that it does not. See Hadix v. Johnson, 133 F.3d 940, 942–43 (6th Cir.1998); Dougan v. Singletary, 129 F.3d 1424, 1426 (11th Cir.1997); Inmates of Suffolk County Jail v. Rouse, 129 F.3d 649, 656–57 (1st Cir.1997); Benjamin v. Jacobson, 124 F.3d 162, 170–73 (2d Cir.1997); Gavin v. Branstad, 122 F.3d 1081, 1087 (8th Cir.1997); Plyler v. Moore, 100 F.3d 365, 371–72 (4th Cir.1996), cert. denied, 117 S.Ct. 2460 (1997). With some variations, the predominant thread of analysis was that, although consent decrees are final judgments for some purposes, *see* Rufo v. Inmates of the Suffolk County Jail, 112 S.Ct. 748, 764 (1992), they remain open to alteration as equity requires and thus are not final judgments for separation-of-powers purposes. *Cf.* Benjamin v. Jacobson, *supra*, 124 F.3d at 170–73 (holding that, even if a consent decree were a final judgment, the PLRA's termination provision would remain consistent with *Plaut* because it does not terminate underlying consent decrees, but merely precludes future enforcement in the federal courts). The Ninth Circuit, however, recently reached the contrary conclusion that the PLRA mandates the reopening of consent decrees in contravention of *Plaut*. See Taylor v. United States, ___ F.3d ___ (9th Cir.1998)(reasoning that because the PLRA does not purport to alter the underlying constitutional law upon which consent decrees are based, the statutory directive to terminate relief constitutes a forbidden reopening of final judgments).

Page 107.   Add a new Paragraph (8):

(8) *Orders to Negotiate and to Mediate.* The Indian Gaming Regulatory Act, central aspects of which were held unconstitutional under the Eleventh Amendment in Seminole Tribe of Florida v. Florida, 517 U.S. 44 (1996), p. 62, *infra,* included elaborate provisions designed to promote agreements between states and Indian tribes concerning the permissible scope of gambling activities on tribal lands. The statute imposed an obligation on the states to negotiate in good faith and, to enforce this obligation, authorized suits in federal court for a judicial order directing the parties "to conclude * * * a compact within a 60–day period", § 2710(d)(7)(B)(iii). If no compact was agreed to within 60 days, the court was authorized to appoint a mediator. If the state refused to accept the mediator's proposed solution, the mediator was directed to notify the Secretary of the Interior, who would then "prescribe * * * procedures" under which covered gambling activities could be conducted. Dissenting in the Semi-

nole case, Justice Stevens questioned whether "the obviously dispensable involvement of the judiciary in the intermediate stages of a procedure" that may be finally resolved only as the result of a determination by the Secretary of the Interior "is a proper exercise of judicial power" (pp. 99). The majority opinion, although impliedly rejecting this challenge, offered no explicit response.

Justice Stevens is surely correct that a federal court, under the Indian Gaming Regulatory Act, lacked authority to decide the terms on which gambling should be permitted on tribal lands. On the other hand, the court *was* authorized to provide a conclusive determination of the question whether the parties, as required by the statute, had negotiated in good faith; and, as a remedy for breach of that obligation, it was empowered to appoint a mediator with at least some independent authority. Compare the practice contemplated by this statutory scheme with the long-accepted notion under the National Labor Relations Act that an employer or union may be ordered by a court to bargain in good faith but ordinarily may not be required to enter into an agreement. Should the exercise of such a conjunction of issue-determining and remedial powers be impermissible under Article III?

Page 114.   Add a footnote 1a at the end of Paragraph (4):

1a.   Congress amended 31 U.S.C. § 1304 in 1996, to provide that payment of judgments against the United States should be made by the Secretary of the Treasury, rather than the Comptroller General. General Accounting Office Act of 1996, Pub.L.No. 104–316, 110 Stat. 3826, § 202(m)(1996).

Page 122.   Add a footnote 3a at the end of the third paragraph of Paragraph (4):

3a.   Is the threat of "collusion" in framing consent decrees likely to be particularly acute in mass tort litigation? See Coffee, *Class Wars: The Dilemma of the Mass Tort Class Action,* 95 Colum.L.Rev. 1343 (1995), arguing that as a result of recent legal developments, corporate defendants often prefer to be sued in class actions (in order to establish an upper limit on liability, for example), and sometimes collude with accommodating plaintiffs' attorneys to arrange for such suits to be filed—and then settled on favorable terms—by nominal plaintiffs (pp. 1349–52). Among his suggestions for possible reforms, Coffee proposes imposition of various restrictions on the terms and procedures by which plaintiffs' attorneys can settle class actions, and he would allow courts to accept settlements only in class actions satisfying the "commonality" and other requirements of Rule 23 of the Federal Rules of Civil Procedure (pp. 1453–57).

The Supreme Court addressed related issues concerning Rule 23 in Amchem Products, Inc. v. Windsor, 117 S.Ct. 2231 (1997). After holding that the existence of a settlement agreement was "relevant to class certification", the Court ruled that elements of Rule 23 "designed to protect absentees by blocking unwarranted or overbroad class definition * * * demand undiluted, even heightened, attention in the settlement context", since there is no opportunity for the court "to adjust the class, informed by proceedings as they unfold" (p. 2248).

SECTION 3.   SOME PROBLEMS OF STANDING TO SUE

———

SUBSECTION A: PLAINTIFFS' STANDING

———

Page 136.   Add to footnote 1:

Pushaw, *Justiciability and Separation of Powers: A Neo–Federalist Approach,* 81 Corn. L.Rev. 394 (1996), argues that modern justiciability doctrines stem largely from the inventions of Justice Frankfurter, who relied on flimsy historical evidence in claiming that original constitutional understandings sharply limited judicial interference with the political branches (pp. 458–63). Although the Burger and Rehnquist Courts have continued to make historical claims in support of stringent justiciability doctrines, Pushaw argues that "federalist" constitutional theory in fact requires judicial review "coordinate with legislative and executive authority" (p. 471) to ensure that the political branches stay within the bounds of law. Standing should be available wherever Congress grants it in statutory cases, and "[a]t least one person must have standing to bring a claim under every constitutional provision" (p. 485).

Page 141.   Add to Paragraph (2):

The Court was also critical of Flast in Lewis v. Casey, 116 S.Ct. 2174 (1996), which held that prison inmates lack standing to complain about inadequate access to law libraries and other impediments to access to the courts in the absence of a showing that the inadequacies impede presentation of non-frivolous legal challenges to their convictions or confinement. In an opinion concurring in part and dissenting in part, Justice Souter argued that the Court's precedents established a right of access to legal materials needed to file even frivolous claims. And under Flast, he maintained, there was standing to claim a denial of access in such cases, since the disputes would be presented " 'in an adversary context and in a form historically viewed as capable of judicial resolution' "(p. 2203)(quoting Flast). Writing for a five-member majority, Justice Scalia responded that "Flast erred in assuming that assurance of 'serious and adversarial treatment' was the only value protected by standing" (p. 2181 n.3). Somewhat more particularly, "Flast failed to recognize that this doctrine has a separation-of-powers component, which keeps courts within certain traditional bounds vis-a-vis the other branches, concrete adverseness or not. That is where the 'actual injury' requirement comes from" (*id.*).

Does Lewis v. Casey establish a reasonable threshold requirement for plaintiffs who want to challenge their denial of access to prison libraries? Imagine a case involving prisoners who want access to a prison library in order to determine, in the first instance, whether they have colorable legal claims. If they are denied all access to the library, Lewis appears to hold that, in order to have standing to challenge their exclusion, they must establish that their legal claims are at least not frivolous. But how could they be expected to make such a showing if they are denied access to a law library or other sources of legal assistance?

Page 143.   Add to footnote 11:

See also Bennett v. Spear, 117 S.Ct. 1154 (1997)(in order to survive a motion to dismiss, plaintiffs bear only a "relatively modest" burden of pleading facts adequate to establish causation and redressability, as well as injury; more specific facts must be " 'set forth' by affidavit or other evidence" to survive a motion for summary judgment).

Page 144. Add to Paragraph (4)(b)

The Court returned to issues involving "injury" and "generalized griev-ances" in FEC v. Akins, 118 S.Ct. 1777 (1998), also discussed p. 14 *infra*. In an opinion by Justice Breyer, the Court upheld (6–3) the standing of a group of voters to challenge a determination by the Federal Election Commission ("FEC") that the American Israel Public Affairs Committee is not a "political committee" as defined by the Federal Election Campaign Act of 1971 and, therefore, had not violated the Act and was not required to make disclosures concerning its membership, contributions, and expenditures. Citing Public Citizen v. Dep't. of Justice, Fourth Edition p. 144, and Havens Realty Corp. v. Coleman, Fourth Edition p. 172, Justice Breyer's majority opinion found that the plaintiffs' "inability to obtain information"—which they alleged had to be disclosed under the statute—constituted the injury-in-fact that is required for standing by Article III (p. 1784). The Court distinguished United States v. Richardson, Fourth Edition p. 143, as resting crucially on a determination that there was no "nexus" between taxpayer status and the plaintiff's asserted right to information under the Statement and Accounts Clause; in this case, by contrast, Congress had expressly conferred a right to sue on all citizens "aggrieved" by the FCC's dismissal of their complaints and thus mooted any "nexus" requirement, as well as overcoming all prudential objections to stand-ing.

The "strongest argument" against standing in Akins, the Court said, was "that this lawsuit involves only a 'generalized grievance' " (p. 1785). According to the Court, however, the prohibition against standing in cases of generalized grievances, properly understood, applies only "where the harm at issue is not only widely shared, but is also of an abstract and indefinite nature—for example, harm to the 'common concern for obedience to law' " (*id.*). The Court continued: "Often the fact that an interest is abstract and the fact that it is widely shared go hand in hand. But their association is not invariable, and where a harm is concrete, though widely shared, the Court has found 'injury in fact' ". * * * [That standing may exist in cases involving widely shared injuries] seems particularly obvious where (to use a hypothetical example) large numbers of individuals suffer the same common-law injury (say, a widespread mass tort), or where large numbers of voters suffer interference with voting rights conferred by law. We conclude that similarly, the informational injury at issue here * * * is sufficiently concrete and specific" to satisfy the standing requirements of Article III (p. 1786).

Justice Scalia's dissent (joined by Justices O'Connor and Thomas) argued that United States v. Richardson, which also involved an asserted injury arising from "the Government's unlawful refusal to place information within the public domain", was not persuasively distinguishable (p. 1790). "[T]he Court is wrong to think that generalized grievances have only concerned us when they are abstract. One need go no further than Richardson to prove that—unless the Court believes that deprivation of information is an abstract injury, in which event this case could be disposed of on that much broader ground" (p. 1791). Justice Scalia continued: "What is noticeably lacking in the Court's discussion of our generalized-grievance jurisprudence is all reference to two words that have figured in it prominently: 'particularized' and 'undifferentiated'. 'Particu-larized' means that 'the injury must affect the plaintiff in a personal and individual way.' If the effect is 'undifferentiated and common to all members of the public,' the plaintiff has a generalized grievance that must be pursued by political rather than judicial means" (*id.*).

When the demand for particularity and differentiation were taken into account, Justice Scalia reasoned, the mass tort and voting rights cases cited by the majority failed to justify standing in the case of an alleged deprivation of information. In the mass tort and voting right cases, "each individual suffers a particularized and differentiated harm. * * * One voter suffers the deprivation of his franchise, another the deprivation of hers. With the generalized grievance, on the other hand, the injury or deprivation is not only widely shared but it is undifferentiated. The harm caused to Mr. Richardson [and Mr. Akins] * * * was precisely the same as the harm caused to everyone else: unavailability of [information]" (*id.*).

How persuasive is the distinction that Justice Scalia draws? Just as "one voter suffers the deprivation of his franchise, another the deprivation of hers", why doesn't one citizen suffer the deprivation of his right to information, another the deprivation of her right to information?

An obvious difference between Richardson and Akins is that Congress specifically authorized standing in the latter case, but not in the former. In cases involving injuries that are widely shared, how much, if anything, should turn on whether Congress has authorized standing? See p. 14, *infra*.

Page 148.   Add to footnote 21:

See also Steel Co. v. Citizens for a Better Environment, 118 S.Ct. 1003, 1016–20 (1998)(denying standing due to absence of redressability).

Page 149.   Add to footnote 22:

See also Clinton v. New York, 118 S.Ct. ___ (1998), in which the Court relied on Associated General Contractors and Bryant v. Yellen in upholding the standing of a farmers' cooperative to challenge the President's "cancellation", under the Line Item Veto Act, of a statutory provision granting favorable tax treatment to third parties selling processing facilities to farmers' cooperatives. The Court characterized the relevant injury as the deprivation of a "bargaining chip" in sales negotiations that inflicted "sufficient likelihood of economic injury to establish standing" (p. ___). Justice Scalia, joined by Justice O'Connor, dissented, arguing that under Allen v. Wright and Simon v. Eastern Kentucky Welfare Rights Org., "the speculative nature of a third party's response to changes in federal tax law defeats standing" (p. ___).

For an argument that the Court's standing holdings in Bakke and Associated General Contractors are "racially suspicious" and fit a broader pattern of suspicious standing decisions, see Spann, *Color-Coded Standing*, 80 Corn.L.Rev. 1422 (1995).

Page 149.   Add to Paragraph (5)(d):

The Court avoided the justiciability issues posed by a class suit on behalf of plaintiffs who had been exposed to toxic substances but had not yet become sick, as well as others who had manifest more concrete injuries, in Amchem Products, Inc. v. Windsor, 117 S.Ct. 2231 (1997). The Court, per Justice Ginsburg, held that there was no certifiable class under Fed.R.Civ.Pro. 23. Because class certification issues were "antecedent to the existence of Article III issues", the Court had no occasion to reach the latter explicitly, although it was "mindful" "that Rule 23's requirements must be interpreted in keeping with Article III constraints" (p. 2244). *Cf.* Note, 109 Harv.L.Rev. 1066, 1083 (1996)(arguing that "Article III does not erect a per se barrier against" suits by plaintiffs who have been exposed to a toxic substance but not yet manifested physical injury, including those participating in class actions, but suggestions that individualized assessment will likely reveal many such actions to be unripe "or otherwise defective for prudential reasons").

Page 151.   Add to footnote 24:

But compare Lewis v. Casey, 116 S.Ct. 2174, 2181 n. 3 (1996), which asserts that "Flast erred" in failing to recognize that standing "doctrine has a separation-of-powers component, which keeps courts within certain traditional bounds vis-a-vis the other branches".

Page 152.   Add to Paragraph (6):

Stearns, *Standing Back from the Forest: Justiciability and Social Choice,* 83 Cal.L.Rev. 1309 (1995), argues that, viewed through the lens of "social choice theory", standing doctrine is an important complement to the doctrine of stare decisis. Stare decisis performs the important function of preventing the Supreme Court from rendering inconsistent and thus destabilizing decisions over time. But stare decisis creates an incentive for ideological litigants to seek to determine the "path" of the law by bringing cases at early or otherwise opportune moments. According to Stearns, standing doctrine "renders the inevitable path dependency of legal doctrine * * * more fair by preventing ideological litigants from manipulating the path in which cases are presented for consideration" (p. 1315). See also Stearns, *Standing and Social Choice: Historical Evidence,* 144 U.Pa.L.Rev. 309 (1995)(arguing that standing doctrine acquired its current structure during an era in which a substantively divided Supreme Court knew that it was likely to render "arbitrary" decisions not supported by any stable majority in cases that it decided on the merits).

Page 157.   Add a new Paragraph (10):

(10) *Timing of the Standing Determination.* In Steel Co. v. Citizens for a Better Environment, 118 S.Ct. 1003 (1998), Justice Scalia, in an opinion styled as that of "the Court", rejected the so-called "hypothetical jurisdiction" doctrine, discussed p. 5 above, and also concluded more broadly that, at least outside of narrowly defined and exceptional circumstances, a federal court must resolve Article III standing questions before reaching non-jurisdictional questions. Justice Scalia acknowledged that, under the Court's precedents, a court (i) may sometimes resolve a "merits" question before deciding a question of statutory standing, and (ii) may determine a statutory standing question before resolving a question of Article III standing. But it did not follow, he insisted, that a merits question could be given priority over an Article III standing question (p. 1013 n. 2).

Justice O'Connor (joined by Justice Kennedy), who joined Justice Scalia's opinion, also concurred separately. Quoting the Court's acknowledgment that "several of our decisions 'have diluted the absolute purity of the rule that Article III jurisdiction is always an antecedent question' ", she noted that, in her view, "the Court's opinion should not be read as cataloguing an exhaustive list of circumstances under which federal courts may exercise judgment in 'reserv[ing] difficult questions of ... jurisdiction when the case alternatively could be resolved on the merits in favor of the same party' " (p. 1020). Is Justice O'Connor's view consistent with the Court opinion that she purported to join and for which her vote was necessary to make a majority?

Justice Breyer, concurring in part and concurring in the judgment, acknowledged that federal courts should ordinarily decide standing questions first, but he argued that "[t]he Constitution does not impose a rigid judicial 'order of operations,' when doing so" would require courts to struggle with "intractable" questions that made no difference to the outcome, thereby imposing "unnecessary delay and consequent added cost" (p. 1021).

Justice Stevens, concurring in the judgment in an opinion joined in part by Justices Souter and Ginsburg, concluded that the question whether a plaintiff had stated a cause of action could be as much jurisdictional as the question whether a plaintiff had standing. Standing questions therefore did not need to take absolute priority; the Court had discretion to determine which threshold question to decide first (pp. 1021–27).

How significant is the disagreement among the Justices about the scope and nature of the judicial obligation to resolve standing questions before other questions?

Page 170. Add to Paragraph (1):

Following Lujan, the Court again found an absence of standing, despite a congressional authorization to sue, in Raines v. Byrd, 117 S.Ct. 2312 (1997), discussed p. 16, *infra*, but distinguished Lujan and upheld congressionally conferred standing in FEC v. Akins, *infra*.

Page 173. Add to Paragraph (3):

In FEC v. Akins, 118 S.Ct. 1777 (1998), the Court, in an opinion by Justice Breyer, held (6–3) that it lay within the power of Congress to confer standing on any citizen suffering the "injury" of "inability to receive information" that results from another party's alleged noncompliance with statutory disclosure requirements. At issue was the standing of a group of voters, under a statute authorizing suit by any person "aggrieved" by a Federal Election Commission decision dismissing his or her complaint, to seek review of a Commission ruling that the American Israel Public Affairs Committee is not a "political committee" subject to regulation and reporting requirements under the Federal Election Campaign Act of 1971. The Court appeared to accept that the interest in access to information, which is widely shared and would not have been protected at common law, would fail to satisfy "prudential" standing requirements in the absence of statutory authorization (pp. 1783–84). But congressional action overcame prudential limits, as well as mooting the "nexus" requirement on which the Court had focused in United States v. Richardson, Fourth Edition p. 143, when it found no adequate connection between the plaintiffs' taxpayer status and their claim of access to the CIA budget under the Statement and Account Clause.

Justice Scalia, joined by Justices O'Connor and Thomas, dissented. In his view, the statute's authorization of suit by any "aggrieved party" should not be read to authorize suit by any citizen disappointed by the FEC's failure to take enforcement action. And it was only as a result of the agency's failure to take enforcement action that the plaintiffs suffered their asserted injury of inability to acquire information: "Respondents claim that each of them is elevated to the special status of a 'party aggrieved' by the fact that the requested enforcement action (if it was successful) would have had the effect, among others, of placing certain information in the agency's possession, where respondents, along with everyone else in the world, would have had access to it" (p. 1789).

With respect to the constitutional dimension of the standing issue, Justice Scalia thought that Congress could not confer standing based on "generalized grievances" that were not more "particularized" or differentiated than a generalized denial of access to the same information. He also protested that the Court's contrary decision had potentially large implications: "If today's decision is correct, it is within the power of Congress to authorize any interested person to manage (through the courts) the Executive's enforcement of any law that includes a requirement for the filing and public availability of a piece of paper. This is not the system we have had, and it is not the system we should desire" (p. 1792).

Does Akins suggest that the barriers to congressionally authorized citizen standing established by Lujan v. Defenders of Wildlife, Fourth Edition p. 157, can always or nearly always be surmounted by a properly drafted statute?

Page 177.   Add to Paragraph (5):

Compare the approach taken in National Credit Union Administration v. First National Bank & Trust Co., 118 S.Ct. 927 (1998), which upheld standing under the zone-of-interests test. At issue was whether a bank had standing to challenge a ruling by the National Credit Union Administration (NCUA) that authorized multi-employer credit unions, despite a requirement of the Federal Credit Union Act that federally defined credit unions "shall be limited to groups having a common bond of occupation or association" (p. 930–31). In an opinion by Justice Thomas, the Court emphasized that "for a plaintiff's interests to be arguably within the 'zone of interests' to be protected by a statute, there does not have to be an 'indication of congressional purpose to benefit the would-be plaintiff' " and that it is sufficient if the interest asserted is " 'arguably within the zone of interests to be protected' " (p. 935). Dividing 5–4, the Court found this test to be satisfied. Even if Congress had enacted the restriction on credit union membership to ensure that credit unions remain responsive to their members, rather than to protect banks against competition, "an interest in limiting the markets that federal credit unions can serve" was "one of the interests 'arguably . . . to be protected' " by the statute (p. 935).

Dissenting, Justice O'Connor protested that the Court erred by failing to focus on "whether the common bond provision was intended to protect respondents' commercial interest" (p. 941). In prior cases upholding competitors' standing under the zone-of-interests test, Justice O'Connor argued, Congress had specifically enacted anti-competition provisions, and the injuries complained of therefore fell within the zone of interests that the statutes had sought to protect. By failing to demand a showing that Congress had sought to protect against the type of competitive injury of which the plaintiffs complained, Justice O'Connor asserted, the Court's approach would grant standing to every plaintiff who could establish an Article III injury and thus "render[] the zone-of-interests test ineffectual" (p. 941).

See also Bennett v. Spear, 117 S.Ct. 1154, 1164–65 (1997)(adversely affected citizens have standing to challenge alleged over-regulation under the Endangered Species Act, even if they are not personally subject to regulatory duties; the zone-of-interests test does not turn on the "overall purpose" of the statute, but on the "particular provision of law" aimed at preventing "uneconomic (because erroneous) * * * determinations" upon which the plaintiff relied).

Page 181.   Add to Paragraph (4):

See also Shaw v. Hunt, 517 U.S. 899 (1996)(holding that plaintiffs lack standing to challenge districting legislation as an unconstitutional racial gerrymander when they neither reside within the challenged district nor present specific evidence that they personally have been subjected to a racial classification).

For critical comment on the theory of standing reflected in the Court's racial gerrymandering cases, see Dow, *The Equal Protection Clause and the Legislative Redistricting Cases—Some Notes Concerning the Standing of White Plaintiffs*, 81 Minn.L.Rev. 1123 (1997); Durchslag, *United States v. Hays: An Essay on Standing to Challenge Majority–Minority Districts*, 65 U.Cin.L.Rev. 341 (1997); Note, 49 Stan.L.Rev. 381 (1997). Compare Ely, *Standing to Challenge Pro–Minority Gerrymanders*, 111 Harv.L.Rev. 576, 595 (1997)(arguing that "[t]o favor pro-minority gerrymanders" while opposing standing for the typically white "filler people" who are not members of the racial majority within a district "is to engage in a profound inconsistency, that of supposing the right of a black citizen to cast an effective vote for someone of his own race to be terribly important, while maintaining that withholding from a white citizen the right to cast an effective vote for someone of *his* race doesn't even count as a deprivation").

Page 183. Add to Paragraph (5):

The Court distinguished Coleman v. Miller and held that congressional plaintiffs lacked standing in Raines v. Byrd, 117 S.Ct. 2312 (1997). Plaintiffs, six present and former members of the House and Senate, sought a declaratory judgment that the Line Item Veto Act ("the Act"), which authorizes the President to "cancel" certain spending and tax benefit measures after signing them into law, violates the separation of powers. The Act specifically authorized suit for declaratory and injunctive relief by "[a]ny Member of Congress or any individual adversely affected"; plaintiffs brought suit the day after the Act took effect, claiming that the statute " 'dilute[d] their Article I voting power' " (p. 2316).

Writing for the majority, Chief Justice Rehnquist first emphasized that standing depends on a showing of *"personal injury"* (emphasis in original) and noted that "our standing inquiry has been especially rigorous when reaching the merits of a dispute would force us to decide whether an action taken by one of the other two branches of the Federal Government was unconstitutional" (p. 2317–18). Plaintiffs, the Court then observed, based their claim of standing on a "type of institutional injury"—"a loss of political power"—and did "not claim that they have been deprived of something to which they are *personally* entitled—such as their seats as members of Congress after their constituents had elected *them*" (p. 2318)(emphasis in original). Coleman was not controlling, the Court said: it stands "at most * * * for the proposition that legislators whose votes would have been sufficient to defeat (or enact) a specific legislative act have standing to sue if that legislative action goes into effect (or does not go into effect), on the ground that their votes have been completely nullified" (p. 2319). Although plaintiffs alleged that the Line Item Veto Act diluted the significance of their votes for bills subject to presidential cancellation, there was a "vast difference" between the "level of vote nullification" in this case and that in Coleman.

The concluding section of the Court's opinion specifically noted factors possibly limiting its holding: "We attach some significance to the fact that appellees have not been authorized to represent their respective Houses of Congress, and indeed both Houses actively oppose their suit. * * * [N]or [does the decision] foreclose[] the Act from constitutional challenge (by someone who suffers judicially cognizable injury as a result of the Act). Whether the case would be different if any of these circumstances were different we need not now decide" (p. 2322).

Justice Souter, joined by Justice Ginsburg, concurred in the judgment that the plaintiffs lacked standing. Justice Stevens, dissenting, would have sustained standing and invalidated the Act on the merits. Justice Breyer, who also dissented, argued that the case was not distinguishable from Coleman.

Is the majority's attempted distinction of "personal" and "institutional" injuries consistent with Coleman? If not, is the degree of difference in the "institutional" injuries in the two cases sufficient to support the divergent results, or has Coleman effectively been limited to its facts? Would congressional standing in the D.C. Circuit's "pocket veto" cases, Fourth Edition pp. 182–83, be sustainable under Raines?

Raines joins a lengthening line of cases in which the Court has held congressional grants of standing unconstitutional. See Fourth Edition pp. 169–70. Given that Congress had authorized suit to challenge the Line Item Veto Act by "[a]ny Member of Congress", how could the Court have thought it possibly significant that the specific plaintiffs in Raines had "not been authorized to represent their respective Houses of Congress"?

Page 186.   Add to footnote 11:

In United Food & Commercial Workers Union Local 751 v. Brown Group, Inc., 517 U.S. 544 (1996), the Court held that Congress may displace the third requirement of the Hunt test, and authorize a union to sue for damages on behalf of its members. The Court, per Justice Souter, unanimously found that the first element of the Hunt test directly implemented Article III's injury, causation, and redressability requirements, and that the second was "complementary to the first, for its demand that an association plaintiff be organized for a purpose germane to the subject of its member's claim raises an assurance that the association's litigators will themselves have a stake in the resolution of the dispute" (pp. 555–56). "But once an association has satisfied Hunt's first and second prongs", it was "difficult to see a constitutional necessity for anything more" (p. 556). The third prong, which essentially embodies the "presumption * * * that litigants may not assert the rights of absent third parties" (p. 557), was "judicially fashioned and prudentially imposed" (p. 558) and thus subject to abrogation by Congress.

Page 195.   Add to footnote 11:

See also Campbell v. Louisiana, 118 S.Ct. 1419, 1422–24 (1998)(upholding the third-party standing of a white criminal defendant to raise an equal protection challenge involving discrimination against blacks in selecting grand jurors).

Page 195.   Add a Paragraph (5)(f):

(f) In Miller v. Albright, 118 S.Ct. 1428 (1998), seven members of an otherwise fractured Court agreed that an illegitimate child, born in the Philippines of a Filipino mother and an American father, had standing to assert her father's equal protection claim to be able to transmit American citizenship to his offspring on the same terms as an American mother of an illegitimate child. On the merits, the Court, by a 6–3 vote, rejected the petitioner's constitutional claim.

With respect to third-party standing, Justice Stevens' opinion announcing the judgment of the Court, which was joined only by Chief Justice Rehnquist, noted that the plaintiff clearly had standing to assert her own right to be treated as a citizen; without elaboration, the plurality then cited Craig v. Boren (Fourth Edition p. 193) as establishing that she could rely on her father's asserted equal protection rights to provide the basis for her claim. On the merits, however, Justice Stevens concluded that the discrimination effected by the statute did not offend the Constitution. In an opinion dissenting on the merits, Justice Breyer, joined by Justices Souter and Ginsburg, offered the fullest explanation of why third-party standing should be permitted. He reasoned that the petitioner had suffered injury in fact, "[s]he has a 'close' and relevant relationship" with her father, and "there was 'some hindrance' to her father's asserting his own rights" by virtue of an unappealed dismissal of his complaint for lack of standing (p. 1456). Justice Scalia, whose opinion concurring in the judgment was joined by Justice Thomas, would have found this ground inadequate "[a]s an original matter", but apparently agreed that third-party standing was supportable under the Court's precedents (p. 1447 n.1). He added: "Our law on this subject is in need of what may charitably be called clarification, but I would leave it for another day". Id. On the merits, Justice Scalia found that the suit must fail because the Court lacked authority to "provide the relief requested: conferral of citizenship on a basis other than that prescribed by Congress" (p. 1446).

Justice O'Connor, joined by Justice Kennedy, concurred in the judgment but dissented on the third-party standing issue. She found no sufficient "hindrance" to the father's assertion of his own rights; although the district court had held that the father lacked standing, there was no obstacle to appealing that decision, which then could have been corrected (p. 1444). Justice O'Connor noted, however, that had she agreed that the question whether the statute worked a gender-based discrimination was properly before the Court, she would "not share Justice Stevens' assessment that the provision withstands heightened scrutiny" (p. 1445).

If Justices O'Connor and Kennedy were prepared to say that the challenged statute should have been subjected to heightened scrutiny in a suit by a father of an illegitimate child; and if in such a suit they would have joined Justices Breyer, Souter, and Ginsburg to hold that the statute was invalid and therefore unenforceable in all cases; did it make any sense for Justices O'Connor and Kennedy to vote to deny relief to the petitioner on the ground that she lacked third-party standing?

Page 197. Add to footnote 1:

See also Leavitt v. Jane L., 518 U.S. 137 (1996)(per curiam)(reversing a federal court of appeals decision that held a state statute regulating abortions not separable as a matter of state law despite a provision of the abortion section of the state code providing that anti-abortion legislation should be treated as separable).

SUBSECTION B: DEFENDANTS' STANDING

Page 204. Add to the first paragraph in footnote 2:

See also Hill, *The Puzzling First Amendment Overbreadth Doctrine*, 25 Hofstra L.Rev. 1063, 1074–76 (1997)(suggesting that "saving" constructions should not be "retroactive" with respect to "soft-core" violators who, at the time they engaged in regulated expressive activities, could reasonably have believed that their conduct was constitutionally protected).

Page 210.   Add a footnote 5a at the end of the first sentence of Paragraph (9):

5a.   For criticism of the traditional notion that courts should avoid statutory interpretations that would give rise to hard constitutional questions, see Schauer, *Ashwander Revisited*, 1995 Sup.Ct.Rev. 71, 177–78. According to Schauer, interpretations adopted expressly to avoid constitutional issues intrude on Congress' lawmaking prerogative by effectively "redrafting" legislative enactments (pp. 186–87). By signalling the court's view concerning the ostensibly avoided constitutional issue, such interpretations discourage Congress from legislating again (p. 195). And they achieve their effects in opinions that lack the benefit of a reasoned confrontation with the constitutional issue in its full complexity (pp. 195–96).

Page 210.   Add to footnote 6:

See also Reno v. ACLU, 117 S.Ct. 2329, 2350 (1997)(declining to provide a narrowing construction of parts of a federal statute where the "open-ended character" of the challenged provision, which prohibited transmission of certain "indecent" messages over the internet, gave "no guidance whatever for limiting its coverage").

Page 212.   Add to Paragraph (10):

Dissenting from a denial of certiorari in Janklow v. Planned Parenthood, Sioux Falls Clinic, 517 U.S. 1174 (1996), Justice Scalia, joined by the Chief Justice and Justice Thomas, contended that the circuits were split over the permissibility of facial challenges to abortion legislation. In Justice Scalia's view, United States v. Salerno, Fourth Edition p. 211, had correctly summarized "a long established principle of our jurisprudence" that overbreadth challenges are permissible only in First Amendment cases and that, in all other contexts, a facial challenge could succeed only if the challenger establishes that " 'no set of circumstances exists under which the Act would be valid' "(517 U.S. at 1178, quoting Salerno). Acknowledging, however, that the Court had sent "mixed signals" about whether abortion statutes could be challenged as facially overbroad (*id.*), he would have granted the writ to resolve the question. Justice Stevens, in a separate memorandum, supported the denial of certiorari. He argued that Salerno's "dictum" that "a facial challenge must fail unless there is 'no set of circumstances' in which the challenge could be validly applied" was a "rigid and unwise" departure from the Court's precedents (p. 1175). Indeed, before the "rhetorical flourish" to which Justice Stevens objected, Salerno had stated the "long established" and appropriate principle: " 'The fact that [a legislative Act] might operate unconstitutionally under some conceivable circumstances is insufficient to render it wholly invalid.' "*Id.*, quoting Salerno. Explaining his vote to deny certiorari, Justice Stevens saw "no need for this Court affirmatively to disavow [Salerno's] unfortunate language, in the abortion context or otherwise, until it is clear that a federal court has ignored the appropriate principle and applied the draconian 'no circumstance' dictum to deny relief in a case in which a facial challenge would otherwise be successful" (p. 1176). See also Romer v. Evans, 517 U.S. 620, 643 (1996)(Scalia, J., dissenting)(arguing that the Court erred in invalidating a state constitutional amendment that barred state or local legislation forbidding discrimination against homosexuals; even if the provision were invalid insofar as it affected persons merely of homosexual "orientation"—rather than those who engaged in homosexual conduct[b]—a facial challenge could not succeed under Salerno's "no circumstances" test).

Cf. Washington v. Glucksberg, 117 S.Ct. 2258, 2275, (1997)(holding that a state statute prohibiting physician assisted suicide is not unconstitutional "either on its face, or 'as applied to competent, terminally ill adults who wish to hasten their deaths by obtaining medication prescribed by their doctors' ").

Page 213. Add to Paragraph (11):

In National Endowment for the Arts v. Finley, 118 S.Ct. ___ (1998), the Court rejected a facial void-for-vagueness challenge to a statute calling for federal funding of the arts to "tak[e] into consideration general standards of decency and respect for the diverse beliefs and values of the American public". The Court characterized the statutory terms as "opaque"; observed that "if they appeared in a criminal statute or a regulatory scheme, they could raise substantial vagueness concerns"; and "recognize[d] * * * that artists may conform their speech to what they believe to be the decision-making criteria in order to acquire funding" (p. ___). But the Court concluded that "when the government is acting as patron rather than as sovereign", vagueness was likely to be unavoidable; "if this statute is unconstitutionally vague, then so too are all government programs awarding scholarships and grants on the basis of subjective criteria such as 'excellence' " (p. ___). Justice Souter, dissenting, agreed with the Court that the challenged provision was not unconstitutionally vague, but would have invalidated it on overbreadth grounds, since the "decency and respect criteria may not [permissibly] be employed in the very many instances in which the art seeking a subsidy is neither aimed at children nor meant to celebrate a particular culture" (p. ___).

Is there any principled reason why vague standards for the dispensation of grants for speech and expressive activities should not be as readily subject to facial attack as substantially standardless licensing schemes, discussed at Fourth Edition pp. 203–04 & n.1? How significant is it that substantive First Amendment doctrine makes access to a public forum a presumptive right, but treats access to other facilities and sources of support as subject to governmental discretion?

SECTION 4.   MOOTNESS

Page 222. Add to Paragraph (5):

See also Arizonans for Official English v. Arizona, 117 S.Ct. 1055 (1997)(holding on peculiar facts that, after a claim to injunctive relief became moot, there was no defendant against whom a claim for "nominal damages" might be asserted, and thus no basis for rejecting a suggestion of mootness).

---

b. Justice Scalia argued that the challenged amendment's treatment of those who engaged in homosexual conduct was clearly constitutionally valid in light of Bowers v. Hardwick, 478 U.S. 186 (1986).

Page 223.   Add at the end of the first paragraph:

See also Spencer v. Kemna, 118 S.Ct. 978 (1998)(refusing to presume that collateral consequences attach to a parole revocation and holding a habeas corpus petition moot after the expiration of the sentence for which parole had been revoked), also discussed at p. 142, *infra.*

SECTION 5.   RIPENESS

Page 251.   Add at the end of Paragraph (2)(c):

See also Ohio Forestry Ass'n v. Sierra Club, 118 S.Ct. 1665 (1998)(environmental group's challenge to a resource management plan is not ripe for review when permission to engage in logging has not yet been granted, modifications in the plan remain possible, and plaintiffs have not properly raised claims of immediate harm to their interest in access to undisturbed wilderness).

Page 252.   Add to footnote 2:

Cf. Texas v. United States, 118 S.Ct. 1257 (1998)(suit seeking declaration that preclearance provisions of the Voting Rights Act would not apply if Texas were to implement a state law authorizing sanctions against local school districts is not ripe in the absence of identified, likely imposition of such sanctions).

Page 256.   Add to Paragraph (3):

The Court unanimously distinguished the Williamson County case, and held a takings claim ripe, in Suitum v. Tahoe Regional Planning Agency, 117 S.Ct. 1659 (1997). Because agency regulations conclusively forbade building on Suitum's undeveloped lot, the Court concluded that she did not need to take the futile step of applying for a variance. And although Suitum was entitled to valuable "Transferable Development Rights" (TDRs) that she could sell to other landowners (who were not categorically forbidden to develop their property under applicable regulations), Justice Souter's majority opinion found that she did not need to find a buyer and seek agency approval of the transfer in order for her suit to be ripe; the valuation of her TDRs was "simply an issue of fact about possible market prices" (p. 1668) that the district court was competent to resolve. In an opinion concurring in part and concurring in the judgment, Justice Scalia, joined by Justices O'Connor and Thomas, argued that issues about the value and salability of Suitum's TDRs were not relevant to the question whether she was complaining of "final" agency action that was ripe for judicial review. According to Justice Scalia, those issues were relevant only to the question whether, if a taking were found, Suitum had received constitutionally adequate compensation. Does the difference between the majority and concurring opinions tend to corroborate the view that ripeness determinations are often conceptually connected with merits issues? See Fourth Edition pp. 252–55.

SECTION 6.   POLITICAL QUESTIONS

Page 288.   Substitute the following text for footnote 13:

A few state courts have exercised jurisdiction over claims under the Guarantee Clause. See, *e.g.*, In re Initiative Petition No. 348, State Question No. 640, 820 P.2d 772 (Okla.1991); Cagle v. Qualified Electors of Winston County, 470 So.2d 1208 (Ala.1985). Should state courts be able to exercise jurisdiction over claims that would be treated as nonjusticiable in federal court? On the one hand, federal justiciability doctrines generally are not binding on state courts. On the other, the Supreme Court frequently suggests that, under the separation of powers, the resolution of "political questions" is committed to either Congress or the national executive branch. Is there something unique about claims under the Guarantee Clause? Compare Linde, *Who Is Responsible for Republican Government?*, 65 U.Colo.L.Rev. 709 (1994)(arguing that Guarantee Clause claims are justiciable in state court), with Weinberg, *Political Questions and the Guarantee Clause,* 65 U.Colo.L.Rev. 887 (1994)(arguing that state court jurisdiction is permissible only on the supposition that current Supreme Court jurisprudence is mistaken).

CHAPTER III

THE ORIGINAL JURISDICTION OF THE SUPREME COURT

___

INTRODUCTORY NOTE ON THE POWER OF CONGRESS TO REGULATE THE JURISDICTION

___

Page 296. Add to footnote 6:

Amar's understanding of the original jurisdiction is criticized in Harrison, *The Power of Congress to Limit the Jurisdiction of Federal Courts and the Text of Article III*, 64 U.Chi. L.Rev. 203, 248–49 (1997), and defended against Harrison's criticisms in Pushaw, *Congressional Power Over Federal Court Jurisdiction: A Defense of the Neo–Federalist Interpretation of Article III*, 1997 BYU L.Rev. 847, 890–91 (1997).

Pages 314–16. Add to Paragraph (2):

For an argument that in disputes concerning the interpretation of interstate compacts, state law should presumptively be adopted where the compacting states' laws are in accord, see Note, 111 Harv.L.Rev. 1991 (1998).

CHAPTER IV

CONGRESSIONAL CONTROL OF THE DISTRIBUTION OF JUDICIAL POWER AMONG FEDERAL AND STATE COURTS

SECTION 1. CONGRESSIONAL REGULATION OF FEDERAL JURISDICTION

Page 349. Add to footnote 7:

The amount-in-controversy requirement has now been increased to $75,000.

Page 352. Add to Paragraph (5)(a)(i):

According to Judge Posner, it is widely believed "by the practicing bar that federal judges are, on average (an important qualification), of higher quality than their state counterparts"? Posner, The Federal Courts: Challenge and Reform 216 (2d ed.1996); see also Neuborne, *Parity Revisited: The Uses of a Judicial Forum of Excellence,* 44 DePaul L.Rev. 797 (1995). Is this perception relevant to the parity debate?

Page 353. Add to Paragraph (5)(a)(ii):

But cf. Neuborne, *Parity Revisited: The Uses of a Judicial Forum of Excellence,* 44 DePaul L.Rev. 797, 799 (1995)(noting "a general decline in the ability to win a novel individual rights case anywhere", but maintaining that "a relative institutional advantage for the plaintiff [still] exists in federal court; an advantage resulting from a mix of political insulation, tradition, better resources and superior professional competence").

Page 353. Add at the end of the first paragraph of Paragraph (5)(b):

But cf. Wells, *Behind the Parity Debate: The Decline of the Legal Process Tradition in the Law of Federal Courts,* 71 B.U.L.Rev. 609 (1991); and Wells, *Who's Afraid of Henry Hart?,* 14 Const.Comm. 175 (1997). Professor Wells asserts the central relevance to both legal and policy debates of a "weak parity" thesis, which holds that state courts are sufficiently competent and unbiased so that "a litigant will receive a constitutionally adequate hearing on a federal claim" there (71 B.U.L.Rev. at 610), but also maintains that state courts "are not interchangeable with federal courts", and may sometimes provide a "home court advantage" to state defendants (14 Const.Comm. at 185–86).

Page 367.   Add to footnote 19:

But cf. Felker v. Turpin, 116 S.Ct. 2333, 2341–42 (1996)(Souter, J., joined by Stevens and Breyer, JJ., concurring)(terming it an "open" question whether a statute limiting the Supreme Court's appellate jurisdiction would be unconstitutional if, in practice, it stopped the Court from reviewing "divergent interpretations" of a federal statute).

Page 368.   Add to footnote 21:

The Prison Litigation and Reform Act of 1995 (PLRA), 110 Stat. 1321 (1996), provides in part that "in any civil action with respect to prison conditions, a defendant * * * shall be entitled to the immediate termination of any prospective relief if the relief was approved or granted in the absence of a finding by the court that the relief is narrowly drawn, extends no further than necessary to correct the violation of the Federal right, and is the least intrusive means necessary to correct the violation of the Federal right." 18 U.S.C. § 3626(b)(2). Does this provision impermissibly "prescrib[e] a rule of decision without changing the underlying law"? See Plyler v. Moore, 100 F.3d 365 (4th Cir.1996)(rejecting this suggestion).

Page 370.   Add to Paragraph (3):

For further discussion of the contemporary significance of Klein, compare Sager, *Klein's First Principle: A Proposed Solution*, 86 Geo.L.J. ___ (forthcoming July 1998)(reading Klein broadly as barring Congress from enacting statutes the enforcement of which would require a court to speak and act against its own best judgment on matters of great consequence for the community) with Meltzer, *Courts, Congress, and Constitutional Remedies*, 86 Geo.L.J. ___ (forthcoming July 1998)(arguing that Sager reads Klein too broadly and that his view would unduly restrict Congress' capacity to confer statutory rights that extend beyond the reach of constitutional rights).

Page 370.   Add to Paragraph (4):

The Court again avoided significant constitutional questions about the scope of Congress' power in Felker v. Turpin, 116 S.Ct. 2333 (1996), by holding that a statute withdrawing its certiorari jurisdiction in certain habeas cases had not affected its authority to review the case before it upon a petition for an original writ of habeas corpus under 28 U.S.C. §§ 2241 and 2254. Title I of the Antiterrorism and Effective Death Penalty Act of 1996 ("Act"), Pub.L. 104–132, 110 Stat. 1217, provides that second or "successive" petitions for federal habeas corpus must be dismissed unless authorized (pursuant to stringent statutory criteria) by the court of appeals. In the provision challenged in Felker, the Act further establishes that decisions by the courts of appeals in this "gatekeeping" capacity (116 S.Ct. at 2337) "shall not be appealable and shall not be the subject of a petition for rehearing or for a writ of certiorari." Upon being denied authorization to file a successive petition by the court of appeals, Turpin filed a document styled "Petition for Writ of Habeas Corpus, for Appellate or Certiorari Review * * *, and for Stay of Execution" with the Supreme Court. After hearing the case on an expedited schedule at the end of the 1995 Term, the Court, per Rehnquist, C.J., held unanimously that the Act's preclusion of certiorari review of the court of appeals' "gatekeeping" decisions did not offend Article III, § 2.

Following the principle of statutory interpretation established by Ex parte Yerger, Fourth Edition p. 358 n. * * *, which disfavors implied repeals of Supreme Court appellate jurisdiction, the Court first found that the Act did not withdraw its authority to entertain original habeas petitions under § 2241. Because the Court thus retained jurisdiction to review the court of appeals' gatekeeping decisions in cases such as Felker, the claim that Congress had violated Article III, § 2, was "obviate[d]" (p. 2339). (The Court did not advert to issues that might be presented in a case in which the court of appeals authorized a successive petition; there would be no habeas corpus jurisdiction to review such a decision.)

The Court next held that the Act's stringent requirements for the authorization of successive petitions in the lower federal courts, whether or not they formally limited the Court's capacity to issue writs of habeas corpus under § 2241, should "inform our authority to grant such relief as well" (p. 2339). But even with its authority to grant the writ (as well as that of the lower federal courts) sharply circumscribed in cases involving successive petitions, the Court found no violation of the Suspension Clause. "Judgments about the proper scope of the writ" presumptively lie within Congress' domain, and the Act's limits on successive petitions were "well within" the permissible range (p. 2340). In the final section of its opinion, the Court dismissed the original petition for habeas corpus on the ground that the petitioner had failed to meet the Act's standards for authorization of successive petitions, "let alone the requirement" established by the Court's Rule 20.4(a) "that there be 'exceptional circumstances' justifying the issuance of" original writs (*id.*).

Justice Stevens, in a concurring opinion joined by Justices Souter and Breyer, described the Court's response "to the argument that the Act has deprived this Court of appellate jurisdiction in violation of Article III, § 2" as "incomplete" (p. 2341). Other potential devices for Supreme Court review included the All Writs Act, 28 U.S.C. § 1651, and the certification of questions for the Court's review under 28 U.S.C. § 1254(b). In a separate concurring opinion, Justice Souter, joined by Justices Stevens and Breyer, reserved the question that would be presented under Article III, § 2 if the courts of appeals "adopted divergent interpretations of the gatekeeper standard" and if it should turn out, in practice, that "statutory avenues other than certiorari for reviewing a gatekeeping determination were closed" (p. 2341–42).

The Court opinion in Felker does not expressly invoke the maxim that statutes should be construed to avoid difficult constitutional questions, but can the result be explained on any other basis? Consider Tushnet, *"The King of France with Forty Thousand Men": Felker v. Turpin and the Supreme Court's Deliberative Processes*, 1996 Sup.Ct.Rev. 163, 182: "Congress's attempt to speed up executions was rendered almost entirely toothless: Every prospective applicant denied leave to file a second petition by a court of appeals now can file an application for leave to file an original writ in the Supreme Court, instead of filing a petition for certiorari." Doesn't the force of this claim depend on the Court's standard for reviewing original writs?

For further discussion of the Felker case, including its ruling that the challenged statutory provision did not effect an unconstitutional "suspension" of the writ of habeas corpus, see pp. 123, 133 *infra*.

Page 372. Add to footnote 28:

Harrison, *The Power of Congress to Limit the Jurisdiction of Federal Courts and the Text of Article III*, 64 U.Chi.L.Rev. 203 (1997), offers a sustained textual critique of Amar's thesis; see also Velasco, *Congressional Control Over Federal Court Jurisdiction: A Defense of the Traditional View*, 46 Cath.U.L.Rev. 671, 763 (1997)(advancing a textual and historical defense of "the orthodox position that Congress possesses nearly plenary authority to regulate" federal jurisdiction). For a point-by-point response to Professor Harrison, see Pushaw, *Con-*

gressional Power Over Federal Court Jurisdiction: A Defense of the Neo–Federalist Interpretation of Article III, 1997 BYU L.Rev. 847.

Page 379.   Add to footnote 34:

On the pre-*Marbury* history, see Desan, *The Constitutional Commitment to Legislative Adjudication in the Early American Tradition*, 111 Harv.L.Rev. 1381 (1998)(arguing that in New York and certain other colonies in the early nineteenth century, adjudication of claims against the government regularly occurred in the legislature rather than in the courts, with legislators perceived as bound by obligations of "public faith").

Page 379.   Add to footnote 35:

See also Siegel, *Suing the President: Nonstatutory Review Revisited*, 97 Colum.L.Rev. 1612 (1997)(defending judicial power and responsibility to realize the constitutional ideal of a remedy for every legal wrong through the recognition of "nonstatutory" rights to sue for both constitutional and statutory violations).

Page 379.   Add at the end of Paragraph (2):

Issues about possible constitutional limits on congressional authority to preclude judicial review have recently arisen under two statutes involving immigration. The Antiterrorism and Effective Death Penalty Act of 1996 ("AEDPA"), Pub.L.No. 104–132, 110 Stat. 1214, provides: "Any final order of deportation against an alien who is deportable by reason of having committed a criminal offense [within an enumerated category] shall not be subject to review by any court." AEDPA, § 440(a). In addition, § 401(e) of the Act repeals 8 U.S.C. § 1105(a)(10) (1994), the statutory provision that had expressly provided habeas corpus review for aliens held in custody pursuant to a deportation order. Taken together, these provisions could be read to eliminate all judicial review of certain deportation orders. Nonetheless, to avoid the constitutional issues that a total preclusion of judicial review would present, most lower federal courts have distinguished between judicial "review", which the AEDPA clearly restricts and in some cases eliminates, and judicial inquiry on habeas corpus, which these courts have held continues to exist under other statutes, such as 28 U.S.C. § 2241. See, *e.g.*, Williams v. INS, 114 F.3d 82, 83–84 (5th Cir.1997); Fernandez v. INS, 113 F.3d 1151, 1155 (10th Cir.1997); Kolster v. INS, 101 F.3d 785, 790 (1st Cir.1996). Despite holding that federal habeas corpus jurisdiction continues to exist, many courts have ruled that the scope of habeas review must be very narrow in order to effectuate the purposes of the AEDPA. See, *e.g.*, Mbiya v. INS, 930 F.Supp. 609, 611 (N.D.Ga.1996)(limiting habeas review to claims asserting a "fundamental miscarriage of justice"). But see Mojica v. Reno, 970 F.Supp. 130, 163 (E.D.N.Y.1997)(rejecting *Mbiya* standard); Note, 110 Harv.L.Rev. 1850, 1859 (1997)(same).

The Illegal Immigration Reform and Immigrant Responsibility Act of 1996, Pub.L.No. 104–208, 110 Stat. 3009–546 (IIRIRA), goes several steps beyond the AEDPA in demarcating classes of cases not subject to judicial review. In addition, a provision codified at 8 U.S.C. § 1252(g) states that, "[e]xcept as provided in this section and notwithstanding any other provision of law, no court shall have jurisdiction to hear any cause or claim by or on behalf of any alien arising from the decision or action by the Attorney General to commence proceedings, adjudicate cases, or execute removal orders against any alien under this chapter." Some lower courts have held that this provision precludes all forms of judicial review, including review on habeas corpus, except as provided in the IIRIRA itself. See, *e.g.*, Auguste v. Attorney General, 118 F.3d 723, 725–26 (11th Cir.1997), modified on other grounds on rehearing by 140

F.3d 1373 (11th Cir.1998); Yang v. I.N.S., 109 F.3d 1185, 1195–96 (7th Cir.), cert. denied, 118 S.Ct. 624 (1997); see also Charan v. Schiltgen, 1997 WL 135938 (N.D.Cal.1997); Safarian v. Reno, 968 F.Supp. 1101, 1106 (E.D.La. 1997). Other courts, however, relying on Felker v. Turpin, p. 25, *supra*, have concluded that the IIRIRA does not bar habeas jurisdiction with sufficient specificity to overcome the presumption against complete statutory preclusion of judicial review; these courts have, accordingly, continued to uphold habeas corpus jurisdiction of narrow scope, as in the AEDPA context. See, *e.g.*, Goncalves v. Reno, ___ F.3d ___ (1st Cir.1998); Mojica v. Reno, 970 F.Supp. 130, 157–58 (E.D.N.Y.1997); Ozoanya v. Reno, 968 F.Supp. 1, 5–7 (D.D.C.1997).

Scholarly commentary has also argued that the IIRIRA, like the AEDPA, should be interpreted to permit judicial review of certain claims in order to avoid the difficult constitutional questions that a complete withdrawal of jurisdiction would present. See, *e.g.*, Benson, *Back to the Future: Congress Attacks the Right to Judicial Review of Immigration Proceedings,* 29 Conn. L.Rev. 1411 (1997)(discussing various narrowing constructions of the IIRIRA); Note, 111 Harv.L.Rev. 1578 (1998)(defending the courts' reliance on canons of statutory construction to avoid concluding that either the AEDPA or the IIRIRA wholly precludes judicial review). In the absence of a narrowing construction, other scholars have concluded that the preclusion of review effected by the IIRIRA and the AEDPA would violate the Constitution. See, *e.g.*, Neuman, *Habeas Corpus, Executive Detention, and the Removal of Aliens,* 98 Colum.L.Rev. 961 (1998)(arguing that the IIRIRA effects an unconstitutional suspension of the writ of habeas corpus); Fallon, *Applying the Suspension Clause to Immigration Cases,* 98 Colum.L.Rev. 1061 (1998)(questioning the force of Neuman's Suspension Clause claim but arguing alternatively that the IIRIRA's jurisdiction-stripping provisions violate Due Process and Article III insofar as they purport to withdraw all jurisdiction over constitutional claims and questions of law); Cole, *Jurisdiction and Liberty: Habeas Corpus and Due Process as Limits on Congress's Control of Federal Jurisdiction,* 86 Geo.L.J. ___ (forthcoming July 1998)(arguing that IIRIRA violates the Suspension and Due Process Clauses, which require judicial review of agency decisions when liberty is at stake); Meltzer, *Congress, Courts, and Constitutional Remedies,* 86 Geo. L.J. ___ (forthcoming July 1998)(questioning Cole's reliance on the Suspension and Due Process Clauses rather than on Article III and his assertion that the presence of a liberty interest, without more, always requires broad judicial review, but concluding that IIRIRA, if interpreted globally to preclude judicial review of issues of constitutional and statutory law, would be unconstitutional).

SECTION 2.   AUTHORITY TO ALLOCATE JUDICIAL POWER TO NON-ARTICLE III FEDERAL TRIBUNALS

Page 436.   Add to footnote 5:

See also Klein, *The Validity of the Public Rights Doctrine in Light of the Historical Rationale of the Seventh Amendment,* 21 Hast.Const.L.Q. 1013 (1994)(arguing that the public rights exception to the Seventh Amendment is unsound in light of the Amendment's historical foundations in distrust of government).

Page 438. Substitute the following text for the sentence following footnote 2:

Aggrieved parties then have a right of appeal to the court of appeals. 28 U.S.C. § 636(c)(3). (An alternative appellate mechanism, which permitted appeal of a magistrate judge's decision to the district court if all parties consented, was eliminated by the Federal Courts Improvement Act of 1996, 110 Stat. 3847.)

Page 440. Add to Paragraph 3(c):

In the absence of consent, may a district court delegate to a magistrate judge conclusive authority to grant or deny a "certificate of probable cause" necessary to appeal the denial of a habeas corpus petition? For a negative answer, see Jones v. Johnson, 134 F.3d 309, 310–11 (5th Cir.1998).

SECTION 3. FEDERAL AUTHORITY AND STATE COURT JURISDICTION

Page 452. Add to footnote 5:

See also Resnik, *History, Jurisdiction, and the Federal Courts: Changing Contexts, Selective Memories, and Limited Imagination*, 98 W.Va.L.Rev. 171, 255–63 (1995)(suggesting the desirability of a third category of "national courts"—to be established by either Congress or interstate compacts, and staffed primarily by state judges—to handle diversity litigation and other matters of interstate significance arising primarily under state law).

Page 452. Add a footnote 6a at the end of Paragraph 3(a):

6a. On the question of Congress' authority to regulate the procedures and remedial powers of state courts in cases outside the jurisdictional headings of Article III—as, for example, in mass tort cases—see Weinberg, *The Power of Congress Over Courts in Nonfederal Cases,* 1995 BYU L.Rev. 731; Steinman, *Reverse Removal,* 78 Iowa L.Rev. 1029 (1993).

Page 467. Add at the end of the first paragraph of Paragraph 4(b):

The Court reserved the question whether a state court could entertain an action for damages against a sitting President in Clinton v. Jones, 117 S.Ct. 1636 (1997). The Court found unanimously that the President enjoyed no immunity from a suit in federal court based on acts committed before he took office, but stated that "it is not necessary to consider or decide whether a comparable claim might succeed in a state tribunal. If this case were being heard in a state forum, * * * petitioner would presumably rely on federalism and comity concerns, as well as the interest in protecting federal officers from possible local prejudice that underlies the authority to remove certain cases brought against federal officials * * *. Whether those concerns would present a more compelling case for immunity is a question that is not before us" (p. 1642).

Page 476. Add to Paragraph 3(d):

The Court extended the principle of New York v. United States in Printz v. United States, 117 S.Ct. 2365 (1997). Dividing 5–4, the Court, in an opinion by Justice Scalia, held that Congress overstepped constitutional bounds by directing local law enforcement officials to conduct background checks on would-be purchasers of handguns. Just as the federal government may not order the states to legislate, neither may it "command the States' officers, or those of their political subdivisions, to administer or enforce a federal regulatory program" (p. 2384). The Court followed the New York decision in distinguishing Testa: the Supremacy Clause requires state courts to enforce federal law, but does not impose similar obligations on other state officials. FERC, the Court said, "merely imposed preconditions to continued state regulation of an otherwise pre-empted field, * * * and required state administrative agencies to apply federal law while acting in a judicial capacity, in accord with Testa" (p. 2381).

Justice O'Connor, concurring, noted that Congress remained free to enlist states in enforcing federal programs "on a contractual basis", as it does under a number of other statutes. Justice Stevens, joined by Justices Souter, Ginsburg, and Breyer, dissented.

Is the Court's distinction of FERC, based on the notion that the state administrative agency performed a judicial function (even though it was not a judicial agency and not all of its functions were clearly judicial), a persuasive one?

Page 478.   Add to footnote 10:

Cf. Pennsylvania Dep't of Corrections v. Yeskey, 118 S.Ct. 1952 (1998) (assuming that an "unmistakably clear" statement is needed to make the Americans with Disabilities Act applicable to state prisons, but finding the requirement satisfied).

Page 478.   Add a footnote 10a at the end of Paragraph (4):

10a.   The Long Range Plan for the Federal Courts, as approved by the Judicial Conference of the United States, appears at 166 F.R.D. 49 (1996). See also Carrington, *Federal Use of State Institutions in the Administration of Criminal Justice*, 49 S.M.U.L.Rev. 557, 560 (1996)(urging the prosecution of many federal criminal cases in state court and proposing "transfer payments" to compensate the states for increased costs and to "assure that the federal prosecutors would be given * * * cooperation * * * in the conduct of trials").

Page 488.   Add to Paragraph (4):

Compare Johnson v. Fankell, 117 S.Ct. 1800 (1997), which held that a *state* court, in a suit against a state official under § 1983, need not provide an interlocutory appeal from a trial judge's denial of a motion for summary judgment based on qualified immunity. Terming qualified immunity " 'an entitlement not to stand trial or face the other burdens of litigation,' "the Court had held in Behrens v. Pelletier, 516 U.S. 299, 306 (1996), p. 150 *infra*, that in a *federal* court action under § 1983, denials of summary judgment motions based on qualified immunity are immediately appealable "final judgments" under 28 U.S.C. § 1291. Nonetheless, the Court ruled unanimously in Johnson that Idaho procedural rules precluding interlocutory appeals were not preempted in § 1983 actions. "While it is true that the defense [of qualified immunity] has its source in a federal statute (§ 1983), the ultimate purpose of qualified immunity is to protect the state and its officials from the overenforcement of federal rights. The Idaho Supreme Court's application of the State's procedural rules [to bar an interlocutory appeal] in this context is thus less an interference with federal interests than a judgment about how best to balance the competing state interests of limiting interlocutory appeals and providing state officials with immediate review of the merits of their defense" (p. 1805).

The Court also found that the challenged Idaho rules were "not 'outcome determinative' in the sense" used in Felder, since "postponement of the appeal until after final judgment will not affect the ultimate outcome of the case" (pp. 1805–06). (How persuasive is that argument in view of the characterization of the purpose of immunity doctrine quoted above in the Behrens case?) The Court added that "Congress has mentioned nothing about interlocutory appeals in § 1983; rather, the right to an immediate appeal in the federal court system is found in § 1291, which obviously has no application to state courts" (p. 1806 n. 12).

Would the Court's reasoning in Johnson apply if the defendant had been a *federal* officer in a Bivens action who had failed (or for some reason not been able) to remove the case to a federal court?

CHAPTER V

REVIEW OF STATE COURT DECISIONS BY THE SUPREME COURT

SECTION 1. THE ESTABLISHMENT OF THE JURISDICTION

Page 493. Add to footnote 8:

Additional discussion of the pre–1914 cases is found in Hartnett, *Why is the Supreme Court of the United States Protecting State Judges from Popular Democracy?*, 75 Tex.L.Rev. 907, 915–32 (1997), which views the 1914 Act as a mechanism to counteract political pressure faced by state court judges rendering unpopular decisions, and proceeds to take the surprising view that that Act should not have been interpreted as giving state officials the same right as private litigants to seek Supreme Court review of unfavorable state court judgments.

Page 507. Add to Paragraph (2):

See also Graber, *The Passive–Aggressive Virtues: Cohens v. Virginia and the Problematic Establishment of Judicial Power*, 12 Const.Comm. 67 (1995)(suggesting that the Court's ruling on the merits in Cohens—that the state court conviction did not violate federal law—was implausible, but may have reflected the same strategy deployed in Marbury v. Madison: to make politically palatable a striking assertion of federal judicial power by deciding in the end against awarding relief).

SECTION 2. THE RELATION BETWEEN STATE AND FEDERAL LAW

SUBSECTION A: SUBSTANTIVE LAW

Page 540. Add after the third line of Paragraph (4):

See also Pennsylvania v. Labron, 116 S.Ct. 2485 (1996)(per curiam), where the Court ruled that a state court opinion—which rested on the state constitution, but also cited federal precedents in finding a search and seizure violation—did not contain "a 'plain statement' sufficient to tell us 'the federal cases

[were] being used only for the purpose of guidance, and d[id] not themselves compel the result that the court had reached' "(p. 2487, quoting Long). Justice Stevens' dissent (joined by Justice Ginsburg) objected that the state court had not rested "primarily" on federal law, nor was its holding "interwoven" with federal law; thus the Court's ruling "extends Michigan v. Long beyond its original scope" (p. 2490).

Page 561.   Add a new Paragraph (4)(c):

(c) A claim of deprivation of *life* without due process was at issue in Ohio Adult Parole Auth. v. Woodard, 118 S.Ct. 1244 (1998). There a death row inmate challenged the procedures followed by the parole authority, which holds hearings concerning clemency and makes recommendations to the Governor, who in turn possesses the power to grant clemency. The prisoner objected to (1) the notice given (three days before a pre-hearing interview and ten days before the hearing), (2) the refusal to permit him to testify or submit documentary evidence at the hearing, and (3) the refusal to guarantee that his counsel could participate. In ruling against him, Chief Justice Rehnquist (for a plurality of four) declared that Connecticut Board of Pardons v. Dumschat, 452 U.S. 458 (1981), which had held that non-capital prisoners have no entitlement to clemency and hence cannot challenge clemency procedures on due process grounds, was fully applicable to capital cases. He added that state law had not created any entitlement, noting that the Governor had unfettered discretion and that denial of clemency does not impose " 'atypical and significant hardship on the inmate' " but merely requires a prisoner to serve the sentence originally imposed (p. 1251, quoting Sandin v. Connor, 515 U.S. at 484 (Fourth Edition p. 560)). Finally, the plurality rejected the claim that clemency was an integral part of the state's criminal justice system, and hence that due process protections necessarily attached. Evitts v. Lucey, 469 U.S. 387 (1985), which had accepted a similar argument in upholding a right to effective assistance of counsel on a first appeal, was distinguishable, as clemency, unlike an appeal, does not enhance the reliability of adjudication, is entrusted to a different branch of government, and is discretionary and unstructured.

The other five Justices disputed the plurality's suggestion that no procedural protections are ever required in clemency proceedings. Four Justices, in an opinion by Justice O'Connor, concurred in the judgment rejecting the prisoner's claim; she determined that the state's procedures comported with whatever limits the Due Process Clause may impose on clemency proceedings. Justice Stevens' separate opinion would have remanded the case to permit the district court to determine the constitutional adequacy of the procedures.

———

SUBSECTION C: APPLICATION OF LAW TO FACT

———

Page 607.   Add to Paragraph (2):

In Ornelas v. United States, 517 U.S. 690 (1996), a federal prosecution, the Court ruled that a federal court of appeals should engage in de novo review of a district court's application, to the facts of the case, of the Fourth Amendment standards of "probable cause" and "reasonable suspicion". Chief Justice Rehnquist's opinion noted the fluidity of those two standards, which "acquire content only through application. Independent review is therefore necessary if appellate courts are to maintain control of, and to clarify the legal principles" (p. 697). Because the Court cited its earlier decisions in federal and state criminal prosecutions interchangeably, the ruling suggests that Supreme Court review of similar state court decisions should also be de novo.[1]

However, Ornelas does necessarily require *state* appellate courts to review state trial court decisions de novo. See Greene v. Georgia, 519 U.S. 145 (1996)(per curiam)(when reviewing state court convictions, state appellate courts need not follow the standards that govern review by federal habeas corpus courts); *cf.* Johnson v. Fankell, p. 30, *supra* (state appellate courts are not required to permit an interlocutory appeal in circumstances in which federal law permits such an appeal).

SECTION 3.   FINAL JUDGMENTS AND THE HIGHEST STATE COURT

Pages 637–38.   Add to Paragraph (4):

Pennsylvania v. Ritchie was all but overruled in Jefferson v. City of Tarrant, 118 S.Ct. 481 (1997). There a state trial court ruled that a state statute permitting punitive but not compensatory damages in wrongful death suits did not restrict recovery of compensatory damages from municipalities sued under 42 U.S.C. § 1983. The trial court then certified the issue to the Alabama Supreme Court, which accepted certification, held that the state statute did limit recovery of compensatory damages in claims under § 1983, and remanded for further proceedings. After granting plaintiff's petition for a writ of certiorari, the Supreme Court dismissed the writ as improvidently granted, holding that the Alabama Supreme Court's judgment was not final. Although that judgment, if not reversed, would effectively terminate the § 1983 claims (for state law would eliminate any compensatory damages, while § 1983 itself does not authorize recovery of punitive damages in suits against municipalities), Justice Ginsburg's majority opinion noted that on remand the case would proceed to trial on the merits of two state law tort claims. If the plaintiffs were to prevail on those claims but recover less than they might have under § 1983, or to lose on grounds not dispositive of their federal claims, they would be free to seek review of the federal issue. "Even if the Alabama Supreme Court adheres to its interlocutory ruling as 'law of the case,' that determination will in no way limit our ability to review the issue on final judgment" (p. 486, citing, *inter alia*, Fourth Edition p. 642).

---

1. Justice Scalia's lone dissent argued that district courts have the necessary expertise to apply Fourth Amendment standards; that they are closer than the courts of appeals to the facts and the underlying credibility determinations; that individual applications of those standards are so highly fact-bound as rarely to have much precedential value; and that the only purpose of the exclusionary rule—to deter the police—will not be compromised by deferential review.

Justice Stevens' dissent protested that the case was indistinguishable from Ritchie—a decision from which he had dissented but which, he argued, governed until squarely overruled (a course he advocated). In response, the Court acknowledged that Ritchie might be read to support the view that plaintiffs "need not present their federal questions to the state courts a second time before obtaining review in this Court" (p. 486). But without sharply distinguishing the present case, the Court noted that in Ritchie it had doubted "whether there would be any subsequent opportunity to raise the federal questions, and we were reluctant to put the [state agency] in the bind of either disclosing a confidential file or being held in contempt. Ritchie is an extraordinary case and we confine it to the precise circumstances the Court there confronted. We now clarify that Ritchie does not augur expansion of the exceptions stated in Cox Broadcasting Corp., and we reject any construction of Ritchie that would contradict this opinion" (p. 487).

CHAPTER VI

THE LAW APPLIED IN CIVIL ACTIONS IN THE DISTRICT COURTS

SECTION 1. PROCEDURE

Page 668.   Add a new footnote 17a at the end of Paragraph (7)(a):

17a.   For discussion of the question whether the 1988 amendments should be taken either as restricting the scope of the Court's rulemaking powers or as codifying the Court's existing view of that scope, see Note, 111 Harv.L.Rev. 2294 (1998).

Page 668.   Add to footnote 18:

Cf. The Federal Courts Improvement Act of 1996, Pub.L.No. 104–317, § 608, 110 Stat. 3847, which further extended the deadline for congressionally-authorized studies relating to judicial administration to June 30, 1997.

Though the CJRA has now expired, Congress decided to make permanent 28 U.S.C. § 476(a), which requires that the Director of the Administrative Office of the United States Courts prepare a semiannual report listing certain delayed matters on each judicial officer's docket. See Pub.L.No. 105–53 (1997).

For a persuasive argument that while the CJRA's sunset provisions are ambiguous as to whether all of the Act's *programs* have expired, a fair reading of the Act (considered in the light of Congress' failure to renew it) leads to the conclusion that they have, see Tobias, *The Judicial Conference Report and the Conclusion of Federal Civil Justice Reform*, 175 F.R.D. 351 (1998).

For retrospectives on the CJRA, see Symposium, *Evaluation of the Civil Justice Reform Act*, 49 Ala.L.Rev. 1 (1997); Cavanagh, *The Civil Justice Reform Act of 1990: Requiescat in Pace,* 173 F.R.D. 565 (1997). The RAND Institute conducted detailed studies of the effectiveness of various CJRA reforms. See RAND Institute, Just, Speedy, and Inexpensive? An Evaluation of Judicial Case Management Under the CJRA (1996).

Page 669.   Add to Paragraph (7)(b):

For further criticism of the "Balkanization" engendered by the CJRA, see Carrington, *A New Confederacy? Disunionism in the Federal Courts*, 45 Duke L.J. 929 (1996)(arguing, *inter alia*, that the District Court for the Eastern District of Texas' Cost and Delay Reduction Plan, a local rule that was formulated under the CJRA and that deals with fee-shifting and other matters, violates various statutory and constitutional limitations); Chemerinsky & Friedman, *The Fragmentation of Federal Rules*, 46 Mercer L.Rev. 757

(1995)(situating the CJRA in the context of such other areas of the "fragmentation" of rulemaking authority as discovery and alternative dispute resolution).

Complaints about fragmentation have also extended to the rules and practices of the federal appellate courts. For an especially harsh criticism, see Sisk, *The Balkanization of Appellate Justice: The Proliferation of Local Rules in the Federal Circuits,* 68 U.Colo.L.Rev. 1 (1997).

A subcommittee of the Judicial Conference recently recommended various reforms of the rulemaking process, some of which have already been implemented. See Subcommittee on Long Range Planning to the Committee on Rules of Practice, Procedure and Evidence of the Judicial Conference of the United States, *A Self-Study of Federal Judicial Rulemaking,* 168 F.R.D. 679 (1996).

Page 675. Add to Paragraph (2):

The relationship between the Enabling Act and an Act of Congress arose in an unusual context in Henderson v. United States, 517 U.S. 654 (1996). In a provision unchanged since its enactment in 1920, the Suits in Admiralty Act (SAA), 46 U.S.C.App. § 742, permits certain actions in admiralty to be brought against the United States and further states that the plaintiff shall "forthwith" serve a copy of the complaint on the U.S. Attorney and shall mail a copy to the Attorney General. Rule 4 of the Federal Rules of Civil Procedure, however, as enacted by Congress in 1982, 96 Stat. 2527, authorizes an extendable 120-day period for service of process in all cases. In an action under the SAA, service of process was effected in accordance with Rule 4 but (the Court assumed) too late to meet the SAA requirement that service be made "forthwith".

After rejecting the government's argument that the period provided by Rule 4 set only an outer limit for service of process (and could therefore be harmonized with the requirement of the SAA), the Court also rejected the argument that the SAA provision for service was a "jurisdictional" limitation on the government's waiver of sovereign immunity. The Court then went on to hold that the "procedural" provision of Rule 4 governing the time available for service superseded the shorter period specified in the SAA. Observing that the question did not arise squarely under the Enabling Act because Rule 4, as amended, had been enacted by Congress, the Court said: "As the United States acknowledges, * * * a Rule made law by Congress supersedes conflicting laws no less than a Rule this Court prescribes." 517 U.S. at 668.[a]

Note that, despite the argument made by Professor Clinton (Fourth Edition p. 675 n. 3)—that the Enabling Act's delegation of authority to override statutes is unconstitutional—all the Justices assumed that such authority could be exercised in areas not involving subject matter jurisdiction or statutory limitations on the waiver of sovereign immunity.

a. In concurring, Justices Scalia and Kennedy observed that while Congress could condition a waiver of sovereign immunity on strict compliance with such procedural provisions as the time for service, they agreed with the majority that the "forthwith" requirement of the SAA did not impose such a condition. Justice Thomas, joined by the Chief Justice and Justice O'Connor in dissent, argued that the SAA's requirement of service "forthwith" was a jurisdictional limitation on the waiver of sovereign immunity, and thus could not be changed by a rule of procedure promulgated under the Enabling Act and should not be regarded as having been impliedly repealed by Congress in 1982. (On the "sovereign immunity" aspect of the case, see p. 59, *infra.*)

SECTION 2. THE POWERS OF THE FEDERAL COURTS IN DEFINING PRIMARY LEGAL OBLIGATIONS THAT FALL WITHIN THE LEGISLATIVE COMPETENCE OF THE STATES

Page 684. Add to footnote 5:

See also Conant, The Constitution and the Economy: Objective Theory and Critical Commentary, Ch. 7 (1991)(arguing that Swift was a case arising under the interstate-international law merchant ("general commercial law") and not what was then viewed as "the common law").

Page 686. Add a new footnote 11a at the end of Paragraph (6):

11a. For the view that Swift was correctly decided, see Lessig, *Erie-Effects of Volume 110: An Essay on Context in Interpretive Theory*, 110 Harv.L.Rev. 1785, 1787–92 (1997). Professor Lessig argues that Swift comported with the widely-accepted understanding in 1842 that the common law emanated not from courts, but from external sources (in the case of Swift, from the commercial world). By the time of Erie, this understanding of the source of the common law had eroded, rendering obsolete attempts to distinguish between some abstract notion of the common law and the perceptions of the court applying it.

In contrast, Professors Goldsmith and Walt argue that scholars like Lessig have failed adequately to distinguish between the constitutional holding of Erie and prevailing views about legal positivism. Professors Goldsmith and Walt contend that Erie is best understood as grounded not in changes in the understanding of the common law since Swift, but as an exercise in constitutional interpretation. See Goldsmith & Walt, *Erie and the Irrelevance of Legal Positivism*, 84 Va.L.Rev. 673 (1998).

Page 693. Add a new footnote a at the end of the first paragraph in Paragraph (1):

a. For a discussion of the various techniques that a federal court sitting in diversity may employ in resolving unclear questions of state law, see Clark, *Ascertaining the Laws of the Several States: Positivism and Judicial Federalism after Erie*, 145 U.Pa.L.Rev. 1459 (1997). Professor Clark argues that certification of difficult questions to the state's highest court best respects the role of the state courts in a federal judicial system.

SECTION 3. ENFORCING STATE-CREATED OBLIGATIONS— EQUITABLE REMEDIES AND PROCEDURE

Page 713. Add to footnote 7:

For an analysis of the history of the Federal Arbitration Act that supports Justice Thomas' dissent in Allied–Bruce Terminix, see Comment, 1 Harv. Negotiation L.Rev. 169 (1996).

In Doctor's Associates, Inc. v. Casarotto, 517 U.S. 681 (1996), the Court once again reaffirmed Southland, and also limited the scope of the Volt decision (Fourth Edition p. 712, note 6). In Doctor's Associates, a state court, relying on Volt, had declined to enforce an arbitration clause because it did not comply with a state law requirement that such a clause must be "typed in underlined capital letters on the first page of the contract." With only Justice Thomas dissenting (on the ground that the Federal Arbitration Act (FAA) does not apply in the state courts), the majority held this state-law provision preempted by § 2 of the Federal Act. Volt was distinguished on the ground that the state rule in that case "determined only the efficient order of proceedings; it did not affect the enforceability of the arbitration clause itself" and thus would not frustrate the purposes of the FAA (p. 688).

For a stinging critique of the line of cases of which Doctor's Associates is the most recent, see Carrington & Haagen, *Contract and Jurisdiction*, 1996 Sup.Ct.Rev. 331. The authors fault the decisions on a number of grounds; the most relevant to this chapter is that "the Court has completely federalized a body of law that was until recently regarded as an appropriate subject for the exercise of state sovereignty" (p. 332).

Page 713.   Add a new footnote 8a at the end of Paragraph (4):

8a. For discussion of the role of state law in determining the scope of discretion to entertain a declaratory judgment action in a diversity case, see p. 111, *infra*.

Page 719.   Add a new Paragraph (4a):

(4a) *The Gasperini Decision.* Difficult questions of the judge-jury relationship in diversity suits were at issue in Gasperini v. Center for Humanities, Inc., 116 S.Ct. 2211 (1996), a case involving the standard for district and appellate court review of the amount of a jury award. Under a New York law enacted in 1986 (N.Y. Civ. Prac. Law & Rules § 5501(c)), appellate courts are empowered to review the size of a jury verdict and to order a new trial when the award "deviates materially from what would be reasonable compensation"—a standard that the Supreme Court recognized as inviting more rigorous judicial review of awards than the prior "shock the conscience" test followed in both state and federal courts in New York. In a diversity action brought in a New York federal court for the loss of certain slide transparencies, the jury awarded the plaintiff $450,000; the district court (without comment) denied the defendant's motion to set aside the verdict as excessive; and the Second Circuit, after holding that § 5501(c) governed the controversy, reversed and remanded the case for a new trial unless the plaintiff agreed to a reduced award of $100,000.

On certiorari, the Supreme Court first considered whether New York law should apply under the Erie doctrine, and held that it should. Writing for the majority, Justice Ginsburg ruled that if New York had a "statutory cap" on damage awards, that cap would clearly control in a diversity case. She then stated that § 5501 did not differ from such a cap in its substantive objective (of controlling jury awards) but only in its use of a procedural technique to be applied on a case-by-case basis. Given the aims of Erie, its doctrine "precludes a recovery in federal court significantly larger than the recovery that would have been tolerated in state court" (p. 2214).

The Court then addressed the question whether the federal interest in the allocation of authority between judge and jury, especially as reflected in the Seventh Amendment, served in any way to undercut or modify the obligation to follow state law. The Court noted that, under New York precedent, § 5501 governed the standard to be applied by trial judges as well by appellate courts, and held that the application of that standard by a federal trial judge would not run afoul of the Seventh Amendment. In light of the "re-examination clause" of that Amendment, however, appellate review, while not entirely precluded, was limited to the question whether the district court's determination was an abuse of discretion. The Court concluded that this resolution accommodated both the interests served by the Erie doctrine and those reflected in the

Seventh Amendment, and ordered the case returned to the district court for its review of the award under the New York standard.[7]

Justice Scalia, joined by the Chief Justice and Justice Thomas, disagreed with the majority at every critical point. The bulk of his opinion was devoted to the argument that, under the Seventh Amendment, appellate courts may not review (even for abuse of discretion) district court refusals to set aside civil jury awards as contrary to the weight of the evidence. He went on to argue that the decision was also a major departure from precedent in holding that a state's allocation of authority between judges and juries must be followed by federal courts in diversity cases. Quoting Byrd, Justice Scalia contended that "changing the standard by which trial judges review jury verdicts does disrupt the federal system, and is plainly inconsistent with 'the strong federal policy against allowing state rules to disrupt the judge-jury relationship in federal court' "(p. 2237). The analogy to a statutory cap on damages was misleading because of the difference "between a rule of law * * * [that] would ordinarily be imposed upon the jury in the trial court's instructions, and a rule of review, which simply determines how closely the jury verdict will be scrutinized for compliance with the instructions" (p. 2238). Under the Court's holding, he warned, even a state rule that allowed a defendant to select the lesser of two jury awards would have to be followed in federal court.

How significant is the Gasperini decision with respect to the largely unresolved questions of the governing standards in diversity cases for directed verdicts, new trials based on the weight of the evidence, and appellate review of jury determinations? Assuming that the Seventh Amendment itself does not bar application of the New York standard in a federal trial court, does the Supreme Court's decision undercut the effort in Byrd to preserve the federal system as "an independent system for administering justice" (356 U.S. at 537)? Does the Court embrace the analysis in Hanna that is discussed in Fourth Edition pp. 727–28, Paragraph (2)? Or even the outcome-determinative analysis of York? (For affirmative answers to the last question, see *The Supreme Court, 1995 Term—Leading Cases*, 110 Harv.L.Rev. 135, 256, 265–66 (1996); Floyd, *Erie Awry: A Comment on Gasperini v. Center for Humanities , Inc.*, 1997 BYU L.Rev. 267, 303–304. Professor Floyd's analysis also criticizes other aspects of the decision.) Does the Byrd rationale play a larger role in the Court's holding as to the scope of *appellate* review?

For an analysis of Gasperini in the context of a comprehensive discussion of the Erie doctrine, see Rowe, *Not Bad for Government Work: Does Anyone Else Think the Supreme Court Is Doing A Halfway Decent Job in Its Erie–Hanna Jurisprudence?*, 73 Notre Dame L.Rev. 963 (1998). Professor Rowe, taking his academic colleagues to task for their "hypercritical[]" approach to the Supreme Court's efforts, concludes that "in addition to being reasonably sensitive to federalist concerns and the nuances of a somewhat complex area," the Court's doctrine has been "fairly comprehensible and workable in its broad outlines" and "remarkably stable * * * over three decades" (pp. 1014–15). As

7. The Court also rejected the argument that the result reached with respect to the standard to be applied by the trial court was in conflict with Fed.R.Civ.P. 59. See p. 41, *infra*.

Justice Stevens, dissenting in part, agreed with the Court's Erie analysis, but would have affirmed the judgment of the court of appeals on the grounds that (a) the Seventh Amendment did not preclude an appellate court from applying the New York standard, and (b) the Second Circuit had properly done so.

for the Gasperini decision, it has left the "basic framework for analysis * * * very much intact", although it does suggest a greater willingness to construe potentially applicable Federal Rules to avoid "direct conflicts" with state policies and to "preserve Byrd interest analysis in a subset of cases involving judge-made federal procedural rules" (p. 1014).

Page 728.   Add to footnote 2:

Especially thorny problems arise when federal courts must decide whether to apply federal or state ethical rules to the conduct of lawyers in federal cases—problems compounded by the widely varied approaches of the federal courts to the question of whether to adopt local rules governing this subject (and if so, in what form), as well as by the relative inaccessibility of those rules. For an exhaustive survey and excellent analysis, see Mullenix, *Multiforum Federal Practice: Ethics and Erie*, 9 Geo.J. Legal Ethics 89 (1995)(arguing for the formulation of uniform federal standards of professional responsibility and for the separation of the courts' disciplinary and dispute-resolution functions).

Page 730.   Add to Paragraph (4):

In Gasperini v. Center for Humanities, Inc., more fully discussed at p. 24, *supra,* Justice Scalia ended his dissent by contending that the result reached (with respect to the standard to be applied by the district court) was squarely in conflict with Fed.R.Civ.P. 59, which allows a new trial "for any of the reasons for which new trials have heretofore been granted in actions at law in the courts of the United States". That provision, in his view, clearly imposed a federal standard. The majority (quoting the statement in the Fourth Edition p. 729 that the Court has "continued since Hanna to, interpret the federal rules to avoid conflict with important state regulatory policies") responded that Rule 59 did not preclude reference to the only appropriate source of law for determining whether damages are excessive—the state law governing the cause of action. (116 S.Ct. at 2224 n. 22). And Justice Stevens added that Rule 59 "hardly constitutes a command that federal courts must always substitute federal limits on the size of judgments for those set by the several States in cases founded upon state law causes of action. Even at the time of [Rule 59's] adoption, federal courts were bound to apply state statutory law in such cases" (p. 2226, note 1).

Does this dispute between majority and dissent echo the dispute (discussed above) over the question whether the relevant standard of review of a jury award is analogous for Erie purposes to the applicability of a state imposed cap on the size of an award?

Page 731.   Add to footnote 9:

Some circuits have held that state rules of evidence can control even beyond matters of privilege. See, *e.g.*, Hottle v. Beech Aircraft Corp., 47 F.3d 106 (4th Cir.1995)(holding that a state rule barring the introduction of evidence of a party's internal practices to prove negligence was sufficiently bound up with substantive state policy to require its application in federal court).

SECTION 4.   THE EFFECT OF STATE LAW (AND OF PRIVATE AGREEMENT) ON THE EXERCISE OF FEDERAL JURISDICTION

Page 739.   Add a new footnote 3a at the end of Paragraph (4):

3a.   In City of Chicago v. International College of Surgeons, 118 S.Ct. 523 (1997), the Supreme Court held that the college's state court suit contesting local administrative action on federal constitutional grounds could be removed in its entirety to federal court, notwithstanding the fact that the complaint also contained state law claims requiring on-the-record review of the administrative proceedings.

Justice O'Connor, writing for a majority of seven, denied that Stude or other decisions suggested that federal district courts could never review state administrative action. Rather, to the extent that these decisions "might be read to establish limits on the scope of federal jurisdiction [they] address only whether a cause of action for judicial review of a state administrative decision is within the district court's original jurisdiction under the diversity statute" (p. 532). Given the existence of original jurisdiction over the federal claim in the case, then, the supplemental jurisdiction statute (28 U.S.C. § 1367) allowed the district court to take jurisdiction over related state law claims as to which original jurisdiction might be lacking (although the district court, in its discretion, might decide not to exercise such jurisdiction). (For further discussion of the use of § 1367 in this case, see p. 54, *infra*.)

Justice Ginsburg, joined in dissent by Justice Stevens, denied that the supplemental jurisdiction statute was designed to "embrace the category of [state law] appellate business at issue here" (p. 535).

CHAPTER VII

FEDERAL COMMON LAW

SECTION 1. DEFINING PRIMARY OBLIGATIONS

Page 754. Add a new footnote 1a at the end of Paragraph (2):

1a. In Murphy v. FDIC, 61 F.3d 34 (D.C.Cir.1995), the court ruled that D'Oench Duhme's specific holding had been statutorily displaced by an enactment that expressly protects the FDIC in specified circumstances. The ruling rested heavily on the Supreme Court's refusal, in O'Melveny & Myers v. FDIC, 512 U.S. 79 (1994), Fourth Edition p. 765 note 6, to supplement a detailed statutory scheme with a federal common law rule. But a number of courts have refused to follow Murphy, treating the question whether a federal statutory scheme displaces a *pre-existing* federal common law rule, like that of D'Oench Duhme, differently from the question whether such a scheme precludes supplementation by a *new* federal common law rule, as in O'Melveny. See, *e.g.*, Young v. FDIC, 103 F.3d 1180, 1188–89 (4th Cir.1997) & cases cited.

Pages 757–58. Add to footnote 6:

Professor Clark, in *Federal Common Law: A Structural Reinterpretation*, 144 U.Pa.L.Rev. 1245 (1996), offers a view that bears at least a kinship with that of Professor Hill. Clark suggests that much federal common law concerns matters that the Constitution's structure places beyond state legislative competence, and hence does not raise federalism concerns. In such areas, judge-made law is justifiable as long as it furthers a basic aspect of the constitutional scheme—such as equality of right between the states (in interstate disputes) or protection of the constitutional prerogatives of the federal political branches (in foreign relations matters). He argues that in only some admiralty cases (prize cases and certain private maritime claims) do the states lack legislative competence so as to permit federal lawmaking, and suggests, more tentatively, that in cases, like Clearfield, involving federal proprietary interests, common law rules cannot be justified because they do not further basic aspects of the constitutional scheme.

Page 765. Add to Paragraph (5):

In Atherton v. FDIC, 117 S.Ct. 666 (1997), the Resolution Trust Company brought suit, as receiver of a failed bank, against bank officers and directors for misconduct. The Court unanimously ruled that absent any federal statutory regulation, state law rather than federal common law would provide the applicable rules of decision. Unlike the Kimbell Foods opinion, here the Court did not suggest that federal common law governs the matter and then proceed to the question whether state law should be incorporated as the federal rule of decision; instead, Justice Breyer's opinion asked simply whether there is a need to displace state law with a federal rule of decision. (Compare the Fourth Edition p. 768 note 10.) On the question of need, the Court's discussion echoed Kimbell Foods, and stressed that " 'a significant conflict between some federal policy or interest and the use of state law ... must first be specifically shown' "before federal common law is fashioned (p. 670, quoting Wallis v. Pan American Petroleum Corp., 384 U.S. 63, 68 (1966), Fourth Edition p. 781). The

Court proceeded to rule that a federal statute providing that directors or officers may be liable for gross negligence did not preclude liability under state law for less culpable conduct (*e.g.*, simple negligence).

Page 768. Add to Paragraph (7)(d):

When questions of state law arise in federal question actions, courts have followed different approaches in determining which state's law applies. Some follow Klaxon Co. v. Stentor Elec. Mfg. Co., Fourth Edition p. 695, and apply the choice-of-law rules of the forum state; others have fashioned federal common law to govern choice of law. See Recent Case, 109 Harv.L.Rev. 1156 (1996).

Page 784. Add a new Paragraph (7):

(7) *Federally Protected Interests in Privately–Created Property Rights.* A case similar to those in Paragraph (6) of this Note (see Fourth Edition pp. 783–84), but in which federal law, rather than creating a proprietary interest, regulates its incidents once it has been privately created, is Boggs v. Boggs, 117 S.Ct. 1754 (1997). There, a decedent purported to bequeath to her two sons her community property interest in her husband's undistributed pension plan benefits. The husband subsequently remarried, and upon his death his second wife claimed his pension benefits, contending that the purported transfer by the first wife was invalid under ERISA. By a 5–4 vote, the Supreme Court agreed.

Justice Kennedy's opinion for the Court framed the question as one of preemption. He deemed it unnecessary to rely on ERISA's express preemption clause, instead ruling that application of state community property law to uphold the claim of the two sons would conflict with federal purposes. As to one aspect of the dispute—competing claims to the husband's annuity—the Court relied on a section of ERISA providing that (absent a waiver from the participant's spouse) a pension payable to a married participant must be in the form of a "joint and survivor annuity," under which a surviving spouse is entitled to at least 50% of the amount payable during the couple's joint lives. Concluding that this provision sought to ensure a steady income stream to surviving spouses, the Court ruled that federal policy would be impaired if the first wife's purported bequest of community property rights were permitted to diminish the second wife's pension benefits.

Relying on two other ERISA provisions, the Court also found a conflict between federal statutory purposes and the sons' claims respecting other retirement-related benefits. The first provision, which recognizes community property interests in certain domestic relations orders, was read as impliedly precluding other community property claims like those at issue in the instant dispute. The second provision, which precludes assignment or alienation of pension plan benefits, was interpreted as precluding the first wife's purported transfer. "Community property laws have, in the past, been pre-empted in order to ensure implementation of a federal statutory scheme. Free v. Bland is of particular relevance here" (p. 1766).[1]

---

1. Justice Breyer's dissent (joined in full by Justice O'Connor and in part by the Chief Justice and Justice Ginsburg) stressed that the two sons had not sued the pension fund, but rather had sought an accounting that would occur only after the death of their father. Justice Breyer noted that although the sons' claim for an accounting might be

Page 800. Add to footnote 9:

The approach of Mobil Oil v. Higginbotham was re-affirmed and extended in Zicherman v. Korean Air Lines, 116 S.Ct. 629 (1996) and Dooley v. Korean Air Lines Co., 118 S.Ct. 1890 (1998). In both cases, the Court unanimously refused to authorize a survival action under general maritime law for non-pecuniary losses, viewing the Death on the High Seas Act (which authorizes recovery only of pecuniary losses) as the exclusive source of recovery for death on the high seas.

In Yamaha Motor Corp., U.S.A. v. Calhoun, 516 U.S. 199 (1996), a suit on behalf of a 12 year-old girl killed in a jet-ski accident while on vacation in Puerto Rico, the Court ruled unanimously that the federal action recognized in Moragne did not oust all state wrongful death remedies. The refusal in Offshore Logistics to permit supplemental state law remedies was based on Congress' having prescribed a comprehensive remedy for seamen. Here, by contrast, there was no comprehensive remedy for non-seafarers (persons, like the decedent, protected neither as seamen under the Jones Act nor as longshore workers under the Longshore and Harbor Workers' Compensation Act). The only relevant congressional disposition, § 7 of the Death on the High Seas Act, 46 U.S.C.App. § 767, states: "The provisions of any State statute giving or regulating rights of action or remedies for death shall not be affected by this chapter". The Court found that variations in supplemental state remedies posed no threat to federal maritime policy.

For critical discussion, see Friedell, *Searching for a Compass: Federal and State Law Making Authority in Admiralty*, 57 La.L.Rev. 825 (1997).

Page 802. Add to Paragraph (2):

Not infrequently, federal legislation includes express preemption clauses. These clauses can pose difficult interpretive issues, including whether there should be implied preemption of state law apart from the scope of the preemption clause. See, *e.g.,* Boggs v. Boggs, p. 44, *supra,* where the Court displaced state law in reliance on implied preemption principles without deciding the reach of ERISA's express preemption clause. See generally Stabile, *Preemption of State Law by Federal Law: A Task for Congress or the Courts?*, 40 Vill.L.Rev. 1 (1995), arguing forcefully that congressional efforts to specify preemptive effect tend to serve statutory purposes poorly while often displacing state law inappropriately. Stabile advocates leaving the reach of preemption to the courts, which would decide particular questions in light of statutory purposes rather than seeking to rest upon express or implied congressional intention to preempt.

Page 805. Add to Paragraph (5):

For criticism of the consensus view that in complex litigation ordinary choice-of-law practices should be replaced by adoption of a single rule of decision, see Kramer, *Choice of Law in Complex Litigation*, 71 N.Y.U.L.Rev. 547 (1996). Kramer argues, *inter alia,* that choice of law is not a mere procedural doctrine, but is "as substantive as it gets" (p. 569), and thus that choice of law principles applicable in individual litigation should not be discarded when consolidation occurs.

based on the first wife's community property interest, Louisiana law might permit them to collect only nonpension community assets of equivalent value to the pension benefits— thus leaving intact the second wife's annuity. And ERISA's anti-alienation provision, Justice Breyer argued, sought "to prevent plan beneficiaries from prematurely divesting themselves of the funds they will need for retirement, not to prevent application of the property laws that define the legal interest in those funds" (p. 1772).

Pages 807–10.   Add to Paragraphs (2)–(5):

Should customary international law (CIL)—which is found not in treaties but rather in the consistent practice of nations, followed from a sense of legal obligation—be viewed by American courts seeking to determine its content as a kind of federal common law? Most courts and scholars addressing that question have thought so, and have found that CIL is presumptively incorporated into the legal system and given effect as federal law. That "modern position" is powerfully challenged, however, in Bradley & Goldsmith, *Customary International Law as Federal Common Law: A Critique of the Modern Position*, 110 Harv.L.Rev. 815 (1997). They argue, *inter alia*, that treating CIL as federal common law is inconsistent with Erie, noting particularly Erie's positivist insistence that law be associated with a particular sovereign and its realist recognition that judicial decision-making is a form of lawmaking. They also suggest that the modern position departs from constitutional norms of democratic self-governance—a concern magnified as CIL has evolved to embrace a nation's relations not only with other nations but also with its citizens (as, for example, with human rights law), and thus to be more likely to conflict with domestic law.

The status of CIL has important implications for both state and federal courts. Rejection of the modern position would imply that federal courts may entertain suits under the Alien Tort Statute, 28 U.S.C. § 1350, only insofar as that statute, or the Torture Victim Protection Act, see Fourth Edition p. 810, creates a federal cause of action or authorizes federal courts to fashion federal common law. As for state courts, rejection of the modern position would free them from what might otherwise be posited as an obligation under the Supremacy Clause to follow CIL—as, for example, if a criminal defendant were to contend that the state's otherwise constitutional death penalty violates CIL.

Bradley & Goldsmith's position is vigorously criticized in Koh, *Is International Law Really State Law?*, 111 Harv.L.Rev. 1824 (1998); Neuman, *Sense and Nonsense About Customary International Law: A Response to Professors Bradley and Goldsmith*, 66 Ford.L.Rev. 371 (1997); Stephens, *The Law of Our Land: Customary International Law as Federal Law After Erie*, 66 *id.* 393; Goodman & Jinks, *Filartaga's Firm Footing: International Human Rights and Federal Common Law*, 66 *id.* 463. Bradley & Goldsmith defend themselves in *The Current Illegitimacy of International Human Rights Litigation*, 66 *id.* 319, and in *Federal Courts and the Incorporation of International Law*, 111 Harv. L.Rev. 2260 (1998).

Would rejection of the broad claim that CIL is a form of federal common law leave room for a narrower federal common law of foreign relations—one shaped by American federal interests and looking to CIL only as one possible source of an appropriate federal rule of decision? That question is addressed in Goldsmith, *Federal Courts, Foreign Affairs, and Federalism*, 83 Va.L.Rev. 1617 (1997), which challenges the premise that foreign affairs constitute an inherently federal enclave in which federal common lawmaking is appropriate. Professor Goldsmith contends, *inter alia*, that the Sabbatino decision represented a sharp break with nearly 200 years of practice. And because any distinction between foreign and domestic matters is increasingly problematic in the face of growing global integration, he argues that permitting the federal judiciary (in which the interests of states are not represented) to fashion common law threatens to invade the states' traditional domains. He also argues that the affirmative case for such lawmaking is commonly exaggerated: Congress and the President have adequate means to monitor and, when necessary, to override state practices affecting foreign relations, while the federal courts lack the capacity to determine when international interests call for preempting state law.

What does the last argument suggest about the capacity (quite apart from the inclination) of state courts—or even state legislatures—to shape state law in a fashion conducive to harmonious foreign relations? Should state courts be free, for example, to deny foreign governments, their heads of state, or their diplomats immunity from suit—except to the extent that a federal enactment confers such immunity? What should a federal (or state) court do when the federal executive branch urges that national interests call for a federal common law rule? Does Professor Goldsmith convince you that Sabbatino was wrong?

Page 810.   Add to footnote 6:

Commentators continue to debate the proper interpretation of § 1350. Compare Sweeney, *A Tort Only in Violation of the Law of Nations*, 18 Hast.Int'l & Comp.L.Rev. 445 (1995)(reading the statutory phrase "tort only", against the background of prize law, as reaching only cases in which the legality of the capture was not in issue and suit was only for damages for a wrong related to the capture—thereby falling outside the admiralty jurisdiction), with Dodge, *The Historical Origins of the Alien Tort Statute: A Response to the "Originalists"*, 19 *id.* 221 (1996)(defending Filartiga's interpretation of § 1350 as a dynamic provision providing a federal remedy for all torts in violation of the law of nations).

SECTION 2.   ENFORCING PRIMARY OBLIGATIONS

SUBSECTION A: CIVIL ACTIONS BY THE FEDERAL GOVERNMENT

Page 818.   Add to Paragraph (4):

For a thorough argument that the Executive Branch needs no statutory authority to bring suit to enforce the Fourteenth Amendment, see Yackle, *A Worthy Champion for Fourteenth Amendment Rights: The United States in Parens Patriae*, 92 Nw.U.L.Rev. 111 (1997). Challenging the reasoning of the contrary decisions, Yackle argues, *inter alia*, that (a) the executive branch does have standing to sue, in part by analogy to a state's capacity to bring *parens patriae* actions to vindicate rights of its citizens, and (b) rather than requiring a clear statement to permit suit, courts should require a clear statement to foreclose executive action to vindicate constitutional rights.

A far narrower view is taken in Monaghan, *The Protective Power of the Presidency*, 93 Colum.L.Rev. 1 (1993), which advocates recognition of a general presidential power "to preserve, protect, and defend the personnel, property and instrumentalities of the national government" that encompasses a limited right to initiate protective litigation (p. 61).[1] Efforts by the President (acting without statutory authorization) to enforce Fourteenth Amendment rights against the states fall outside the scope of this protective power, and thus Monaghan endorses the lower court holdings denying authority to bring such

---

1.   Monaghan notes but does not answer the question whether in a genuine emergency the President possesses a broader authority to act without statutory authorization.

actions. Moreover, Monaghan asserts that proper invocation of the protective power ordinarily depends upon there being a pre-existing prohibition against the conduct in question. Thus, while In re Debs, Fourth Edition p. 815, might otherwise exemplify the protective power, he argues that the Court there erred in treating the strike as violative of federal law. He similarly criticizes the government's position in New York Times v. United States, Fourth Edition p. 817, on the ground that "no source outside the President's will * * * was cited as rendering the decision to publish illegal" (p. 72).

Subsection B: Private Civil Actions

Page 828.   Add to Paragraph (8)(e):

For further discussion of whether courts should formulate federal rules of decision to protect against "overenforcement" of § 1983, in situations in which a state has power (which it has chosen not to exercise) to confer such protection under its own law, see Johnson v. Fankell, p. 30, *supra*.

Page 829.   Add to Paragraph (10):

Mikva & Pfander, *On the Meaning of Congressional Silence: Using Federal Common Law to Fill the Gap in Congress's Residual Statute of Limitations*, 107 Yale L.J. 393 (1997), advocate a presumption that § 1658's four-year period governs federal actions even when brought under statutes enacted before December 1, 1990 (when § 1658 took effect). Congress' failure to make § 1658 expressly applicable to actions under earlier enactments stemmed, they suggest, from concern about disrupting settled expectations—and thereby attracting opposition from interest groups. However, the authors view § 1658 as a congressional acknowledgment that borrowing state law was no longer a sensible approach. They contend, furthermore, that the ordinary reasons for deferring to state law—respecting traditional areas of state control and facilitating intrastate uniformity—have little force as to limitations periods; the rights of action are federal, and the variety of possible state law analogies makes intrastate uniformity of little importance. As support for the appropriateness of federal common lawmaking that borrows a provision of an otherwise inapplicable statute, they cite Moragne v. State Marine Lines, Inc., Fourth Edition p. 791. Thus, they conclude that the four-year period should govern suits under pre–1990 enactments unless application of that period would disrupt settled expectations—which are more likely to exist where precedent (1) has already selected a period from *federal* law, or (2) looks to borrowing state law periods longer than four years.

Page 841.   Add to Paragraph (2):

In Morse v. Republican Party of Virginia, 517 U.S. 186 (1996), five Justices found an implied right of action under § 10 of the Voting Rights Act. The suit challenged the Republican Party of Virginia's imposition of a registration fee for delegates to a nominating convention for the party's candidate for the U.S. Senate. Plaintiffs claimed, *inter alia*, that the fee constituted a poll tax prohibited by § 10 of the Act. Justice Stevens, joined by Justice Ginsburg, reasoned: "While [the district court's refusal to imply a private action] might have been correct if the Voting Rights Act had been enacted recently, it fails to give effect to our cases holding that our evaluation of congressional action 'must take into account its contemporary legal context' "(pp. 230–21, quoting Cannon, and citing Merrill Lynch, Pierce, Fenner & Smith, Fourth Edition p. 841). He also stressed two factors the Court had noted when ruling, in Allen v. State Bd. of Elections, 393 U.S. 544 (1969), that private parties may enforce the pre-clearance requirements of § 5 of the Act: first, achievement of the Act's goals could be hampered were enforcement authority limited to the Attorney General; and second, the Attorney General, in whom the expressly vested enforcement authority, urged the Court to uphold a private right of action. Justice Stevens added that Congress had ratified the Court's interpretation of § 5, and that the Court had also entertained private suits to enforce § 2 of the Act (a result supported by the legislative history of amendments to the Act).

Justice Breyer (joined by Justices O'Connor and Souter), concurring in the judgment, wrote separately on the substantive issue whether political parties were subject to regulation under the Act, but agreed that Congress intended to create a private right of action under § 10.

Justice Thomas' dissent (joined by the Chief Justice and Justices Scalia and Kennedy) argued that while § 5 of the Act creates substantive rights that benefit voters, § 10 does not do so; rather than banning poll taxes, it merely authorizes the Attorney General to sue to challenge poll taxes that violate the Constitution. "Thus, § 10 confers no rights upon individuals and its remedial scheme is limited to suit by the Attorney General" (p. 288). Justice Thomas continued: "I am unpersuaded by the maxim that Congress is presumed to legislate against the backdrop of our 'implied cause of action' jurisprudence. That maxim is relevant to but one of the three [sic] factors that were established for determining the existence of private rights of action in Cort v. Ash". The ultimate inquiry " 'is whether Congress intended to create the private remedy asserted' "(quoting Transamerica Mortgage Advisors, Inc., Fourth Edition p. 845). That inquiry begins with the statutory language, and § 10's express authorization only of suits by the Attorney General "precludes the inference that Congress intended the availability of implied causes of action under that section" (*id.*).

Page 842. Add to footnote 10:

See also Pierce, *Agency Authority to Define the Scope of Private Rights of Action*, 48 Admin.L.Rev. 1 (1996)(arguing that agencies should be held to have power to issue rules specifying the scope of private rights of action).

Page 845. Add to Paragraph (6):

The implied right of action for Title IX violations recognized in Cannon was given a narrow scope in Gebser v. Lago Vista Ind. School Dist., 118 S.Ct. 1989 (1998)(5–4), a case raising the question whether or in what circumstances a school district that receives federal funds (and hence is subject to Title IX) is liable for damages when one of its employees (a high school teacher) sexually harasses a student.

The Court (per O'Connor, J.) began by stressing that it was dealing with a right of action not expressly conferred by statute but rather judicially implied, giving it "a measure of latitude to shape a sensible remedial scheme that best comports with the statute" (p. 1996). In exercising that latitude, the Court noted that Title IX (unlike, for example, Title VII) does not expressly make an entity liable for the acts of its agents, and that in 1972, when Title IX was enacted, the principal civil rights statutes were limited to provision of injunctive or equitable relief. The Court also relied heavily on the fact that a federal agency may not invoke Title IX's express remedy—a funding cut-off—until it has first advised the "appropriate person" of the entity's failure to comply and has determined that voluntary compliance cannot be secured. "It would be unsound, we think, for a statute's express system of enforcement to require notice to the recipient and an opportunity to come into voluntary compliance while a judicially implied system of enforcement permits substantive liability without regard to the recipient's knowledge or its corrective actions upon receiving notice" (p. 1999) The foregoing considerations led the majority to announce the rule that in cases not involving an official policy of the recipient, "a damages remedy will not lie under Title IX unless an official who at a minimum has authority to address the alleged discrimination and to institute corrective measures on the recipient's behalf has actual knowledge of discrimination in the recipient's programs and fails adequately to respond" (*id.*). The Court added that "the response must amount to deliberate indifference to discrimination" to avoid the risk that a recipient could be liable "not for its own official decision but instead for its employees' individual actions", noting that "[c]omparable considerations led to our adoption of a deliberate indifference standard for claims under § 1983 alleging that a municipality's actions in failing to prevent a deprivation of federal rights was the cause of the violation" (*id.*). (For discussion of the decisions under § 1983, see pp. 99–100, *infra.*)

Justice Stevens' vigorous dissent (joined by Justices Souter, Ginsburg, and Breyer) contended, *inter alia,* that the Court's holding was at odds with agency law and would provide incentives for responsible officials to remain in the dark about wrongdoing; that private damages relief should not be precluded solely because an administrative cut-off of funds is unavailable; and that the standard announced by the Court would be exceedingly difficult to satisfy. He raised the possibility that a recipient of funds contesting a claim for damages could raise an affirmative defense that it had adopted and vigorously enforced a policy designed to prevent sexual harassment (a position endorsed in a separate dissent by Justice Ginsburg, joined by Justices Souter and Breyer), but noted that the facts in this case did not support any such defense.

SUBSECTION C: REMEDIES FOR CONSTITUTIONAL VIOLATIONS

Page 852.   Add to Paragraph (4)(c):

In Seminole Tribe of Florida v. Florida, 517 U.S. 44 (1996), a casual dictum stated that the Supreme Court "is empowered to review a question of federal law arising from a state court decision *where a State has consented to suit*" (p. 71 n. 14; emphasis added). Neither Reich nor McKesson was cited. For criticism of any suggestion that, absent consent, a state court has no remedial obligation, see Meltzer, *The Seminole Decision and State Sovereign Immunity,* 1996 Sup.Ct.Rev. 1, 57–60; Monaghan, *The Sovereign Immunity "Exception",* 110 Harv.L.Rev. 102, 125 n. 161 (1996). Compare Vázquez, *What is Eleventh*

Amendment Immunity?, 106 Yale L.J. 1683 (1997)(offering a reinterpretation of Reich and McKesson, in light of the Seminole dictum, as recognizing a monetary remedy for constitutional harm only against state officials rather than against the state itself).

Two Terms later, in Newsweek, Inc. v. Florida Dep't of Revenue, 118 S.Ct. 904 (1998), the Court, in a routine and unanimous per curiam opinion, ruled that the Florida state courts were obliged to provide the taxpayer with a refund remedy for collection of an unconstitutional tax. No mention was made of the state's having consented to suit in its own courts. Indeed, the state courts had refused to provide a refund remedy, holding that the taxpayer had an adequate prepayment remedy. In reversing, the Court followed McKesson (which also arose in Florida) and Reich in holding that where longstanding state practice permitted a refund action, the state courts could not turn around and rule that taxpayers relying on that practice could seek only whatever pre-payment remedies might exist.[1]

Page 856.   Add to footnote 9:

In Idaho v. Coeur d'Alene Tribe, 117 S.Ct. 2028 (1997), discussed at pp. 60–62, *infra*, Justice Souter's dissent (joined by Justices Stevens, Ginsburg, and Breyer) declared that the state court remedial obligation recognized in General Oil Co. v. Crain is not limited to cases in which a remedy is unavailable in federal court. He added that Crain's holding was not undermined by the per curiam decision in Musgrove: the Court's decision there, he said, may have rested on the view that the state court's dismissal was based on a valid state law regarding the timing, but not the existence, of state remedies. In a footnote, Justice Souter reported that quite apart from any federal obligation, all fifty states permit private suit in state court for declaratory and injunctive relief "in circumstances where relief would be available in federal court under [Ex parte] Young" (p. 2058 n.15, citing cases from every state). The other opinions in Coeur d'Alene did not address these questions.

---

1. Professor Woolhandler offers an iconoclastic view of the tax refund cases, rooted in her understanding of historical practice. See Woolhandler, *The Common Law Origins of Constitutionally Compelled Remedies*, 107 Yale L.J. 77 (1997). States, she contends, are presumptively obliged to maintain tort-like remedies against government *officials* alleged to have deprived someone of liberty or property in violation of federal law. But in her view, "state assertions of sovereign immunity in state court were historically respected" (p. 152), and absent state consent to be sued as an entity, the Court required the state only to maintain tort remedies against individual officers. She acknowledges that Reich v. Collins affirms that "a denial by a state court of a recovery of taxes exacted in violation of the laws or Constitution of the United States by compulsion is itself in contravention of the Fourteenth Amendment, the sovereign immunity States traditionally enjoy in their own courts notwithstanding" (513 U.S. at 109–10; internal quotation omitted), but struggles to read Reich as nonetheless resting in the end on consent.

CHAPTER VIII

THE FEDERAL QUESTION JURISDICTION OF THE DISTRICT COURTS

SECTION 1. INTRODUCTION

Page 878. Add to footnote 2:

Professor Woolhandler contends that, prior to the Civil War, the federal courts served as a forum for the vindication of federal rights to a greater extent than most commentators have supposed. Contending that "diversity jurisdiction served as an early form of federal question jurisdiction", she argues that federal courts sitting in diversity during the pre-Civil War era often declined to follow state rules that militated against the vindication of a federal (and often constitutional) right. See Woolhandler, *The Common Law Origins of Constitutionally Compelled Remedies*, 107 Yale L.J. 77, 162 (1997).

SECTION 2. THE SCOPE OF THE CONSTITUTIONAL GRANT OF FEDERAL QUESTION JURISDICTION

Page 899. Add to Paragraph (1):

On the potential effects of the Red Cross decision on other congressionally chartered organizations, see Maistrellis, *American National Red Cross v. S.G. & A.E.: An Open Door to the Federal Courts for Federally Chartered Corporations*, 45 Emory L.J. 771 (1996).

Page 903. Add a new footnote 3a at the end of the first paragraph:

3a. A recent amendment to the FSIA, adding subsection (a)(7) to 28 U.S.C. § 1605, bars any foreign state "designated as a state sponsor of terrorism" from claiming sovereign immunity in an action arising from a terrorist act, provided that the claimant was a United States national at the time of the act in question and that (if the act occurred within the territory of the defendant state) the defendant had been afforded a reasonable opportunity to arbitrate the claim. See Antiterrorism and Effective Death Penalty Act of 1996, Pub.L.No. 104–132, § 221, 110 Stat. 1214.

Page 905. Add to footnote 4:

In the wake of Gutierrez de Martinez, may a federal court set aside certification, yet retain jurisdiction by reinstating the original state law tort action? In an opinion relying heavily on the reasoning of the Gutierrez de Martinez plurality, the Fifth Circuit recently said yes, citing grounds of judicial economy, convenience, and fairness. See Garcia v. United States, 88 F.3d 318 (5th Cir.1996).

SECTION 3.   THE SCOPE OF THE STATUTORY GRANT OF FEDERAL QUESTION JURISDICTION

Page 928.   Add to the beginning of footnote 4:

Professor Oakley, in a Reporter's Memorandum in the ALI Federal Judicial Code Revision Project, argues that Shoshone is better understood by considering portions of § 2325 not quoted in the decision. He notes that the statute provided for a grant of a federal mining patent only after the potential patentee staked a claim, and allowed time for adverse claims to be filed so that any controversy could be "settled by a court of competent jurisdiction". In other words, he contends, the statute did not confer a federal right (and thus a basis for federal question jurisdiction) until after non-federal judicial processes had been invoked or the time period for bringing such claims had expired. See ALI, Federal Judicial Code Revision Project, Tentative Draft No. 2, at 138 (1998).

Page 933.   Add to Paragraph (3)(e):

For a recent case relying in part on the suggestion (in footnote 12 of Merrell Dow) of the relevance of the degree of "federal interest" in determining federal question jurisdiction—even in the absence of a congressionally created cause of action—see Ormet Corp. v. Ohio Power Co., 98 F.3d 799 (4th Cir.1996)(upholding jurisdiction in suit involving emission allowances on ground that state-by-state resolution would undermine efficacy of environmental regulation).

Page 947.   Add a new Paragraph (1)(c):

In Textron Lycoming Reciprocating Engine Division, Avco Corp. v. UAW, 118 S.Ct. 1626 (1998), the Court expressed doubts that federal question jurisdiction exists in a situation, converse to that in Skelly Oil, where the declaratory judgment complaint asserts a nonfederal defense to a potential federal claim. The plaintiff in Textron (allegedly in anticipation of a potential action by Textron under § 301 of the Taft–Hartley Act for breach of a collective bargaining agreement) sought a declaration that the agreement was voidable. The Court, after ruling that the plaintiff's claim did not fall within § 301, noted that it has never spoken to the converse-Skelly situation, and that some language in Skelly "suggests that the declaratory-judgment plaintiff must himself have a federal claim" (p. 1630). The Court did not rule on the question, however, as it decided that the declaratory plaintiff had failed to present a justiciable case or controversy.

Would the well-pleaded complaint rule support federal question jurisdiction in such a case? Do you agree with Justice Breyer (who, in an opinion concurring in the result, reached the declaratory judgment question not decided by the majority) that federal jurisdiction would exist because the relevant question in declaratory judgment cases is the character of the threatened action?

SECTION 4.   FEDERAL QUESTION REMOVAL

Page 950. Add to footnote 2:

In Rivet v. Regions Bank of Louisiana, 118 S.Ct. 921 (1998), the Court appears to have overruled the holding of Moitie on the issue of removal. Addressing the "enigmatic footnote" in that case, the Court stated that Moitie "did not create a preclusion exception to the rule * * * that a defendant could not remove on the basis of a federal defense" (p. 926). The unanimous holding of the Rivet case was that a state court action that had been removed on the basis that the state claim was precluded by a prior federal judgment should have been remanded to the state court.

Page 953. Add to Paragraph (4):

In 1996, Congress overruled the Supreme Court's decision in the Primate case by amending § 1442(a)(1) to authorize removal by the United States and by federal agencies, as well as by federal officers. See Federal Courts Improvement Act of 1996, Pub. L. No. 104–317, § 206, 110 Stat. 3847. (At the time of the Primate decision, the relevant language of § 1442 (a) provided for removal of any action brought "against * * * [a]ny officer of the United States or any agency thereof, or person acting under him, for any act under color of such office * * *.")

SECTION 5.   SUPPLEMENTAL (PENDENT) JURISDICTION

Page 972.   Substitute the following text for Paragraph (10)(c):

Although § 1367 is not made explicitly applicable to cases originating in a state court and then removed, the Court in City of Chicago v. International College of Surgeons, 118 S.Ct. 523 (1997)(also discussed at p. 42, *supra*, and p. 145, *infra*), squarely held that federal courts may exercise supplemental jurisdiction under § 1367 over state claims in removed cases.

Justice Ginsburg, joined in dissent by Justice Stevens, did not disagree with this aspect of the holding but argued that review of state administrative findings (which the plaintiff was seeking in connection with the state claims in the case) is appellate in nature, and that § 1367 should not be used as a vehicle for such "cross-system appeals" absent explicit authorization by Congress (pp. 534–35). See also ALI, Federal Judicial Code Revision Project, Tentative Draft No. 2, at xx (1998)(arguing that whatever its merits, the majority's view could cause a "far-reaching change in the historic function of the district courts").

Page 973.   Add to Paragraph (10)(e):

In support of the Ninth Circuit's reasoning in Executive Software, see Corey, *The Discretionary Exercise of Supplemental Jurisdiction Under the Supplemental Jurisdiction Statute*, 1995 BYU L.Rev. 1263 (considering various ways that § 1367(c) and Gibbs standards could interact and recommending the

Executive Software approach as most consistent with the legislative purpose of § 1367).

Section 1367(c) clearly indicates that a federal court may refuse to exercise supplemental jurisdiction, but leaves open the question whether the court may remand the *entire* case to state court, or only the state law claims. See In re City of Mobile, 75 F.3d 605 (11th Cir.1996)(holding that a federal court must retain jurisdiction over properly removed federal claims); Borough of West Mifflin v. Lancaster, 45 F.3d 780 (3d Cir.1995)(same).

Page 973.   Add a new Paragraph (11):

(11) *Proposed ALI Revision of § 1367.* In 1998, as the first phase of a new study of the Judicial Code, the American Law Institute approved a proposal to revise the supplemental jurisdiction statute. The approved proposal, with some minor modifications, appears in ALI, Federal Judicial Code Revision Project, Tentative Draft No. 2 (1998). The proposal includes the following notable features:

• Introducing what the Reporter described as an approach that is "claim-specific" (defined in this context in terms both of a particular pair of parties and a particular legal theory) rather than "action-specific" (defined as a judicial proceeding for relief of a civil nature).

• Ratifying the decisions holding that § 1367 overrules the Zahn case (see p. 145, *infra*), and expanding supplemental jurisdiction to embrace other instances in which the only bar to the supplemental claim is lack of the requisite amount in controversy.

• Reinstating to its pre–§ 1367 status the then-prevailing law of supplemental jurisdiction as it related to claims by intervenors.

• Retaining, but slightly narrowing, the present scope of district court discretion to decline the exercise of supplemental jurisdiction.

• Overruling the decision in City of Chicago v. International College of Surgeons, 118 S.Ct. 523 (1997)(described at p. 54, *supra*), with respect to its holding that supplemental jurisdiction may extend to claims that are "appellate" and not "original" in character. See the discussion in Tentative Draft No.2, at xix-xx.

Page 973.   Add a new Paragraph (12):

(12) *Cross-References.* For discussion of the availability of supplemental jurisdiction outside the scope of § 1367, and of limitations on that availability, see Fourth Edition pp. 1566–67 note 5; p. 145, *infra*. For a recently enacted limitation on the availability of supplemental jurisdiction over certain domestic relations matters, see The Violence Against Women Act of 1994, discussed at p. 113, *infra*.

SECTION 6.   RELATED HEADS OF JURISDICTION

Page 987.   Add a new footnote 8a at the end of the second paragraph of Paragraph (5)(e):

8a.   But see United States ex. rel. Riley v. St. Luke's Episcopal Hospital, 982 F.Supp. 1261 (S.D.Tex.1997)(holding that qui tam plaintiffs do not satisfy the injury-in-fact prerequisite for standing under Article III, and that Congress cannot, consistently with the principle of separation of powers, confer standing on such plaintiffs by assigning to them the right of the United States to pursue a legal claim).

CHAPTER IX

SUITS CHALLENGING OFFICIAL ACTION

SECTION 1. SUITS CHALLENGING FEDERAL OFFICIAL ACTION

SUBSECTION B: THE SOVEREIGN IMMUNITY OF THE UNITED STATES AND ASSOCIATED REMEDIAL PROBLEMS

Page 1001. Add to footnote *:

In the 1997 Term, the Supreme Court reaffirmed its prior holdings that an Indian Tribe is subject to suit only where Congress has authorized the suit or the Tribe has waived its immunity. Kiowa Tribe v. Manufacturing Technologies, Inc., 118 S.Ct. 1700 (1998).

Page 1002. Add a new footnote 3a at the end of Paragraph (1)(b):

3a. For a forceful revisionist argument attacking conventional notions of the role and significance of sovereign immunity in American law, see Pfander, *Sovereign Immunity and the Right to Petition: Toward a First Amendment Right to Pursue Judicial Claims Against the Government*, 91 Nw.U.L.Rev. 899 (1997). Professor Pfander contends that the First Amendment right to petition was derived from the right as it existed in Virginia, under which citizens were entitled to present to *both* the judiciary and the legislature claims against the state. This history, he concludes, undermines the wide-ranging doctrine of sovereign immunity constructed by the Supreme Court.

Page 1017. Add a new Paragraph (3)(a):

(3)(a) *The Impact of Idaho v. Coeur d'Alene Tribe*. The continuing significance of the Lee decision, and its relationship to Ex parte Young, was a subject of contention in Idaho v. Coeur d'Alene Tribe, 117 S.Ct. 2028 (1997), a case discussed in detail at pp. 60–62, *infra*. That case involved a federal court suit by the Tribe (and several members) against Idaho officials, seeking declaratory and injunctive relief on the basis of a claim of ownership of certain submerged and related lands. (The claim was based on an 1873 federal Executive Order later ratified by Congress. The specific relief requested included a declaration of entitlement to exclusive use and occupancy of the lands in question, a declaration of the invalidity of all state regulation of the lands, and an injunction against any violation of the plaintiffs' rights in the lands.)

The Court held, 5–4, that the action against the state officers was barred by the Eleventh Amendment. In an opinion announcing the judgment of the Court but joined in full only by Chief Justice Rehnquist, Justice Kennedy hardly mentioned the Lee decision. A narrower concurring opinion by Justice O'Connor, joined by Justices Scalia and Thomas, acknowledged the relevance of Lee, but distinguished it on the ground that while the official defendants in Lee had been held to have no right to possess the land, the government retained the right to regulate the use of the land; in Coeur d'Alene, on the other hand, the Tribe sought a declaration that "the lands are not within the State's sovereign jurisdiction" (p. 2044). "Whatever distinction can be drawn between possession and ownership of real property in other contexts, it is not possible to make such a distinction for submerged lands" (*id.*).

Speaking for four dissenters, Justice Souter found the force of the Lee decision inescapable. Whether or not the question involves the ownership of submerged lands, Lee in his view "illustrates that an issue of property title is no different from any other legal or constitutional matter that may have to be resolved in deciding whether the officer of an immune government is so acting beyond his authority as to be amenable to suit without necessarily implicating his government" (p. 2050).

The Lee holding appears to survive this decision, since at least seven Justices clearly regarded it as still good law. But how successful was the effort of the three concurring Justices to distinguish it? (The question is further discussed below, at pp. 61–62.)

Page 1024. Add to Paragraph (5):

The significance of the suggestion in the Lee case that a judgment against government officers does not bind the government itself arose in Idaho v. Coeur d'Alene Tribe, discussed briefly above and more fully at pp. 60–62, *infra*. Once again, this aspect of Lee did not enter into the discussion in Justice Kennedy's opinion. But Justice O'Connor concluded that while the suggestion made sense in Lee, it was not helpful in Coeur d'Alene because of the inevitable impact of a decision for the Tribe on the rights of the state. In Lee, she said, "[a] court could find that the officials had no right to remain in possession, thus conveying all the incidents of ownership to the plaintiff, while not formally divesting the State of its title" (p. 2044). In Coeur d'Alene, on the other hand, a ruling in the Tribe's favor "in practical effect, would be indistinguishable from an order granting the Tribe title to submerged lands" (*id.*).

Interestingly, the dissent did not challenge Justice O'Connor's interpretation of Lee, but found that it did not undermine either the applicability or the value of the Lee rationale in the Coeur d'Alene context: "[W]e have of course drawn the jurisdictional line short of ultimately quieting title (which would run directly against the State itself as putative title-holder and not against its officers) or limiting the affected government in any subsequent quiet title action" (pp. 2051–52). Recognizing that the plaintiff's success in a case like Lee was an "aspersion" on the government's claim of title, Justice Souter contended that this effect was preferable to the two alternatives: either compelling the state itself to appear (a result prohibited by the Eleventh Amendment) or "leaving the individual powerless to seek any federal remedy for violation of a federal right, [a result that] would deplete the federal judicial power to a point the Framers could not possibly have intended, given a history of officer liability riding tandem with sovereign immunity extending back to the Middle Ages" (p. 2053).

Would it have been inappropriate for the dissenters to have gone one step further—to have acknowledged that a judgment in cases like Lee, especially in view of modern notions of preclusion (and the doctrine that a party who conducts litigation for another is bound by the result), effectively deprives the government of title, just as the result in a case like Osborn v. Bank of the United States (Fourth Edition pp. 883, 1016) operated to deny the state the constitutional power to levy the tax in issue against the Bank? If that is not the true import of a decision like Lee, can the government simply put different officers in charge of the land after the decision and insist on relitigating the relevant issues?

Page 1028. Add to footnote 5:

Compare Eastern Enterprises v. Apfel, 118 S.Ct. 682 (1998), in which a plurality of four Justices concluded that a federal district court action for declaratory and injunctive relief, based on a "taking" claim, was not premature because in the particular circumstances, it could not be said that monetary relief under the Tucker Act was "an available remedy" (p. ___). The remaining five Justices did not reach this issue because of their view that the case should not be considered as arising under the Takings Clause.

Page 1041. Add to Paragraph (1)(b):

In Henderson v. United States, 517 U.S. 654 (1996), discussed at p. 37, *supra,* the majority read the statutory waiver of sovereign immunity in the Suits in Admiralty Act (SAA) as not conditioned on compliance with the SAA's provision for service of the complaint "forthwith". (The majority then held that the service requirement of the SAA had been superseded by the more liberal service provisions of Fed.R.Civ.P. 4.) Justice Thomas, dissenting, argued, *inter alia,* that the majority's interpretation "is irreconcilable with our sovereign immunity jurisprudence" (p. 673), under which any ambiguity in the breadth of a waiver "must always be resolved in favor of the Government" (p. 675).

Justice Thomas' dissent in Henderson foreshadowed the Court's 5–4 decision, only a short time later, in Lane v. Pena, 116 S.Ct. 2092 (1996). After Lane's enrollment at the federal Merchant Marine Academy had been terminated because of his recently diagnosed diabetic condition, he brought an action alleging violation of § 504 of the Rehabilitation Act and seeking reinstatement and damages. The lower courts held that Lane was entitled to reinstatement, but not to damages, and the Supreme Court affirmed. Although conceding the force of Lane's arguments that the federal government had waived its immunity from damages actions in the Rehabilitation Act, and acknowledging that alternative readings of the relevant statutory provisions were less than satisfactory, the majority nevertheless found lacking the requisite "unequivocal expression" of congressional intent to grant such a waiver (p. 2096–97).

SECTION 2. SUITS CHALLENGING STATE OFFICIAL ACTION

SUBSECTION A: THE ELEVENTH AMENDMENT AND STATE SOVEREIGN IMMUNITY

Page 1048. Add to footnote 3:

See also Pfander, *History and State Suability: An "Explanatory" Account of the Eleventh Amendment,* 83 Cornell L.Rev. 1269 (1998)(contending, on the basis of an exhaustive historical study, that (a) the purpose of the Eleventh Amendment was to explain that Article III should not be read to authorize federal jurisdiction in suits against states to enforce obligations incurred under the Articles of Confederation, and (b) the Amendment left intact the federal courts' power "to enforce the Constitution against the states prospectively" (p. 1278)).

Page 1051. Add a new footnote 11a at the end of the first paragraph of Paragraph (4)(a):

11a. The Court's subsequent forays into the Eleventh Amendment in the admiralty context have not been models of clarity. In Florida Department of State v. Treasure Salvors, Inc., 458 U.S. 670 (1982), it was determined that the Eleventh Amendment did not preclude a federal district court from issuing a warrant, directed against state officials, for property from a wreckage that was the subject of an in rem admiralty suit. But at the same time, the opinion for a plurality of four Justices suggested that the Eleventh Amendment might bar adjudication of the state's ownership of the wreckage.

The Court revisited the issue of state sovereign immunity in the admiralty context in California v. Deep Sea Research, 118 S.Ct. 1464 (1998). That case held that the Eleventh Amendment did not bar federal jurisdiction over an in rem admiralty suit where the state did not possess the res to which it claimed title. The Court concluded that because of the state's lack of possession, any intimations from Treasure Salvors that the Eleventh Amendment barred the adjudication of the state's interest in the property were inapposite.

Page 1058. Add a new Paragraph (10):

(10) *Continuation of the Debate: The Seminole Decision and its Implications.* For the most recent revisiting of the Hans decision, its rationale and implications, see Seminole Tribe of Florida v. Florida, and the following Note, *infra.*

Page 1065. Add a new footnote 2a at the end of Paragraph (3)(a):

2a. In a later article, Professor Woolhandler notes that prior to Young, federal court actions against state officials were frequently based on diversity jurisdiction, even when they raised federal questions, and the remedies imposed by the federal courts in adjudicating those questions were regarded as being based in state law. See Woolhandler, *The Common Law Origins of Constitutionally Compelled Remedies,* 107 Yale L.J. 77 (1997).

Thus, she suggests, Young changed the preexisting situation only in that it allowed the remedies imposed in such cases to be forthrightly regarded as federal remedies.

Page 1066. Add a new Paragraph (4):

(4) *Idaho v. Coeur d'Alene Tribe: An Exception for Submerged Lands?*

The continuing force of Ex parte Young was an important issue in Idaho v. Coeur d'Alene Tribe, 117 S.Ct. 2028 (1997), a case also discussed at pp. 57–59, *supra,* and p. 94, *infra.* In this case, the plaintiffs (an Indian Tribe and several of its members) brought a federal court action against state officials and agencies, and the state itself, seeking declaratory and injunctive relief based on a claim of ownership of certain submerged and related lands. (The specific relief requested included a declaration of entitlement to exclusive use and occupancy of the lands in question, a declaration of the invalidity of all state regulation of the lands, and an injunction against any violation of the plaintiffs' rights in the lands.) Plaintiffs' claim rested on an 1873 federal executive order later ratified by Congress. As the case came to the Supreme Court, only the state officers, who had been sued in their individual capacities, remained as defendants, but the majority held (5–4) that suit against them was barred by the Eleventh Amendment.

In what the Justices referred to as the "principal opinion", Justice Kennedy's analysis pursued several themes. In Part II(B)-(D), a portion of his opinion joined only by the Chief Justice and explicitly rejected by the other seven Justices, Justice Kennedy contended that as the doctrine of Ex parte Young had developed over the years, it had become an essentially discretionary doctrine in which the federal courts looked to a variety of factors in striking an appropriate balance—including the questions whether there was an available state forum to vindicate federal interests (as the Court indicated there was in this case), whether there was a special need to call on a federal court to interpret federal law, and whether the suit would severely affect state-federal relationships.[4]

In Part III of the opinion, a part joined by four other Justices, Justice Kennedy emphasized that the suit was "the functional equivalent" of a quiet title action that "would diminish, even extinguish, the State's control over a vast reach of land and waters long deemed by the State to be an integral part of its territory" (p. 2040). He discussed at length the special concern of the state—a concern deeply rooted in English history—for its sovereign control of submerged lands, as well as the extraordinarily intrusive effect on state interests that a judgment for the plaintiffs would have. "Under these particular and special circumstances, we find the Young exception inapplicable" (p. 2043).

In a concurring opinion joined by Justices Scalia and Thomas, Justice O'Connor took pains to separate herself from Justice Kennedy's effort (in Part II of his opinion) to "recharacterize[] and narrow[] much of our Young jurisprudence" (p. 2045). For her, the critical reason for upholding the Eleventh Amendment claim of the defendants was "the importance of submerged lands to state sovereignty * * * [and to its] ability to regulate use of its navigable waters"; the Tribe should therefore not be permitted, simply by suing state officers rather than the state, to use a federal court "to eliminate altogether the State's regulatory power over the submerged lands at issue" (p. 2044).

Justice Souter, writing for four Justices in dissent, argued vigorously that the case was governed by a long tradition of allowing suits for prospective relief against government officers as a means of testing whether those officers were complying with federal law. In his view, cases like United States v. Lee, Fourth Edition p. 1007, made it clear that the tradition embraced disputes over rights to real property. Arguments about "functional equivalent[s]" in this context were not to the point, he insisted, because the proper question is whether in such cases the "aspersion" on the government's title that might result is "a fair price to pay for the jurisdiction to consider individual claims of federal right" (p. 2053). And as for the special state interest relied on by Justice O'Connor, Justice Souter commented that "Idaho indisputably has a significant sovereign interest in regulating its submerged lands, but it has no legitimate sovereign interest in regulating submerged lands located outside state borders" (p. 2054).

---

4. In the course of discussing the need for case-by-case balancing of state and federal interests, Justice Kennedy did not factor into the equation the significance of Congress' decision to provide for federal jurisdiction in a case like Coeur d'Alene—a decision that appears to reflect the national legislature's judgment that such cases are especially suited for adjudication in a federal court.

Given the narrow grounds of the concurrence, it would appear that the force of Ex parte Young (and its ancestor, United States v. Lee) as a fundamental corollary of sovereign immunity doctrine has not been severely undermined by the Coeur d'Alene decision. But is the effort of the concurrence to create a special categorical exception to the Young doctrine a convincing one? If not, how likely is it that it will (a) endure in its present form, (b) give rise to other "categorical" exceptions that eventually erode the rule, or (c) prove sufficiently difficult to defend and apply that it will eventually be abandoned?

Pages 1075–76.   Add a new Paragraph (4)(c):

(c) The foregoing cases (including Milliken v. Bradley) reflect the difficulty of determining where the prospective/retrospective line falls, but also reflect an agreement that this line is critical in determining the availability of specific relief against individuals. But in Idaho v. Coeur d'Alene Tribe, discussed at pp. 57–59, *supra,* a majority held that in the particular circumstances, a claim concededly limited to prospective relief was nonetheless barred by the Eleventh Amendment.

Page 1076.   Add a new footnote 4a at the end of Paragraph (4):

4a.   In Regents of the University of California v. Doe, 117 S.Ct. 900 (1997), the Court unanimously held that the federal government's obligation to indemnify a state agency for any money judgment against it did not in itself divest the agency of its Eleventh Amendment immunity. In a brief opinion, the Court, in referring to the discussion of financial liability in the PATH case (Fourth Edition pp. 1057–58), explained that the critical question in an action against an agency for retroactive compensation was not whether a third party (other than the state) would be ultimately responsible for satisfying a judgment but rather whether the agency is "the kind of entity that should be treated as an arm of the State" (p. 904).

Page 1085.   Substitute for Pennsylvania v. Union Gas and the Note on pp. 1097–1105 the following Principal Case and Note:

SEMINOLE TRIBE OF FLORIDA V. FLORIDA

517 U.S. 44, 116 S.Ct. 1114, 134 L.Ed.2d 252 (1996).
Certiorari to the United States Court of Appeals for the Eleventh Circuit.

■ CHIEF JUSTICE REHNQUIST delivered the opinion of the Court.

The Indian Gaming Regulatory Act provides that an Indian tribe may conduct certain gaming activities only in conformance with a valid compact between the tribe and the State in which the gaming activities are located. 25 U.S.C. § 2710(d)(1)(C). The Act, passed by Congress under the Indian Commerce Clause, imposes upon the States a duty to negotiate in good faith with an Indian tribe toward the formation of a compact, § 2710(d)(3)(A), and authorizes a tribe to bring suit in federal court against a State in order to compel performance of that duty, § 2710(d)(7). We hold that notwithstanding Congress' clear intent to abrogate the States' sovereign immunity, the Indian Commerce Clause does not grant Congress that power, and therefore § 2710(d)(7) cannot grant jurisdiction over a State that does not consent to be sued. We further hold that the doctrine of Ex parte Young, 209 U.S. 123 (1908), may not be used to enforce § 2710(d)(3) against a state official.

I

Congress passed the Indian Gaming Regulatory Act in 1988 in order to provide a statutory basis for the operation and regulation of gaming by Indian tribes. The Act divides gaming on Indian lands into three classes—I, II, and III * * *. Class III gaming—the type with which we are here concerned—* * * includes such things as slot machines, casino games, banking card games, dog racing, and lotteries. It is the most heavily regulated of the three classes. The Act provides that class III gaming is lawful only where it is: ① authorized by an ordinance or resolution that ⓐ is adopted by the governing body of the Indian tribe, ⓑ satisfies certain statutorily prescribed requirements, and ⓒ is approved by the National Indian Gaming Commission; ② located in a State that permits such gaming for any purpose by any person, organization, or entity; and ③ "conducted in conformance with a Tribal–State compact entered into by the Indian tribe and the State under paragraph (3) that is in effect." § 2710(d)(1).

→ reqs of statute

The "paragraph (3)" to which the last prerequisite of § 2710(d)(1) refers is § 2710(d)(3), which describes the permissible scope of a Tribal–State compact, and provides that the compact is effective "only when notice of approval by the Secretary [of the Interior] of such compact has been published by the Secretary in the Federal Register." More significant for our purposes, however, is that § 2710(d)(3) describes the process by which a State and an Indian tribe begin negotiations toward a Tribal–State compact:

> "(A) Any Indian tribe having jurisdiction over the Indian lands upon which a class III gaming activity is being conducted, or is to be conducted, shall request the State in which such lands are located to enter into negotiations for the purpose of entering into a Tribal–State compact governing the conduct of gaming activities. Upon receiving such a request, the State shall negotiate with the Indian tribe in good faith to enter into such a compact."

The State's obligation to "negotiate with the Indian tribe in good faith," is made judicially enforceable by §§ 2710(d)(7)(A)(i) and (B)(i):

State obligated to negotiate in good faith

> "(A) The United States district courts shall have jurisdiction over—
>
> > "(i) any cause of action initiated by an Indian tribe arising from the failure of a State to enter into negotiations with the Indian tribe for the purpose of entering into a Tribal–State compact under paragraph (3) or to conduct such negotiations in good faith. . . .
>
> "(B)(i) An Indian tribe may initiate a cause of action described in subparagraph (A)(i) only after the close of the 180–day period beginning on the date on which the Indian tribe requested the State to enter into negotiations under paragraph (3)(A)."

Sections 2710(d)(7)(B)(ii)-(vii) describe an elaborate remedial scheme designed to ensure the formation of a Tribal–State compact. A tribe that brings an action under § 2710(d)(7)(A)(i) must show that no Tribal–State compact has been entered and that the State failed to respond in good faith to the tribe's request to negotiate * * *. If the district court concludes that the State has failed to negotiate in good faith toward the formation of a Tribal–State compact, then it "shall order the State and Indian tribe to conclude such a compact within a 60–day period." § 2710(d)(7)(B)(iii). If no compact has been concluded 60 days after the court's order, then "the Indian tribe and the State shall each submit to a mediator appointed by the court a proposed compact that represents their last best offer for a compact." The mediator chooses from between the two

tribe must show state failed to respond in good faith

compact → mediator w/ 2 compacts

proposed compacts the one "which best comports with the terms of [the Act] and any other applicable Federal law and with the findings and order of the court," and submits it to the State and the Indian tribe. If the State consents to the proposed compact within 60 days of its submission by the mediator, then the proposed compact is "treated as a Tribal–State compact entered into under paragraph (3)." If, however, the State does not consent within that 60–day period, then the Act provides that the mediator "shall notify the Secretary [of the Interior]" and that the Secretary "shall prescribe . . . procedures . . . under which class III gaming may be conducted on the Indian lands over which the Indian tribe has jurisdiction."

In September 1991, the Seminole Tribe * * * sued the State of Florida and its Governor * * *. * * * [P]etitioner alleged that respondents had * * * violat[ed] the "requirement of good faith negotiation" contained in § 2710(d)(3). Respondents moved to dismiss the complaint, arguing that the suit violated the State's sovereign immunity from suit in federal court. The District Court denied respondents' motion * * * [and on interlocutory appeal, the Eleventh Circuit reversed], holding that the Eleventh Amendment barred petitioner's suit against respondents. * * * The court further held that Ex parte Young does not permit an Indian tribe to force good faith negotiations by suing the Governor of a State. Finding that it lacked subject-matter jurisdiction, the Eleventh Circuit remanded to the District Court with directions to dismiss petitioner's suit.[4]

* * * [W]e granted certiorari, in order to consider two questions: (1) Does the Eleventh Amendment prevent Congress from authorizing suits by Indian tribes against States for prospective injunctive relief to enforce legislation enacted pursuant to the Indian Commerce Clause?; and (2) Does the doctrine of Ex parte Young permit suits against a State's governor for prospective injunctive relief to enforce the good faith bargaining requirement of the Act? * * *

* * * Although the text of the [Eleventh] Amendment would appear to restrict only the Article III diversity jurisdiction of the federal courts, "we have understood the Eleventh Amendment to stand not so much for what it says, but for the presupposition . . . which it confirms." Blatchford v. Native Village of Noatak, 501 U.S. 775, 779 (1991). That presupposition, first observed over a century ago in Hans v. Louisiana, 134 U.S. 1 (1890), has two parts: first, that each State is a sovereign entity in our federal system; and second, that " 'it is inherent in the nature of sovereignty not to be amenable to the suit of an individual without its consent.' " Id., at 13 (emphasis deleted), quoting The Federalist No. 81 * * *. For over a century we have reaffirmed that federal jurisdiction over suits against unconsenting States "was not contemplated by the Constitution when establishing the judicial power of the United States." Hans, supra, at 15 [additional citations omitted].

* * *

II

Petitioner argues that Congress through the Act abrogated the States' immunity from suit. In order to determine whether Congress has abrogated the

4. Following its conclusion that petitioner's suit should be dismissed, the Court of Appeals went on to consider how § 2710(d)(7) would operate in the wake of its decision. The court decided that those provisions of § 2710(d)(7) that were problematic could be severed from the rest of the section, and read the surviving provisions of § 2710(d)(7) to provide an Indian tribe with immediate recourse to the Secretary of the Interior from the dismissal of a suit against a State.

States' sovereign immunity, we ask two questions: first, whether Congress has "unequivocally expressed its intent to abrogate the immunity," Green v. Mansour, 474 U.S. 64, 68 (1985); and second, whether Congress has acted "pursuant to a valid exercise of power." *Ibid.*

A

* * *

* * * [W]e agree * * * that Congress has in § 2710(d)(7) provided an "unmistakably clear" statement of its intent to abrogate. * * *.[9]

B

Having concluded that Congress clearly intended to abrogate the States' sovereign immunity through § 2710(d)(7), we turn now to consider whether the Act was passed "pursuant to a valid exercise of power." Green v. Mansour, 474 U.S. at 68. Before we address that question here, however, we think it necessary first to define the scope of our inquiry.

Petitioner suggests that one consideration weighing in favor of finding the power to abrogate here is that the Act authorizes only prospective injunctive relief rather than retroactive monetary relief. But we have often made it clear that the relief sought by a plaintiff suing a State is irrelevant to the question whether the suit is barred by the Eleventh Amendment. * * * We think it follows a fortiori from this proposition that the type of relief sought is irrelevant to whether Congress has power to abrogate States' immunity. The Eleventh Amendment does not exist solely in order to "prevent federal court judgments that must be paid out of a State's treasury," Hess v. Port Authority Trans–Hudson Corporation, 513 U.S. 30 (1994); it also serves to avoid "the indignity of subjecting a State to the coercive process of judicial tribunals at the instance of private parties," Puerto Rico Aqueduct and Sewer Authority, 506 U.S. at 146 (internal quotation marks omitted).

Similarly, petitioner argues that the abrogation power is validly exercised here because the Act grants the States a power that they would not otherwise have, viz., some measure of authority over gaming on Indian lands. It is true enough that the Act extends to the States a power withheld from them by the Constitution. Nevertheless, we do not see how that consideration is relevant to the question whether Congress may abrogate state sovereign immunity. The Eleventh Amendment immunity may not be lifted by Congress unilaterally deciding that it will be replaced by grant of some other authority.

Thus our inquiry into whether Congress has the power to abrogate unilaterally the States' immunity from suit is narrowly focused on one question: Was the Act in question passed pursuant to a constitutional provision granting Congress the power to abrogate? See, *e.g.*, Fitzpatrick v. Bitzer, 427 U.S. 445, 452–456 (1976). Previously, in conducting that inquiry, we have found authority to abrogate under only two provisions of the Constitution. In Fitzpatrick, we recognized that the Fourteenth Amendment, by expanding federal power at the expense of state autonomy, had fundamentally altered the balance of state and federal power struck by the Constitution. We noted that § 1 of the

---

9. The dissent argues that in order to avoid a constitutional question, we should interpret the Act to provide only a suit against state officials rather than a suit against the State itself. But in light of the plain text of § 2710(d)(7)(B), we disagree with the dissent's assertion that the Act can reasonably be read in that way. * * *

Fourteenth Amendment contained prohibitions expressly directed at the States and that § 5 of the Amendment expressly provided that "The Congress shall have the power to enforce, by appropriate legislation, the provisions of this article." See *id.*, at 453 (internal quotation marks omitted). We held that through the Fourteenth Amendment, federal power extended to intrude upon the province of the Eleventh Amendment and therefore that § 5 of the Fourteenth Amendment allowed Congress to abrogate the immunity from suit guaranteed by that Amendment.

In only one other case has congressional abrogation of the States' Eleventh Amendment immunity been upheld. In *Pennsylvania v. Union Gas Co.*, 491 U.S. 1 (1989), a plurality of the Court found that the Interstate Commerce Clause granted Congress the power to abrogate state sovereign immunity, stating that the power to regulate interstate commerce would be "incomplete without the authority to render States liable in damages." *Union Gas*, 491 U.S. at 19–20. Justice White added the fifth vote necessary to the result in that case, but wrote separately in order to express that he "[did] not agree with much of [the plurality's] reasoning." *Id.*, at 57.

* * * [P]etitioner does not challenge the Eleventh Circuit's conclusion that the Act was passed pursuant to neither the Fourteenth Amendment nor the Interstate Commerce Clause. Instead, * * * petitioner now asks us to consider whether [the Indian Commerce] clause grants Congress the power to abrogate the States' sovereign immunity.[10]

Both parties make their arguments from the plurality decision in *Union Gas*,* and we, too, begin there. We think it clear that Justice Brennan's opinion finds Congress' power to abrogate under the Interstate Commerce Clause from the States' cession of their sovereignty when they gave Congress plenary power to regulate interstate commerce. See *Union Gas*, 491 U.S. at 17 * * *. * * *

Following the rationale of the *Union Gas* plurality, our inquiry is limited to determining whether the Indian Commerce Clause, like the Interstate Commerce Clause, is a grant of authority to the Federal Government at the expense of the States. The answer to that question is obvious. If anything, the Indian Commerce Clause accomplishes a greater transfer of power from the States to the Federal Government than does the Interstate Commerce Clause. This is clear enough from the fact that the States still exercise some authority over interstate trade but have been divested of virtually all authority over Indian commerce and Indian tribes. Under the rationale of *Union Gas*, if the States' partial cession of authority over a particular area includes cession of the immunity from suit, then their virtually total cession of authority over a different area must also include cession of the immunity from suit. * * * We

---

10. [In addition to arguments based on the Eleventh Amendment,] [r]espondents also contend that the Act mandates state regulation of Indian gaming and therefore violates the Tenth Amendment by allowing federal officials to avoid political accountability for those actions for which they are in fact responsible. See *New York v. United States*, 505 U.S. 144 (1992). This argument was not considered below by either the Eleventh Circuit or the District Court, and is not fairly within the question presented. Therefore we do not consider it here.

* [Ed.] Petitioner contends that "there is no principled basis for finding that congressional power under the Indian Commerce Clause is less than that conferred by the Interstate Commerce Clause", while respondents assert that since the Indian Commerce Clause gives Congress *complete* authority over the Indian tribes, the abrogation power is not "necessary" to the exercise of authority under that clause.

agree with the petitioner that the plurality opinion in Union Gas allows no principled distinction in favor of the States to be drawn between the Indian Commerce Clause and the Interstate Commerce Clause.

no distinction commerce / Indiancom. clause

Respondents argue, however, that * * * if we find the rationale of the Union Gas plurality to extend to the Indian Commerce Clause, then "Union Gas should be reconsidered and overruled." * * * [W]e always have treated stare decisis as a "principle of policy," Helvering v. Hallock, 309 U.S. 106, 119 (1940), and not as an "inexorable command," Payne [v. Tennessee], 501 U.S. 808, 828 (1991). "When governing decisions are unworkable or are badly reasoned, 'this Court has never felt constrained to follow precedent.'" *Id.*, at 827 (quoting Smith v. Allwright, 321 U.S. 649, 665 (1944)). Our willingness to reconsider our earlier decisions has been "particularly true in constitutional cases, because in such cases 'correction through legislative action is practically impossible.'" Payne, *supra,* at 828, (quoting Burnet v. Coronado Oil & Gas Co., 285 U.S. 393, 407 (1932)(Brandeis, J., dissenting)).

?: rule 6

The Court in Union Gas reached a result without an expressed rationale agreed upon by a majority of the Court. * * * Justice White, who provided the fifth vote for the result, wrote separately in order to indicate his disagreement with the majority's [sic] rationale, and four Justices joined together in a dissent that rejected the plurality's rationale. Since it was issued, Union Gas has created confusion among the lower courts that have sought to understand and apply the deeply fractured decision. * * *

The plurality's rationale also deviated sharply from our established federalism jurisprudence and essentially eviscerated our decision in Hans. * * * It was well established in 1989 when Union Gas was decided that the Eleventh Amendment stood for the constitutional principle that state sovereign immunity limited the federal courts' jurisdiction under Article III. * * * As the dissent in Union Gas recognized, the plurality's conclusion—that Congress could under Article I expand the scope of the federal courts' jurisdiction under Article III—"contradicted our unvarying approach to Article III as setting forth the exclusive catalog of permissible federal court jurisdiction." Union Gas, 491 U.S. at 39.

UG deviated from jurisprudence

Never before the decision in Union Gas had we suggested that the bounds of Article III could be expanded by Congress operating pursuant to any constitutional provision other than the Fourteenth Amendment. Indeed, it had seemed fundamental that Congress could not expand the jurisdiction of the federal courts beyond the bounds of Article III. Marbury v. Madison, 5 U.S. 137, 1 Cranch 137 (1803). The plurality's citation of prior decisions for support was based upon what we believe to be a misreading of precedent. The plurality claimed support for its decision from a case holding the unremarkable, and completely unrelated, proposition that the States may waive their sovereign immunity, and cited as precedent propositions that had been merely assumed for the sake of argument in earlier cases, see 491 U.S. at 15.

only 14$\underline{\underline{th}}$

The plurality's extended reliance upon our decision in Fitzpatrick v. Bitzer, that Congress could under the Fourteenth Amendment abrogate the States' sovereign immunity was also, we believe, misplaced. Fitzpatrick was based upon a rationale wholly inapplicable to the Interstate Commerce Clause, viz., that the Fourteenth Amendment, adopted well after the adoption of the Eleventh Amendment and the ratification of the Constitution, operated to alter the pre-existing balance between state and federal power achieved by Article III and the Eleventh Amendment. As the dissent in Union Gas made clear,

Fitzpatrick cannot be read to justify "limitation of the principle embodied in the Eleventh Amendment through appeal to antecedent provisions of the Constitution." Union Gas, 491 U.S. at 42 (Scalia, J., dissenting). * * * Reconsidering the decision in Union Gas, we conclude that none of the policies underlying stare decisis require our continuing adherence to its holding. * * * We feel bound to conclude that Union Gas was wrongly decided and that it should be, and now is, overruled.

Stare decisis doesn't apply here

dissent

The dissent makes no effort to defend the decision in Union Gas, but nonetheless would find congressional power to abrogate in this case.[11] Contending that our decision is a novel extension of the Eleventh Amendment, the dissent chides us for "attending" to dicta. We adhere in this case, however, not to mere obiter dicta, but rather to the well-established rationale upon which the Court based the results of its earlier decisions. When an opinion issues for the Court, it is not only the result but also those portions of the opinion necessary to that result by which we are bound. * * * For over a century, we have grounded our decisions in the oft-repeated understanding of state sovereign immunity as an essential part of the Eleventh Amendment. * * * [The Court at this point discussed Principality of Monaco v. Mississippi (Fourth Edition p. 307), Pennhurst State School & Hosp. v. Halderman (Fourth Edition pp. 1052, 1076), and Ex parte New York (Fourth Edition p. 1051).] It is true that we have not had occasion previously to apply established Eleventh Amendment principles to the question whether Congress has the power to abrogate state sovereign immunity (save in Union Gas). But consideration of that question must proceed with fidelity to this century-old doctrine.

The dissent, to the contrary, disregards our case law in favor of a theory cobbled together from law review articles and its own version of historical events. The dissent cites not a single decision since Hans (other than Union Gas) that supports its view of state sovereign immunity, instead relying upon the now-discredited decision in Chisholm v. Georgia, 2 U.S. (2 Dall.) 419 (1793). Its undocumented and highly speculative extralegal explanation of the decision in Hans is a disservice to the Court's traditional method of adjudication.

The dissent mischaracterizes the Hans opinion. That decision found its roots not solely in the common law of England, but in the much more fundamental " 'jurisprudence in all civilized nations.' "Hans, 134 U.S. at 17, quoting Beers v. Arkansas, 61 U.S. (20 How.) 527, 529 (1858); see also The Federalist No. 81 (A. Hamilton)(sovereign immunity "is the general sense and the general practice of mankind"). The dissent's proposition that the common law of England, where adopted by the States, was open to change by the legislature, is wholly unexceptionable and largely beside the point: that common law provided the substantive rules of law rather than jurisdiction. * * * It also is noteworthy that the principle of state sovereign immunity stands distinct from other principles of the common law in that only the former prompted a specific constitutional amendment.

Hans—with a much closer vantage point than the dissent—recognized that the decision in Chisholm was contrary to the well-understood meaning of the Constitution. The dissent's conclusion that the decision in Chisholm was "reasonable," certainly would have struck the Framers of the Eleventh Amend-

---

11. Unless otherwise indicated, all references to the dissent are to the dissenting   opinion authored by Justice Souter.

ment as quite odd: that decision created "such a shock of surprise that the Eleventh Amendment was at once proposed and adopted." Monaco, *supra,* at 325. The dissent's lengthy analysis of the text of the Eleventh Amendment is directed at a straw man—we long have recognized that blind reliance upon the text of the Eleventh Amendment is " 'to strain the Constitution and the law to a construction never imagined or dreamed of.' "Monaco, 292 U.S. at 326, quoting Hans, 134 U.S. at 15. The text dealt in terms only with the problem presented by the decision in Chisholm; in light of the fact that the federal courts did not have federal question jurisdiction at the time the Amendment was passed (and would not have it until 1875), it seems unlikely that much thought was given to the prospect of federal question jurisdiction over the States.

That same consideration causes the dissent's criticism of the views of Marshall, Madison, and Hamilton to ring hollow. The dissent cites statements made by those three influential Framers, the most natural reading of which would preclude all federal jurisdiction over an unconsenting State.[12] Struggling against this reading, however, the dissent finds significant the absence of any contention that sovereign immunity would affect the new federal-question jurisdiction. But the lack of any statute vesting general federal question jurisdiction in the federal courts until much later makes the dissent's demand for greater specificity about a then-dormant jurisdiction overly exacting.[13]

In putting forward a new theory of state sovereign immunity, the dissent develops its own vision of the political system created by the Framers, concluding with the statement that "the Framer's principal objectives in rejecting English theories of unitary sovereignty . . . would have been impeded if a new concept of sovereign immunity had taken its place in federal question cases, and would have been substantially thwarted if that new immunity had been held untouchable by any congressional effort to abrogate it."[14] This sweeping statement ignores the fact that the Nation survived for nearly two centuries without the question of the existence of such power ever being presented to this Court. And Congress itself waited nearly a century before even conferring federal question jurisdiction on the lower federal courts.

12. * * * [T]he dissent quotes selectively from the Framers' statements that it references. The dissent cites the following, for instance, as a statement made by Madison: "the Constitution 'gives a citizen a right to be heard in the federal courts; and if a state should condescend to be a party, this court may take cognizance of it.' "But that statement, perhaps ambiguous when read in isolation, was preceded by the following: "Jurisdiction in controversies between a state and citizens of another state is much objected to, and perhaps without reason. It is not in the power of individuals to call any state into court. The only operation it can have, is that, if a state should wish to bring a suit against a citizen, it must be brought before the federal courts. It appears to me that this can have no operation but this." See

3 J. Elliot, Debates on the Federal Constitution 67 (1866).

13. Although the absence of any discussion dealing with federal question jurisdiction is therefore unremarkable, what is notably lacking in the Framers' statements is any mention of Congress' power to abrogate the States' immunity. * * *

14. This argument wholly disregards other methods of ensuring the States' compliance with federal law: the Federal Government can bring suit in federal court against a State; an individual can bring suit against a state officer in order to ensure that the officer's conduct is in compliance with federal law; and this Court is empowered to review a question of federal law arising from a state court decision where a State has consented to suit.

In overruling Union Gas today, we reconfirm that the background principle of state sovereign immunity embodied in the Eleventh Amendment is not so ephemeral as to dissipate when the subject of the suit is an area, like the regulation of Indian commerce, that is under the exclusive control of the Federal Government. Even when the Constitution vests in Congress complete law-making authority over a particular area, the Eleventh Amendment prevents congressional authorization of suits by private parties against unconsenting States.[16] * * * Petitioner's suit against the State of Florida must be dismissed for a lack of jurisdiction.

III

Petitioner argues that we may exercise jurisdiction over its suit to enforce § 2710(d)(3) against the Governor notwithstanding the jurisdictional bar of the Eleventh Amendment. Petitioner notes that since our decision in Ex parte Young, we often have found federal jurisdiction over a suit against a state official when that suit seeks only prospective injunctive relief in order to "end a continuing violation of federal law." Green v. Mansour, 474 U.S. at 68. The situation presented here, however, is sufficiently different from that giving rise to the traditional Ex parte Young action so as to preclude the availability of that doctrine.

Here, the "continuing violation of federal law" alleged by petitioner is the Governor's failure to bring the State into compliance with § 2710(d)(3). But the duty to negotiate imposed upon the State by that statutory provision does not stand alone. Rather, as we have seen, Congress passed § 2710(d)(3) in conjunction with the carefully crafted and intricate remedial scheme set forth in § 2710(d)(7).

Where Congress has created a remedial scheme for the enforcement of a particular federal right, we have, in suits against federal officers, refused to supplement that scheme with one created by the judiciary. Schweiker v. Chilicky, 487 U.S. 412, 423 (1988) * * *. Here, of course, the question is not whether a remedy should be created, but instead is whether the Eleventh Amendment bar should be lifted, as it was in Ex parte Young, in order to allow a suit against a state officer. Nevertheless, we think that the same general principle applies: therefore, where Congress has prescribed a detailed remedial scheme for the enforcement against a State of a statutorily created right, a court should hesitate before casting aside those limitations and permitting an action against a state officer based upon Ex parte Young.

* * * [After summarizing the statutory scheme described above, the Court continued:] By contrast with this quite modest set of sanctions, an action brought against a state official under Ex parte Young would expose that official

---

16. Justice Stevens understands our opinion to prohibit federal jurisdiction over suits to enforce the bankruptcy, copyright, and antitrust laws against the States. He notes that federal jurisdiction over those statutory schemes is exclusive, and therefore concludes that there is "no remedy" for state violations of those federal statutes.

That conclusion is exaggerated both in its substance and in its significance. First, * * * [w]e have already seen that several avenues remain open for ensuring state compliance with federal law. See supra, at n. [14]. * * * Second, contrary to the implication of Justice Stevens' conclusion, it has not been widely thought that the federal antitrust, bankruptcy, or copyright statutes abrogated the States' sovereign immunity. * * * [T]here is no established tradition in the lower federal courts of allowing enforcement of those federal statutes against the States. * * *

to the full remedial powers of a federal court, including, presumably, contempt sanctions. If § 2710(d)(3) could be enforced in a suit under Ex parte Young, § 2710(d)(7) would have been superfluous; it is difficult to see why an Indian tribe would suffer through the intricate scheme of § 2710(d)(7) when more complete and more immediate relief would be available under Ex parte Young.[17]

Here, of course, we have found that Congress does not have authority under the Constitution to make the State suable in federal court under § 2710(d)(7). Nevertheless, the fact that Congress chose to impose upon the State a liability which is significantly more limited than would be the liability imposed upon the state officer under Ex parte Young strongly indicates that Congress had no wish to create the latter under § 2710(d)(3). Nor are we free to rewrite the statutory scheme in order to approximate what we think Congress might have wanted had it known that § 2710(d)(7) was beyond its authority. If that effort is to be made, it should be made by Congress, and not by the federal courts. We hold that Ex parte Young is inapplicable to petitioner's suit against the Governor of Florida, and therefore that suit is barred by the Eleventh Amendment and must be dismissed for a lack of jurisdiction.

IV

* * * The Eleventh Circuit's dismissal of petitioner's suit is hereby affirmed.

JUSTICE STEVENS, dissenting.

This case is about power—the power of the Congress of the United States to create a private federal cause of action against a State, or its Governor, for the violation of a federal right. In Chisholm v. Georgia, the entire Court—including Justice Iredell whose dissent provided the blueprint for the Eleventh Amendment—assumed that Congress had such power. In Hans v. Louisiana—a case the Court purports to follow today—the Court again assumed that Congress had such power. In Fitzpatrick v. Bitzer and Pennsylvania v. Union Gas Co., the Court squarely held that Congress has such power. In a series of cases beginning with Atascadero State Hospital v. Scanlon, the Court formulated a special "clear statement rule" to determine whether specific Acts of Congress contained an effective exercise of that power. Nevertheless, in a sharp break with the past, today the Court holds that with the narrow and illogical exception of statutes enacted pursuant to the Enforcement Clause of the Fourteenth Amendment, Congress has no such power.

The importance of the majority's decision to overrule the Court's holding in Pennsylvania v. Union Gas Co. cannot be overstated. The majority's opinion does not simply preclude Congress from establishing the rather curious statuto-

---

17. Contrary to the claims of the dissent, we do not hold that Congress cannot authorize federal jurisdiction under Ex parte Young over a cause of action with a limited remedial scheme. We find only that Congress did not intend that result in the Indian Gaming Regulatory Act. Although one might argue that the text of § 2710(d)(7)(A)(i), taken alone, is broad enough to encompass both a suit against a State (under an abrogation theory) and a suit against a state official (under an Ex parte Young theory), subsection (A)(i) of § 2710(d)(7) cannot be read in isolation from subsections (B)(ii)–(vii), which repeatedly refers exclusively to "the State." * * * Similarly the duty imposed by the Act—to "negotiate ... in good faith to enter into" a compact with another sovereign—stands distinct in that it is not of the sort likely to be performed by an individual state executive officer or even a group of officers.

ry scheme under which Indian tribes may seek the aid of a federal court to secure a State's good faith negotiations over gaming regulations. Rather, it prevents Congress from providing a federal forum for a broad range of actions against States, from those sounding in copyright and patent law, to those concerning bankruptcy, environmental law, and the regulation of our vast national economy.

There may be room for debate over whether, in light of the Eleventh Amendment, Congress has the power to ensure that such a cause of action may be enforced in federal court by a citizen of another State or a foreign citizen. There can be no serious debate, however, over whether Congress has the power to ensure that such a cause of action may be brought by a citizen of the State being sued. Congress' authority in that regard is clear.

* * *

I

* * *

In concluding that the federal courts could not entertain Chisholm's action against the State of Georgia, Justice Iredell [dissenting in Chisholm v. Georgia] relied on the text of the Judiciary Act of 1789, not the State's assertion that Article III did not extend the judicial power to suits against unconsenting States. * * *

* * *

For Justice Iredell then, it was enough to assume that Article III permitted Congress to impose sovereign immunity as a jurisdictional limitation; he did not proceed to resolve the further question whether the Constitution went so far as to prevent Congress from withdrawing a State's immunity. Thus, it would be ironic to construe the Chisholm dissent as precedent for the conclusion that Article III limits Congress' power to determine the scope of a State's sovereign immunity in federal court.[4]

* * * Article [III] should not then have been construed, and should not now be construed, to prevent Congress from granting States a sovereign immunity defense in such cases. That reading of Article III, however, explains why the majority's holding in Chisholm could not have been reversed by a simple statutory amendment adopting Justice Iredell's interpretation of the Judiciary Act of 1789. * * *

* * * Chisholm's holding could have been overturned by simply amending the Constitution to restore to Congress the authority to recognize the doctrine. As it was, the plain text of the Eleventh Amendment would seem to go further and to limit the judicial power itself in a certain class of cases. In doing so, however, the Amendment's quite explicit text establishes only a partial bar to a federal court's power to entertain a suit against a State.

4. In two sentences at the end of his lengthy opinion, Justice Iredell stated that his then-present view was that the Constitution would not permit a "compulsive suit against a State for the recovery of money." In light of Justice Iredell's express statement that the only question before the Court was the propriety of an individual's action for assumpsit against a State, an action which, of course, results in a money judgment, this dicta should not be understood to state the general view that the Constitution bars all suits against unconsenting States. * * *

Justice Brennan has persuasively explained that the Eleventh Amendment's jurisdictional restriction is best understood to apply only to suits premised on diversity jurisdiction, see Atascadero State Hospital v. Scanlon, 473 U.S. 234, 247 (1985)(dissenting opinion), and Justice Scalia has agreed that the plain text of the Amendment cannot be read to apply to federal-question cases. See Pennsylvania v. Union Gas, 491 U.S. at 31 (dissenting opinion).[8] Whatever the precise dimensions of the Amendment, its express terms plainly do not apply to all suits brought against unconsenting States.[9] The question thus becomes whether the relatively modest jurisdictional bar that the Eleventh Amendment imposes should be understood to reveal that a more general jurisdictional bar implicitly inheres in Article III.

* * *

diversity cases only ←

II

The majority appears to acknowledge that one cannot deduce from either the text of Article III or the plain terms of the Eleventh Amendment that the judicial power does not extend to a congressionally created cause of action against a State brought by one of that State's citizens. Nevertheless, the majority asserts that precedent compels that same conclusion. I disagree. The majority relies first on our decision in Hans v. Louisiana, which involved a suit by a citizen of Louisiana against that State for a claimed violation of the Contracts Clause. The majority suggests that by dismissing the suit, Hans effectively held that federal courts have no power to hear federal question suits brought by same-state plaintiffs.

Hans does not hold, however, that the Eleventh Amendment, or any other constitutional provision, precludes federal courts from entertaining actions brought by citizens against their own States in the face of contrary congressional direction. * * * Hans instead reflects, at the most, this Court's conclusion that, as a matter of federal common law, federal courts should decline to entertain suits against unconsenting States. Because Hans did not announce a constitutionally mandated jurisdictional bar, one need not overrule Hans, or even question its reasoning, in order to conclude that Congress may direct the federal courts to reject sovereign immunity in those suits not mentioned by the Eleventh Amendment. Instead, one need only follow it.

* * *

Hans doesn't deal w/ congressional action

As * * * [analysis of Justice Bradley's "somewhat cryptic" opinion in the Hans case] demonstrates, Hans itself looked to see whether Congress had displaced the presumption that sovereign immunity obtains. Although the opinion did go to great lengths to establish the quite uncontroversial historical

8. Of course, even if the Eleventh Amendment applies to federal-question cases brought by a citizen of another State, its express terms pose no bar to a federal court assuming jurisdiction in a federal-question case brought by an in-state plaintiff pursuant to Congress' express authorization. As that is precisely the posture of the suit before us, and as it was also precisely the posture of the suit at issue in Pennsylvania v. Union Gas, there is no need to decide here whether Congress would be barred from authorizing out-of-state plaintiffs to enforce federal rights against States in federal court. * * *

9. Under the "plain text" of the Eleventh Amendment, I note that there would appear to be no more basis for the conclusion that States may consent to federal-court jurisdiction in actions brought by out-of-state or foreign citizens, than there would be for the view that States should be permitted to consent to the jurisdiction of a federal court in a case that poses no federal question. * * *

proposition that unconsenting States generally were not subject to suit, that entire discussion preceded the opinion's statutory analysis. Thus, the opinion's thorough historical investigation served only to establish a presumption against jurisdiction that Congress must overcome, not an inviolable jurisdictional restriction that inheres in the Constitution itself.

* * *

* * * [U]nlike in Hans, in this case Congress has, by virtue of the Indian Gaming Regulation Act, affirmatively manifested its intention to "invest its courts with" jurisdiction beyond the limits set forth in the general jurisdictional statute. By contrast, because Hans involved only an implied cause of action based directly on the Constitution, the Judiciary Act of 1875 constituted the sole indication as to whether Congress intended federal-court jurisdiction to extend to a suit against an unconsenting State.

* * * The reasons that may support a federal court's hesitancy to construe a judicially crafted constitutional remedy narrowly out of respect for a State's sovereignty do not bear on whether Congress may preclude a State's invocation of such a defense when it expressly establishes a federal remedy for the violation of a federal right.

* * *

* * * [With respect to Hans], the particular nature of the federal question involved in [that case] renders the majority's reliance upon its rule even less defensible. Hans deduced its rebuttable presumption in favor of sovereign immunity largely on the basis of its extensive analysis of cases holding that the sovereign could not be forced to make good on its debts via a private suit. * * *

In Hans, the plaintiff asserted a Contracts Clause claim against his State and thus asserted a federal right. To show that Louisiana had impaired its federal obligation, however, Hans first had to demonstrate that the State had entered into an enforceable contract as a matter of state law. That Hans chose to bring his claim in federal court as a Contract Clause action could not change the fact that he was, at bottom, seeking to enforce a contract with the State.

* * *

The view that the rule of Hans is more substantive than jurisdictional comports with Hamilton's famous discussion of sovereign immunity in The Federalist Papers. Hamilton offered his view that the federal judicial power would not extend to suits against unconsenting States only in the context of his contention that no contract with a State could be enforceable against the State's desire. He did not argue that a State's immunity from suit in federal court would be absolute. * * *

III

* * * I agree with the majority that in all cases to which the judicial power does not extend—either because they are not within any category defined in Article III or because they are within the category withdrawn from Article III by the Eleventh Amendment—Congress lacks the power to confer jurisdiction on the federal courts. * * *

* * *

The fundamental error that continues to lead the Court astray is its failure to acknowledge that its modern embodiment of the ancient doctrine of sovereign immunity "has absolutely nothing to do with the limit on judicial power contained in the Eleventh Amendment." Pennsylvania v. Union Gas Co., 491 U.S. at 25 (Stevens, J., concurring). It rests rather on concerns of federalism and comity that merit respect but are nevertheless, in cases such as the one before us, subordinate to the plenary power of Congress.

IV

As I noted above, for the purpose of deciding this case, it is not necessary to question the wisdom of the Court's decision in Hans v. Louisiana. Given the absence of precedent for the Court's dramatic application of the sovereign immunity doctrine today, it is nevertheless appropriate to identify the questionable heritage of the doctrine and to suggest that there are valid reasons for limiting, or even rejecting that doctrine altogether, rather than expanding it.

Except insofar as it has been incorporated into the text of the Eleventh Amendment, the doctrine is entirely the product of judge-made law. Three features of its English ancestry make it particularly unsuitable for incorporation into the law of this democratic Nation.

* * * [Justice Stevens described as "absurd" the notion that "the King can do no wrong", and argued that in any event it was an "unacceptable" proposition "on this side of the Atlantic." He then stated that an idea of immunity based on the sovereign's "divine right" could not apply in a society that separates Church and State, and found similarly inapplicable any argument relying on the "indignity" of allowing a commoner to sue the sovereign. He then criticized as both "unsatisfying", and irrelevant to the question of state immunity in a federal court, the argument of Justice Holmes in Kawananakoa v. Polyblank, 205 U.S. 349, 353 (1907), quoted at Fourth Edition p. 1001.]

In this country the sovereignty of the individual States is subordinate both to the citizenry of each State and to the supreme law of the federal sovereign. For that reason, Justice Holmes' explanation for a rule that allows a State to avoid suit in its own courts does not even speak to the question whether Congress should be able to authorize a federal court to provide a private remedy for a State's violation of federal law. In my view, neither the majority's opinion today, nor any earlier opinion by any Member of the Court, has identified any acceptable reason for concluding that the absence of a State's consent to be sued in federal court should affect the power of Congress to authorize federal courts to remedy violations of federal law by States or their officials in actions not covered by the Eleventh Amendment's explicit text.

While I am persuaded that there is no justification for permanently enshrining the judge-made law of sovereign immunity, I recognize that federalism concerns—and even the interest in protecting the solvency of the States that was at work in Chisholm and Hans—may well justify a grant of immunity from federal litigation in certain classes of cases. Such a grant, however, should be the product of a reasoned decision by the policymaking branch of our Government. For this Court to conclude that time-worn shibboleths iterated and reiterated by judges should take precedence over the deliberations of the Congress of the United States is simply irresponsible.

V

Fortunately, and somewhat fortuitously, a jurisdictional problem that is unmentioned by the Court may deprive its opinion of precedential significance. The Indian Gaming Regulatory Act establishes a unique set of procedures for resolving the dispute between the Tribe and the State. If each adversary adamantly adheres to its understanding of the law, if the District Court determines that the State's inflexibility constitutes a failure to negotiate in good faith, and if the State thereafter continues to insist that it is acting within its rights, the maximum sanction that the Court can impose is an order that refers the controversy to a member of the Executive Branch of the Government for resolution. 25 U.S.C. § 2710(d)(7)(B). As the Court of Appeals interpreted the Act, this final disposition is available even though the action against the State and its Governor may not be maintained. (The Court does not tell us whether it agrees or disagrees with that disposition.) In my judgment, it is extremely doubtful that the obviously dispensable involvement of the judiciary in the intermediate stages of a procedure that begins and ends in the Executive Branch is a proper exercise of judicial power. It may well follow that the misguided opinion of today's majority has nothing more than an advisory character. [With respect to this suggestion, see Fourth Edition, Chap. II, Sec. 2.] Whether or not that be so, the better reasoning in Justice Souter's far wiser and far more scholarly opinion will surely be the law one day.*

For these reasons, as well as those set forth in Justice Souter's opinion, I respectfully dissent.

■ JUSTICE SOUTER, with whom JUSTICE GINSBURG and JUSTICE BREYER join, dissenting.

* * * [T]he Court today holds for the first time since the founding of the Republic that Congress has no authority to subject a State to the jurisdiction of a federal court at the behest of an individual asserting a federal right. * * *

* * *

I

It is useful to separate three questions: (1) whether the States enjoyed sovereign immunity if sued in their own courts in the period prior to ratification of the National Constitution; (2) if so, whether after ratification the States were entitled to claim some such immunity when sued in a federal court exercising jurisdiction either because the suit was between a State and a nonstate litigant who was not its citizen, or because the issue in the case raised a federal question; and (3) whether any state sovereign immunity recognized in federal court may be abrogated by Congress.

* * * [Justice Souter here stated that the answer to the first question is not clear and that the Hans Court had premised its answer to the second on erroneous reasoning.]

The Court's answer today to the third question is likewise at odds with the Founders' view that common law, when it was received into the new American legal systems, was always subject to legislative amendment. * * *

* * *

* [Ed.] For discussion of Justice Stevens'
suggestion in this paragraph of his dissent,
see pp. [8–9], *supra.*

A

* * *

Whatever the scope of sovereign immunity might have been in the Colonies * * * or during the period of Confederation, the proposal to establish a National Government under the Constitution drafted in 1787 presented a prospect unknown to the common law prior to the American experience: the States would become parts of a system in which sovereignty over even domestic matters would be divided or parcelled out between the States and the Nation, the latter to be invested with its own judicial power and the right to prevail against the States whenever their respective substantive laws might be in conflict. With this prospect in mind, the 1787 Constitution might have addressed state sovereign immunity by eliminating whatever sovereign immunity the States previously had, as to any matter subject to federal law or jurisdiction; by recognizing an analogue to the old immunity in the new context of federal jurisdiction, but subject to abrogation as to any matter within that jurisdiction; or by enshrining a doctrine of inviolable state sovereign immunity in the text, thereby giving it constitutional protection in the new federal jurisdiction.

The 1787 draft in fact said nothing on the subject, and it was this very silence that occasioned some, though apparently not widespread, dispute among the Framers and others over whether ratification of the Constitution would preclude a State sued in federal court from asserting sovereign immunity as it could have done on any matter of nonfederal law litigated in its own courts. As it has come down to us, the discussion gave no attention to congressional power under the proposed Article I but focused entirely on the limits of the judicial power provided in Article III. * * *

* * * It may have been reasonable to contend (as we will see that Madison, Marshall, and Hamilton did) that Article III would not alter States' pre-existing common-law immunity despite its unqualified grant of jurisdiction over diversity suits against States. But then, as now, there was no textual support for contending that Article III or any other provision would "constitutionalize" state sovereign immunity, and no one uttered any such contention.

B

The argument among the Framers and their friends about sovereign immunity in federal citizen-state diversity cases * * * ended when this Court, in Chisholm v. Georgia, chose between the constitutional alternatives of abrogation and recognition of the immunity enjoyed at common law. The 4-to-1 majority adopted the reasonable (although not compelled) interpretation that the first of the two Citizen–State Diversity Clauses abrogated for purposes of federal jurisdiction any immunity the States might have enjoyed in their own courts, and Georgia was accordingly held subject to the judicial power in a common-law assumpsit action by a South Carolina citizen suing to collect a debt. The case also settled, by implication, any question there could possibly have been about recognizing state sovereign immunity in actions depending on the federal question (or "arising under") head of jurisdiction as well. * * *

* * * [Justice Souter here discusses Justice Iredell's dissent, referring also to Justice Stevens' discussion of that dissent.]

C

The Eleventh Amendment, of course, repudiated Chisholm * * *. There are two plausible readings of this provision's text. Under the first, it simply repeals the Citizen–State Diversity Clauses of Article III for all cases in which the State appears as a defendant. Under the second, it strips the federal courts of jurisdiction in any case in which a state defendant is sued by a citizen not its own, even if jurisdiction might otherwise rest on the existence of a federal question in the suit. Neither reading of the Amendment, of course, furnishes authority for the Court's view in today's case * * *.

The history and structure of the Eleventh Amendment convincingly show that it reaches only to suits subject to federal jurisdiction exclusively under the Citizen–State Diversity Clauses.[8] In precisely tracking the language in Article III providing for citizen-state diversity jurisdiction, the text of the Amendment does, after all, suggest to common sense that only the Diversity Clauses are being addressed. If the Framers had meant the Amendment to bar federal question suits as well, they could not only have made their intentions clearer very easily, but could simply have adopted the first post-Chisholm proposal, introduced in the House of Representatives by Theodore Sedgwick of Massachusetts on instructions from the Legislature of that Commonwealth. Its provisions would have had exactly that expansive effect:

"No state shall be liable to be made a party defendant, in any of the judicial courts, established, or which shall be established under the authority of the United States, at the suit of any person or persons, whether a citizen or citizens, or a foreigner or foreigners, or of any body politic or corporate, whether within or without the United States." Gazette of the United States 303 (Feb. 20, 1793).

* * *

Congress took no action on Sedgwick's proposal, however, and the Amendment as ultimately adopted two years later could hardly have been meant to limit federal question jurisdiction, or it would never have left the states open to federal question suits by their own citizens. * * *

It should accordingly come as no surprise that the weightiest commentary following the amendment's adoption described it simply as constricting the scope of the Citizen–State Diversity Clauses. * * * [Discussion of Cohens v. Virginia and Osborn v. Bank of the United States omitted.]

The good sense of this early construction of the Amendment as affecting the diversity jurisdiction and no more has the further virtue of making sense of this Court's repeated exercise of appellate jurisdiction in federal question suits brought against states in their own courts by out-of-staters. Exercising appellate jurisdiction in these cases would have been patent error if the Eleventh Amendment limited federal question jurisdiction, for the Amendment's unconditional language ("shall not be construed") makes no distinction between trial and appellate jurisdiction. And yet, again and again we have entertained such

---

8. The great weight of scholarly commentary agrees. * * * As one scholar has observed, the literature is "remarkably consistent in its evaluation of the historical evidence and text of the amendment as not supporting a broad rule of constitutional immunity for states." Jackson, *The Supreme Court, the Eleventh Amendment, and State Sovereign Immunity,* 98 Yale L.J. 1, 44, n. 179.

appellate cases, even when brought against the State in its own name by a private plaintiff for money damages. * * *

* * *

II

* * * Hans v. Louisiana * * * was indeed a leap in the direction of today's holding, even though it does not take the Court all the way. * * * Although the Court invoked a principle of sovereign immunity to cure what it took to be the Eleventh Amendment's anomaly of barring only those state suits brought by noncitizen plaintiffs, the Hans Court had no occasion to consider whether Congress could abrogate that background immunity by statute. * * * [But since, as shown below, Hans was wrongly decided,] [i]t follows that the Court's further step today of constitutionalizing Hans's rule against abrogation by Congress compounds and immensely magnifies the century-old mistake of Hans itself and takes its place with other historic examples of textually untethered elevations of judicially derived rules to the status of inviolable constitutional law.

[handwritten margin note: Hans was wrong!]

[handwritten margin note: mistake (!) of Hans]

A

* * *

* * * The Court [in Hans] rested its opinion on avoiding the supposed anomaly of recognizing jurisdiction to entertain a citizen's federal question suit, but not one brought by a noncitizen. There was, however, no such anomaly at all. As already explained, federal question cases are not touched by the Eleventh Amendment, which leaves a State open to federal question suits by citizens and noncitizens alike. If Hans had been from Massachusetts the Eleventh Amendment would not have barred his action against Louisiana.

Although there was thus no anomaly to be cured by Hans, the case certainly created its own anomaly in leaving federal courts entirely without jurisdiction to enforce paramount federal law at the behest of a citizen against a State that broke it. It destroyed the congruence of the judicial power under Article III with the substantive guarantees of the Constitution, and with the provisions of statutes passed by Congress in the exercise of its power under Article I: when a State injured an individual in violation of federal law no federal forum could provide direct relief. * * *

[handwritten margin note: → fed w/o power to enforce fed law]

How such a result could have been threatened on the basis of a principle not so much as mentioned in the Constitution is difficult to understand. But history provides the explanation. * * * Hans was one episode in a long story of debt repudiation by the States of the former Confederacy after the end of Reconstruction. * * * Given the likelihood that a judgment against the State could not be enforced, it is not wholly surprising that the Hans Court found a way to avoid the certainty of the State's contempt.

* * *

B

The majority does not dispute the point that Hans v. Louisiana had no occasion to decide whether Congress could abrogate a State's immunity from federal question suits. * * *

* * *

The majority * * * would read the "rationale" of Hans and its line of subsequent cases as answering the further question whether the "postulate" of sovereign immunity that "limits and controls" the exercise of Article III jurisdiction, Monaco [v. Mississippi, 292 U.S.] at 322, is constitutional in stature and therefore unalterable by Congress. It is true that there are statements in the cases that point toward just this conclusion. * * * These statements, however, are dicta * * * [and] are counterbalanced by many other opinions that have either stated the immunity principle without more, or have suggested that the Hans immunity is not of constitutional stature. * * *

The most damning evidence for the Court's theory that Hans rests on a broad rationale of immunity unalterable by Congress, however, is the Court's proven tendency to disregard the post-Hans dicta in cases where that dicta would have mattered. If it is indeed true that "private suits against States [are] not permitted under Article III (by virtue of the understanding represented by the Eleventh Amendment)," Union Gas, 491 U.S., at 40 (Scalia, J., concurring in part and dissenting in part), then it is hard to see how a State's sovereign immunity may be waived any more than it may be abrogated by Congress. * * *

waiver/
abrogation

If these examples were not enough to distinguish Hans's rationale of a pre-existing doctrine of sovereign immunity from the post-Hans dicta indicating that this immunity is constitutional, one would need only to consider a final set of cases: those in which we have assumed, without deciding, that congressional power to abrogate state sovereign immunity exists even when § 5 of the Fourteenth Amendment has an [no?] application. * * * Although the Court in each of these cases failed to find abrogation for lack of a clear statement of congressional intent, the assumption that such power was available would hardly have been permissible if, at that time, today's majority's view of the law had been firmly established. * * *

* * *

III

Three critical errors in Hans weigh against constitutionalizing its holding as the majority does today. The first we have already seen: the Hans Court misread the Eleventh Amendment. It also misunderstood the conditions under which common-law doctrines were received or rejected at the time of the Founding, and it fundamentally mistook the very nature of sovereignty in the young Republic that was supposed to entail a State's immunity to federal question jurisdiction in a federal court. While I would not, as a matter of stare decisis, overrule Hans today, an understanding of its failings on these points will show how the Court today simply compounds already serious error in taking Hans the further step of investing its rule with constitutional inviolability against the considered judgment of Congress to abrogate it.

A

* * *

* * * [The sovereign immunity] doctrine's common-law status in the period covering the Founding and the later adoption of the Eleventh Amendment should have raised a warning flag to the Hans Court and it should do the same for the Court today. For although the Court has persistently assumed that the common law's presence in the minds of the early Framers must have

functioned as a limitation on their understanding of the new Nation's constitutional powers, this turns out not to be so at all. One of the characteristics of the
Founding generation, on the contrary, was its joinder of an appreciation of its
immediate and powerful common-law heritage with caution in settling that
inheritance on the political systems of the new Republic. * * * An examination
of the States' experience with common-law reception will shed light on subsequent theory and practice at the national level, and demonstrate that our
history is entirely at odds with Hans's resort to a common-law principle to limit
the Constitution's contrary text.

1

* * * [Justice Souter here discusses the widespread extent to which
reception of English common law in the states was subject to limitation and
adaptation in the light of local circumstances.]

2

* * * [Justice Souter here describes and emphasizes the significance of the
lack of any provision for the reception of English common law at the national
level.]

B

Given the refusal to entertain any wholesale reception of common law,
given the failure of the new Constitution to make any provision for adoption of
common law as such, and given the protests already quoted that no general
reception had occurred, the Hans Court and the Court today cannot reasonably
argue that something like the old immunity doctrine somehow slipped in as a
tacit but enforceable background principle. The evidence is even more specific,
however, that there was no pervasive understanding that sovereign immunity
had limited federal question jurisdiction.

1

As I have already noted briefly, the Framers and their contemporaries did
not agree about the place of common-law state sovereign immunity even as to
federal jurisdiction resting on the Citizen–State Diversity Clauses. Edmund
Randolph argued in favor of ratification on the ground that the immunity
would not be recognized, leaving the States subject to jurisdiction. Patrick
Henry opposed ratification on the basis of exactly the same reading. On the
other hand, James Madison, John Marshall, and Alexander Hamilton all appear
to have believed that the common-law immunity from suit would survive the
ratification of Article III, so as to be at a State's disposal when jurisdiction
would depend on diversity. This would have left the States free to enjoy a
traditional immunity as defendants without barring the exercise of judicial
power over them if they chose to enter the federal courts as diversity plaintiffs
or to waive their immunity as diversity defendants. See [3 Elliot's Debates] at
533 (Madison: the Constitution "gives a citizen a right to be heard in the
federal courts; and if a state should condescend to be a party, this court may
take cognizance of it");[39] id., at 556 (Marshall: "I see a difficulty in making a
state defendant, which does not prevent its being plaintiff"). * * *

39. The Court accuses me of quoting
this statement out of context, but the additional material included by the Court makes
no difference. I am conceding that Madison,

* * * [Justice Souter here quotes from and discusses Hamilton's view of sovereignty in two Federalist Papers: Nos. 32 and 81. He concludes from these materials that Hamilton did not address the question of a state's immunity "when a congressional statute not only binds the States but even creates an affirmative obligation on the State as such, as in this case". Thus, he contends, Hamilton "is no authority for the Court's position."]

* * *

2

We said in Blatchford v. Native Village of Noatak, 501 U.S. 775, 779 (1991), that "the States entered the federal system with their sovereignty intact," but we surely did not mean that they entered that system with the sovereignty they would have claimed if each State had assumed independent existence in the community of nations, for even the Articles of Confederation allowed for less than that. While there is no need here to calculate exactly how close the American States came to sovereignty in the classic sense prior to ratification of the Constitution, it is clear that the act of ratification affected their sovereignty in a way different from any previous political event in America or anywhere else. For the adoption of the Constitution made them members of a novel federal system that sought to balance the States' exercise of some sovereign prerogatives delegated from their own people with the principle of a limited but centralizing federal supremacy.

* * *

Given this metamorphosis of the idea of sovereignty in the years leading up to 1789, the question whether the old immunity doctrine might have been received as something suitable for the new world of federal question jurisdiction is a crucial one. The answer is that sovereign immunity as it would have been known to the Framers before ratification thereafter became inapplicable as a matter of logic in a federal suit raising a federal question. * * *

* * * [In light of] the Framers' general concern with curbing abuses by state governments, it would be amazing if the scheme of delegated powers embodied in the Constitution had left the National Government powerless to render the States judicially accountable for violations of federal rights. * * *

Today's majority discounts this concern. Without citing a single source to the contrary, the Court dismisses the historical evidence regarding the Framers' vision of the relationship between national and state sovereignty, and reassures us that "the Nation survived for nearly two centuries without the question of the existence of [the abrogation] power ever being presented to this Court." But we are concerned here not with the survival of the Nation but the opportunity of its citizens to enforce federal rights in a way that Congress provides. * * * In the end, is it plausible to contend that the plan of the convention was meant to leave the National Government without any way to render individuals capable of enforcing their federal rights directly against an intransigent state?

Hamilton, and Marshall all agreed that Article III did not of its own force abrogate the states' pre-existing common-law immunity, at least with respect to diversity suits. None of the statements offered by the Court, however, purports to deal with federal question jurisdiction or with the question whether Congress, acting pursuant to its Article I powers, could create a cause of action against a State. * * *

C

* * * [In this section, Justice Souter develops the theme that the majority's decision, "constitutionalizing common-law rules at the expense of legislative authority," cannot be squared with the Framers' "abhorrence" of the notion that any common law rules received into the new legal systems would be beyond legislative power to change or reject. He concludes by analogizing the decision to the "practice in the century's early decades that brought this Court to the nadir of competence that we identify with Lochner v. New York, 198 U.S. 45 (1905)."]

IV

The Court's holding that the States' Hans immunity may not be abrogated by Congress leads to the final question in this case, whether federal question jurisdiction exists to order prospective relief enforcing IGRA against a state officer [the Governor], who is said to be authorized to take the action required by the federal law. * * *. The answer to this question is an easy yes, the officer is subject to suit under the rule in Ex parte Young, and the case could, and should, readily be decided on this point alone.

A

* * *

* * * [T]he rule we speak of under the name of Young is so far inherent in the jurisdictional limitation imposed by sovereign immunity as to have been recognized since the Middle Ages. For that long it has been settled doctrine that suit against an officer of the Crown permitted relief against the government despite the Crown's immunity from suit in its own courts and the maxim that the king could do no wrong. * * *

B

* * *

The decision in Ex parte Young, and the historic doctrine it embodies, * * * plays a foundational role in American constitutionalism, and while the doctrine is sometimes called a "fiction," the long history of its felt necessity shows it to be something much more estimable, as we may see by considering the facts of the case. "Young was really and truly about to damage the interest of plaintiffs. Whether what he was about to do amounted to a legal injury depended on the authority of his employer, the state. If the state could constitutionally authorize the act then the loss suffered by plaintiffs was not a wrong for which the law provided a remedy.... If the state could not constitutionally authorize the act then Young was not acting by its authority." Orth, Judicial Power of the United States, at 133. The doctrine we call Ex parte Young is nothing short of "indispensable to the establishment of constitutional government and the rule of law." C. Wright, Law of Federal Courts 292 (4th ed. 1983).

A rule of such lineage, engendered by such necessity, should not be easily displaced, if indeed it is displaceable at all, for it marks the frontier of the enforceability of federal law against sometimes competing state policies. We have in fact never before inferred a congressional intent to eliminate this time-honored practice of enforcing federal law. That of course does not mean that the intent may never be inferred, and where, as here, the underlying right is one of statutory rather than constitutional dimension, I do not in theory reject the Court's assumption that Congress may bar enforcement by suit even against a state official. But because in practice, in the real world of congressional legislation, such an intent would be exceedingly odd, it would be equally odd for this Court to recognize an intent to block the customary application of Ex parte Young without applying the rule recognized in our previous cases, which have insisted on a clear statement before assuming a congressional purpose to "affect the federal balance," United States v. Bass, 404 U.S. 336, 349 (1971). * * *

C

There is no question that by its own terms Young's indispensable rule authorizes the exercise of federal jurisdiction over [the Governor]. Since this case does not, of course, involve retrospective relief, Edelman's limit is irrelevant, and there is no other jurisdictional limitation. Obviously, for jurisdictional purposes it makes no difference in principle whether the injunction orders an official not to act, as in Young, or requires the official to take some positive step, as in Milliken or Quern. Nothing, then, in this case renders Young unsuitable as a jurisdictional basis for determining on the merits whether the petitioners are entitled to an order against a state official under general equitable doctrine. The Court does not say otherwise, and yet it refuses to apply Young. There is no adequate reason for its refusal.

* * *

1

* * *

The Bivens issue in [Schweiker v.] Chilicky [relied on by the majority] * * * is different from the Young issue here in every significant respect. Young is not an example of a novel rule that a proponent has a burden to justify affirmatively on policy grounds in every context in which it might arguably be recognized; it is a general principle of federal equity jurisdiction that has been recognized throughout our history and for centuries before our own history began. * * * One cannot intelligibly generalize from Chilicky's standards for imposing the burden to justify a supplementary scheme of tort law, to the displacement of Young's traditional and indispensable jurisdictional basis for ensuring official compliance with federal law when a State itself is immune from suit.

2

Next, the Court suggests that it may be justified in displacing Young because Young would allow litigants to ignore the "intricate procedures" of IGRA in favor of a menu of streamlined equity rules from which any litigant could order as he saw fit. But there is no basis in law for this suggestion, and the strongest authority to reject it. Young did not establish a new cause of action and it does not impose any particular procedural regime in the suits it permits. It stands, instead, for a jurisdictional rule by which paramount federal law may be enforced in a federal court by substituting a non-immune party (the state officer) for an immune one (the State itself). Young does no more and furnishes no authority for the Court's assumption that it somehow preempts procedural rules devised by Congress for particular kinds of cases that may depend on Young for federal jurisdiction.

* * *

3

The Court's third strand of reasoning for displacing Ex parte Young is a supposed inference that Congress so intended. Since the Court rests this inference in large part on its erroneous assumption that the statute's procedural limitations would not be applied in a suit against an officer for which Young provided the jurisdictional basis, the error of that assumption is enough to show the unsoundness of any inference that Congress meant to exclude Young's application. But there are further reasons pointing to the utter implausibility of the Court's reading of the congressional mind.

IGRA's jurisdictional provision reads as though it had been drafted with the specific intent to apply to officer liability under Young. * * * The door is so obviously just as open to jurisdiction over an officer under Young as to jurisdiction over a State directly that it is difficult to see why the statute would have been drafted as it was unless it was done in anticipation that Young might well be the jurisdictional basis for enforcement action.

But even if the jurisdictional provision had spoken narrowly of an action against the State itself (as it subsequently speaks in terms of the State's obligation), that would be no indication that Congress had rejected the application of Young. An order requiring a "State" to comply with federal law can, of course, take the form of an order directed to the State in its sovereign capacity. But as Ex parte Young and innumerable other cases show, there is nothing incongruous about a duty imposed on a "State" that Congress intended to be effectuated by an order directed to an appropriate state official. * * *

It may be that even the Court agrees, for it falls back to the position that only a State, not a state officer, can enter into a compact. This is true but wholly beside the point. The issue is whether negotiation should take place as required by IGRA and an officer (indeed, only an officer) can negotiate. * * *

Finally, one must judge the Court's purported inference by stepping back to ask why Congress could possibly have intended to jeopardize the enforcement of the statute by excluding application of Young's traditional jurisdictional rule, when that rule would make the difference between success or failure in the federal court if state sovereign immunity was recognized. Why would Congress have wanted to go for broke on the issue of state immunity in the event the State pleaded immunity as a jurisdictional bar? Why would Congress not have wanted IGRA to be enforced by means of a traditional doctrine giving federal courts jurisdiction over state officers, in an effort to harmonize state sovereign immunity with federal law that is paramount under the Supremacy Clause? There are no plausible answers to these questions.

D

There is, finally, a response to the Court's rejection of Young that ought to go without saying. Our long-standing practice is to read ambiguous statutes to avoid constitutional infirmity. * * *

V

Absent the application of Ex parte Young, I would, of course, follow Union Gas in recognizing congressional power under Article I to abrogate Hans immunity. Since the reasons for this position, as explained in Parts II–III, *supra,* tend to unsettle Hans as well as support Union Gas, I should add a word about my reasons for continuing to accept Hans's holding as a matter of stare decisis.

The Hans doctrine was erroneous, but it has not previously proven to be unworkable or to conflict with later doctrine or to suffer from the effects of facts developed since its decision (apart from those indicating its original errors). I would therefore treat Hans as it has always been treated in fact until today, as a doctrine of federal common law. For, as so understood, it has formed one of the strands of the federal relationship for over a century now, and the stability of that relationship is itself a value that stare decisis aims to respect.

In being ready to hold that the relationship may still be altered, not by the Court but by Congress, I would tread the course laid out elsewhere in our cases. The Court has repeatedly stated its assumption that insofar as the relative positions of States and Nation may be affected consistently with the Tenth Amendment, they would not be modified without deliberately expressed intent. * * *

When judging legislation passed under unmistakable Article I powers, no further restriction could be required. Nor does the Court explain why more could be demanded. In the past, we have assumed that a plain statement requirement is sufficient to protect the States from undue federal encroachments upon their traditional immunity from suit. It is hard to contend that this rule has set the bar too low, for (except in Union Gas) we have never found the requirement to be met outside the context of laws passed under § 5 of the Fourteenth Amendment. The exception I would recognize today proves the rule, moreover, because the federal abrogation of state immunity comes as part of a regulatory scheme which is itself designed to invest the States with regulatory powers that Congress need not extend to them. This fact suggests to me that the political safeguards of federalism are working, that a plain statement rule is an adequate check on congressional overreaching, and that today's abandonment of that approach is wholly unwarranted.

There is an even more fundamental "clear statement" principle, however, that the Court abandons today. John Marshall recognized it over a century and a half ago in the very context of state sovereign immunity in federal question cases:

"The jurisdiction of the Court, then, being extended by the letter of the constitution to all cases arising under it, or under the laws of the United States, it follows that those who would withdraw any case of this description from that jurisdiction, must sustain the exemption they claim on the spirit and true meaning of the constitution, which spirit and true meaning must be so apparent as to overrule the words which its framers have employed." Cohens v. Virginia, 6 Wheat. at 379–380.

Because neither text, precedent, nor history supports the majority's abdication of our responsibility to exercise the jurisdiction entrusted to us in Article III, I would reverse the judgment of the Court of Appeals.

NOTE ON CONGRESSIONAL POWER TO ABROGATE STATE IMMUNITY AND ON STATE CONSENT TO SUIT IN FEDERAL COURT

A. Abrogation

(1) *The Continuing Historical Debate.*

(a) The debate over the meaning and purpose of the Eleventh Amendment and over the precise scope and implications of the Hans decision continues sharply to divide the Court. In Seminole, by far the more elaborate historical analysis appears in the dissents, and particularly in that of Justice Souter. But the majority does more than rest on precedent; it invokes and relies on its very different version of the relevant history.

Especially when there is such sharp disagreement over historical questions, how great a role should they play—and how great a role do you believe they play in fact—in determining the vote of each Justice? For a Justice who believes *both* in "originalism" and in the importance of focusing on the particular language of positive law in interpreting that law, do those considerations come into conflict in this case?

(b) The disagreement between majority and dissent, and to a lesser extent, between the two dissenting opinions, is striking with respect to the rationale and holding of Hans. Look again at the Hans decision, Fourth Edition p. 1041. Granted that Justice Bradley's opinion is not a model of lucidity, and that it could have rested on narrow grounds (especially in light of the tenuous nature of the "federal" claim of impairment of contract), can it reasonably be read—as the dissenters contend—as stating only a rule of "federal common law"?[1] Bear in mind, in thinking about this question, that explicit recognition of true federal common law (as distinct from the "general" law of Swift v. Tyson) is in large part a twentieth century development.

(c) Would it then have been more candid, and at least as effective, for the dissenters to have urged that Hans should be squarely overruled to the extent that it posits a constitutional limitation that does not fall within the four corners of the Eleventh Amendment and yet lies beyond the power of Congress to override? Or is it possible to view Hans as articulating a concept of constitutionally protected state sovereign immunity analogous to the concept of constitutional preemption under the "dormant Commerce Clause", *i.e.,* one that Congress itself has the authority to affect in particular cases? Could such a concept be reasonably viewed as a kind of "constitutional common law"?

(2) *Twentieth Century Decisions on the Power of Congress to Abrogate State Sovereign Immunity in the Federal Courts.*

(a) *Fitzpatrick.* As both sides in Seminole acknowledge, the first decision dealing squarely with the power of Congress to abrogate state immunity was Fitzpatrick v. Bitzer, 427 U.S. 445 (1976), a Title VII federal court action

---

1. Meltzer, *The Seminole Decision and State Sovereign Immunity,* 1996 Sup.Ct.Rev. 1, 24–28, quotes extensively from Justice Bradley's opinion—including his statement that "cognizance of suits and actions unknown to the law, and forbidden by the law, was not contemplated by the Constitution when establishing the judicial power of the United States", concludes that Bradley's opinion clearly contains an "alternative constitutional holding" (p. 27), and suggests that Justice Souter's view of the Hans decision as resting only on federal common law may have been animated at least in part by a desire to "foreclose the response" that he was no different from the majority in his willingness to overrule precedent (p. 28).

CT's retirement plan discriminated against male employees

retro!

alleging that Connecticut's retirement plan discriminated against male employees. (Title VII regulates any "person" employing the requisite number of employees in interstate commerce; in 1972 Congress amended the definition of "person" to include state and local "governments, governmental agencies, [and] political subdivisions.") The Supreme Court, per Rehnquist, J., held that the Eleventh Amendment did not bar an award of retroactive retirement benefits and attorney's fees under Title VII, to be paid from the state treasury. Here, the Court said, "the 'threshold fact of congressional authorization' * * * is clearly present" (p. 452).

The 1972 amendment was enacted pursuant to Congress' power under § 5 of the Fourteenth Amendment. That Amendment as a whole represented a "shift in the federal-state balance [that] has been carried forward by more recent decisions of this Court," and past decisions had "sanctioned intrusions by Congress, acting under the Civil War Amendments, into the judicial, executive, and legislative spheres of autonomy previously preserved to the States" (p. 455). Justice Rehnquist continued (p. 456):

"It is true that none of these previous cases presented the question of the relationship between the Eleventh Amendment and the enforcement power granted to Congress under § 5 of the Fourteenth Amendment. But we think that the Eleventh Amendment, and the principle of state sovereignty which it embodies, are necessarily limited by the enforcement provisions of § 5 of the Fourteenth Amendment. In that section Congress is expressly granted authority to enforce 'by appropriate legislation' the substantive provisions of the Fourteenth Amendment, which themselves embody significant limitations on state authority. When Congress acts pursuant to § 5, not only is it exercising legislative authority that is plenary within the terms of the constitutional grant, it is exercising that authority under one section of a constitutional Amendment whose other sections by their own terms embody limitations on state authority. We think that Congress may, in determining what is 'appropriate legislation' for the purpose of enforcing the provisions of the Fourteenth Amendment, provide for private suits against States or state officials which are constitutionally impermissible in other contexts."

Note that the majority in Seminole does not question the continued vitality of Fitzpatrick. Is it readily apparent why the authority granted by § 5 of the Fourteenth Amendment is different from the authority to regulate state activity under other provisions of the Constitution? To what extent is it relevant that the Fourteenth Amendment was adopted *after* the Eleventh? *Cf.* 44 Liquormart, Inc. v. Rhode Island, 517 U.S. 484, 515–16 (1996)(holding that state authority recognized in the Twenty-first Amendment, relating to the regulation of "intoxicating liquors", does not "diminish the force" of the First Amendment as it applies to the states.)[2]

2. Meltzer, note 1, *supra*, at 20–24, criticizes the Court's distinction between abrogation under § 5 and abrogation pursuant to Article I on several grounds. With respect to the "temporal argument", he notes the long-established practice of viewing an amended enactment as a whole and observes that the argument rests in significant part on the purely stylistic convention of reproducing constitutional amendments after the text of the original document. He then points out that the Civil War and its aftermath had a profound impact on all aspects of constitutional theory and practice—an impact not limited to the post-Civil War amendments—and that the distinction drawn by the Court is especially ironic, coming as it did in a case involving Indian affairs, where the limitation on state sovereignty is particularly stringent.

(b) *Quern and the "Clear Statement" Rule.* In a lengthy dictum in Quern v. Jordan, 440 U.S. 332 (1979), Fourth Edition p. 1075, the Court rejected the view that § 1983 should be interpreted to make states suable in federal court: "[Section] 1983 does not explicitly and by clear language indicate on its face an intent to sweep away the immunity of the States; nor does it have a history which focuses directly on the question of state liability and which shows that Congress considered and firmly decided to abrogate the Eleventh Amendment immunity of the States" (p. 345).

The Court's insistence on a clear statement (in the text of the relevant statute) of congressional intent to abrogate state immunity was reemphasized, and made even more rigorous, in several decisions prior to Seminole, *e.g.,* Atascadero State Hosp. v. Scanlon, 473 U.S. 234 (1985), and Dellmuth v. Muth, 491 U.S. 223 (1989). These decisions continue to be relevant in construing congressional action under § 5 of the Fourteenth Amendment. Even though what has been called a "super clear statement rule" may on occasion frustrate the implementation of legislative purpose, can it be defended on the basis that Congress should be required to face directly its political responsibility in deciding to override state interests? See, *e.g.,* Gregory v. Ashcroft, 501 U.S. 452 (1991)(holding that a federal law prohibiting mandatory retirement did not apply to appointed state judges).[3]

Assuming that the case for a clear statutory statement of intent to subject a state to substantive liability is a strong one (on grounds of federalism and political accountability), is it appropriate to impose a *second* clear statement rule with respect to abrogation of state immunity to federal court suit? In light of the statutory grant of general federal question jurisdiction, and the understandable view that a state's own courts may constitute a less desirable forum for the litigation of claims against that state, why shouldn't ordinary techniques of statutory interpretation be sufficient to resolve the issue of abrogation in cases where legislative power to abrogate still exists?

(c) *Union Gas.* Pennsylvania v. Union Gas, holding (in the context of environmental regulation) that Congress can abrogate state immunity from federal court suit in the exercise of its power under the Commerce Clause—and that it did so in the environmental statutes there at issue—is set forth as a principal case in the Fourth Edition at p. 1085. For present purposes it is noteworthy that in casting a critical vote, Justice White concluded that Congress had not in fact sought to abrogate state immunity but that it had the

---

3. In contrast to the approach in these decisions, the Fitzpatrick rationale was applied in the absence of a "clear statement" in Hutto v. Finney, 437 U.S. 678 (1978), discussed at Fourth Edition p. 1074. Hutto was a lawsuit under 42 U.S.C. § 1983 in which injunctive relief against state officials had been awarded. Plaintiffs sought attorney's fees under the Civil Rights Attorney's Fees Awards Act of 1976, 42 U.S.C. § 1988, which provides that in actions to enforce certain federal civil rights statutes (including § 1983), a court may award prevailing parties reasonable attorney's fees "as part of the costs". The Act does not specify that fees may be awarded against a state, but the Senate and House reports did say that fees may be collected, *inter alia,* "from the State", and the House report cited Fitzpatrick. The Court concluded that Congress intended to make states vulnerable to liability for attorney's fees in § 1983 actions, and that because § 1983 enforces the Fourteenth Amendment, the case fell within the principle of Fitzpatrick. (After Seminole, would such attorney's fees be available in a § 1983 action that was based on a violation of a federal right *not* grounded in the Fourteenth Amendment— *e.g.,* a violation of a federal requirement in a welfare program?)

power to do so.[4] On the latter point, Justice White (who did refer in his cryptic opinion to Article I in general but not to the commerce power in particular) declined to endorse any specific theory advanced by the plurality, stating only that he concurred in Justice Brennan's conclusion but did not agree "with much of his reasoning."

Under the circumstances, was it surprising that the Union Gas decision had such a short life? Must Justice White, in refusing to articulate any rationale, accept at least some of the blame? Or was the newly constituted majority determined to overrule Union Gas in any event?

(d) *Seminole.* Wasn't the majority correct that the Union Gas and Seminole decisions had to stand or fall together? Is there any principled basis for distinguishing between the power of Congress under the Commerce Clause and its power under the Indian Commerce Clause?[5]

As suggested above (in Paragraph (1)), there is considerable tension between the notion that state sovereign immunity is constitutionally protected beyond any textually supported reading of the Eleventh Amendment, and the power of Congress to abrogate that immunity. Several commentators argued (prior to Seminole), however, that such authority to abrogate should exist under Article I because the immunity in question is designed to curb the power of appointed federal judges, not politically accountable legislators. See, *e.g.,* Tribe, *Intergovernmental Immunities in Litigation, Taxation, and Regulation: Separation of Powers Issues in Controversies About Federalism,* 89 Harv.L.Rev. 682 (1976); Nowak, *The Scope of Congressional Power to Create Causes of Action Against State Government and the History of the Eleventh and Fourteenth Amendments,* 75 Colum.L.Rev. 1413 (1975). But see Meltzer, note 1, *supra,* at 16–20 (pointing out that Article III's judicial power has never been understood to be subject to congressional expansion, and that the Tribe–Nowak arguments "cannot easily explain why a state is immune from the exercise of original jurisdiction by the district courts but not from Supreme Court appellate jurisdiction to review state judgments" (p. 19)).

(3) *The Consequences of the Seminole Decision.*

(a) Footnote 4 of the Seminole opinion notes the conclusion of the court of appeals that as a result of its decision, the Tribe had immediate recourse to the Secretary of the Interior. Does the Supreme Court's holding, then, end up effectively *reducing* state participation in the process unless the state is willing to waive its immunity from suit?[6]

(b) Doesn't the result in Seminole increase the significance of the determination whether a particular legislative effort to abrogate state immunity falls

---

4. Justice Scalia, on the other hand, concluded that Congress had intended to abrogate state immunity but lacked the constitutional power to take such action.

5. Is there any principled basis for distinguishing between the Commerce Clause and other powers of Congress under Article I? Compare, *e.g.,* Diaz–Gandia v. Dapena–Thompson, 90 F.3d 609 (1st Cir.1996) (upholding abrogation of state immunity in the Veterans' Reemployment Rights Act as a valid exercise of Congress' war power), with, *e.g.,* Matter of Estate of Fernandez, 123 F.3d 241 (5th Cir.1997) (holding that Congress lacks authority to abrogate state sovereign immunity in the exercise of its bankruptcy power).

6. *Cf.* United States v. The Spokane Tribe of Indians, 139 F.3d 1297 (9th Cir. 1998) (suggesting that Congress would not have enacted IGRA absent the provisions struck down in Seminole, and that as a result the pre-IGRA prohibition of state regulation of gambling on tribal lands will often be applicable).

within congressional power under section 5 of the Fourteenth Amendment? Fitzpatrick may have been an easy case in this regard, but what of a decision by Congress to prohibit the imposition of mandatory retirement (or the hiring of child labor) by employers engaged in commerce or activities affecting commerce, and to extend that prohibition to states acting as employers? *Cf.* City of Boerne v. Flores, 117 S.Ct. 2157 (1997)(in holding unconstitutional the Religious Freedom Restoration Act, the Court stated that while Congress' power under section 5 extends to the creation of remedies, it does not include the power to alter substantive rights).[7] In dealing with this issue, how significant is the presence or absence of a congressional reference to the constitutional source of its authority to enact a particular statute?

(4) *Congressional Options After Seminole.*

(a) *State Court Suits.* Is one alternative available to Congress—*whenever* it wants to subject a state to suit pursuant to a valid regulation of state activity—to permit an aggrieved plaintiff to sue the state in a state court? The Court has on several occasions confirmed that the Eleventh Amendment does not apply in state courts, *e.g.,* Nevada v. Hall, 440 U.S. 410 (1979)(Fourth Edition p. 1056), Hilton v. South Carolina Pub. Ry. Comm'n, footnote 15, *infra,* but what if the state interposes a claim of sovereign immunity? See the Court's suggestion in footnote 14 of the Seminole opinion that state "consent[]" is a condition of amenability to suit in state court (and note that the Chief Justice, who wrote that opinion, dissented in Nevada v. Hall). Compare *Note on the Obligation of State Courts to Enforce Federal Law,* Fourth Edition p. 472; *Note on Remedies for Federal Constitutional Rights,* Fourth Edition p. 849.

Alternatively, what if the state seeks to remove the state court suit under § 1441 and then moves to dismiss under the Eleventh Amendment? Is the case one within the original jurisdiction of the district court if the action is barred in its entirety by the Eleventh Amendment? If it is barred in part by that amendment?

---

7. For examples of lower court decisions after City of Boerne dealing with the question of abrogation of state immunity to federal court suit, see, *e.g.,* Clark v. California, 123 F.3d 1267 (9th Cir.1997)(upholding, as a valid exercise of authority under § 5, abrogation of state immunity in the Americans with Disabilities Act (ADA) and the Rehabilitation Act); Coolbaugh v. Louisiana, 136 F.3d 430 (5th Cir.1998)(same holding with respect to the ADA); and Goshtasby v. Board of Trustees of the University of Illinois, 141 F.3d 761 (7th Cir.1998)(same holding under the Age Discrimination in Employment Act (ADEA)); Kimel v. Florida Bd. of Regents, 139 F.3d 1426 (11th Cir.1998)(holding, 2–1, that Congress did not abrogate state immunity in the ADEA but—by a different 2–1 vote—that Congress did successfully abrogate state immunity in the ADA); Aaron v. Kansas, 115 F.3d 813 (10th Cir.1997) (holding invalid Congress' abrogation of state immunity under the Fair Labor Standards Act because that Act was passed as an exercise of the commerce power; congressional intent to act pursuant to § 5 will not be inferred in the absence of a clear indication of such an intent); In re Creative Goldsmiths, 119 F.3d 1140 (4th Cir.1997) (holding invalid congressional abrogation of state immunity in the Bankruptcy Act); Chavez v. Arte Publico Press, 139 F.3d 504 (5th Cir.1998)(holding invalid congressional abrogation of state immunity in the Copyright and Lanham Acts).

For a pre-Boerne decision upholding abrogation under the Patent Act on the ground that the abrogation was a valid exercise of authority under § 5 to protect property rights, see College Sav. Bank v. Florida Prepaid Postsecondary Educ. Expense Bd., 948 F.Supp. 400 (D.N.J.1996).

See generally Note, 111 Harv.L.Rev. 1542 (1998)("Boerne will not [and should not] result in a major constriction of Congress's power to abrogate state immunity from suit * * *. [Deference to congressional fact-finding] maintains a role for Congress in the protection of nonsuspect classes.").

Some light—but not a great deal—was shed on the questions in the last paragraph by the unanimous decision in Wisconsin Dep't of Corrections v. Schacht, 118 S.Ct. 2047 (1998). Schacht had filed a state court suit against the Wisconsin Department of Corrections and several of its employees, in both their "personal" and "official" capacities, complaining that his dismissal as a prison guard violated various federal rights. After removing the case to federal court, defendants moved to dismiss the claims against the Department and against the employees "in their official capacity" on Eleventh Amendment grounds. The district court granted the motion and dismissed the claims, and considering the remaining "personal capacity" claims against the employees on the merits, awarded summary judgment to the defendants on those claims.

Schacht appealed only from the grant of summary judgment, and the court of appeals, raising the question *sua sponte*, ruled that the presence in the case of one or more claims that were barred by the Eleventh Amendment deprived the federal court of jurisdiction over the entire case, and ordered that the case be returned to the state court.

A unanimous Supreme Court reversed, holding that the presence in an otherwise removable case of one or more claims barred by the Eleventh Amendment does not deprive the federal court of jurisdiction to hear the remaining claims. In an opinion by Justice Breyer, the Court reasoned that "[t]he Eleventh Amendment does not automatically destroy original jurisdiction. Rather, * * * [it] grants the State a legal power to assert a sovereign immunity defense should it choose to do so" (p. 2052). The defense can be waived, and if the state does not raise it, the court may also choose to ignore it. Thus at the time of removal, the case as a whole fell within the federal court's original jurisdiction, and the state's later invocation of the Eleventh Amendment "did not destroy removal jurisdiction over the entire case" (p. 2053).

The Court went on to conclude that remand of the entire action was not required by the provision of § 1447(c) requiring remand when, in a removed case, it appears that the court lacks subject-matter jurisdiction. Stating that it had never decided whether Eleventh Amendment immunity is "a matter of subject matter jurisdiction", the Court reasoned that § 1447(c) could not require remand of the *entire* case when there was, at most, a lack of subject-matter jurisdiction with respect to fewer than all the claims before the court.

Justice Kennedy, concurring in the opinion, wrote separately to suggest the possibility—not considered below and not argued or briefed by the parties—that by removing the case to a federal court, the state may have waived its Eleventh Amendment immunity.

The question of waiver is discussed below, in part B of this Note. But assuming that Justice Kennedy's suggestion is not adopted, and that a state does not lose an Eleventh Amendment defense by removal to a federal court, does Schacht cast any light on the question of the appropriate remedy if that defense is upheld? The district court dismissed the claims that were thought to be barred; the court of appeals ordered the entire case remanded. Did Justice Breyer, for the Supreme Court, leave up in the air the question of dismissal or remand of claims barred by the Eleventh Amendment by declining to decide whether or not an Eleventh Amendment defense goes to subject matter jurisdiction? If it does, then remand would seem not only appropriate but mandatory. But if not, isn't dismissal the correct remedy, just as in the case of any other successful non-jurisdictional defense? (Note that if dismissal is the appropriate remedy, any effort to sue a state on a federal claim in a state court will inevitably fail unless Congress specifically precludes removal—something it has rarely done in federal question cases.)

(b) *Suits by the United States.* Another alternative apparently available to Congress is to vest the United States with authority to bring a federal court action to enforce the law against a state. See Fourth Edition p. 1051. But *cf.* footnote 13, *infra* (raising the question of the possible limits on "parens patriae" actions). Could Congress also circumvent the limitation on its abrogation power by authorizing individuals or other entities to sue in the name of the United States (as in a *qui tam* action) to compel state compliance with a federal duty, or to seek compensation for a state's violation of such a duty? See Siegel, *The Hidden Source of Congress's Power to Abrogate State Sovereign Immunity,* 73 Tex.L.Rev. 539 (1995)(arguing that such authority does exist).

(c) *A Remedy Under Ex parte Young.* Historically, the limitations imposed by the doctrine of governmental immunity could be circumvented by a suit for injunctive relief against the appropriate governmental officer, and in Ex parte Young, the Court appeared to recognize a federal common law basis for such relief, even in the absence of a traditional right of action under received tort law doctrines. See Fourth Edition pp. 1058–66. Moreover, the principle of that decision was implicitly incorporated in the statutory provision for injunctive relief against state officers embodied in 42 U.S.C. § 1983, and has been applied even when the relief sought required the officer defendant to take action that could be taken only in an official capacity. See, *e.g.,* Milliken v. Bradley, 433 U.S. 267 (1977), Fourth Edition p. 1073. (Compare also the traditional remedy in habeas corpus—an order to release the prisoner.)

Did the majority in Seminole retreat from this approach when it held that the Ex parte Young rationale was not available to permit the Tribe to obtain an order against the responsible state officers requiring them to negotiate in good faith? To the extent that such an injunctive remedy is not constitutionally required—and surely it is not in the case of a statutory right—Congress may certainly bar a private remedy against a state officer in spite of Ex parte Young and § 1983. See Fourth Edition pp. 376–78, 844, 1134–36. But if, as in Seminole, Congress has authorized a federal court action against a state that turned out to be unavailable because of the Court's decision to overrule its own recent precedent, wouldn't Congress plainly have preferred enforceability against state officers to the absence of *any* judicial remedy? (In any event, isn't it now open to Congress to authorize a federal court to utilize a Young remedy?)

With respect to the elaborate statutory scheme relied on by the Seminole majority as a basis for holding the Young remedy unavailable, isn't that common law remedy sufficiently flexible to be subject to adaptation to specific statutory limitations imposed by the legislature? Perhaps the Young doctrine may not be used to compel a state to enter into a contract, but Congress in IGRA stopped short of such coercion; rather, the core of IGRA's approach is to impose a requirement on the state (acting through its officers, of course) to bargain in good faith.[8]

Meltzer, note 1, *supra,* at 36–41, argues that the Seminole Tribe "should have been afforded a declaratory or injunctive remedy against Governor Chiles" (p. 39) under the rationale of Young and the specific statutory remedy afforded

---

8. As the Seminole majority observed in footnote 10, the state's argument that the statutory scheme also violated the Tenth Amendment was not considered by the Court.

by § 1983, and that the Court's preclusion of such a claim rests on a "mischaracterization" of Young, "a disregard of § 1983, and a misapplication of familiar principles of congressional primacy in shaping remedies for federal statutory violations" (p. 41).

The treatment of Young by the majority in Seminole may have been a result of the majority's desire to reach the underlying question of the power of abrogation, but it was viewed by some observers as signaling a broader retreat from the scope and significance of the Young decision in the vindication of federal rights. Some light (but less than full illumination) was shed on this question by the disposition in the 1996 Term of Idaho v. Coeur d'Alene Tribe, 117 S.Ct. 2028 (1997), a case discussed at pp. 57–59, *supra*. In holding the Young doctrine inapplicable to the federal court suit in that case, Justice Kennedy, joined by the Chief Justice, clearly supported an interpretation of the doctrine that would have required a case-by-case balancing of the various state and federal interests in allowing a federal court disposition of the controversy. But that view was rejected by the remaining seven Justices, with the four dissenters strongly adhering to a broader view of the availability of Young in a suit against state officers, and the three concurring Justices essentially limiting their conclusion as to the inapplicability of Young to the special case of a dispute over the state's title and ability to regulate submerged and related lands.

(d) *Consent.* A final alternative approach (referred to in the opinions in the Schacht case, *supra*) is that of "consent" or "waiver" by the state. That approach and its limits are dealt with in Part B of this Note.

(5) *The Seminole Decision Viewed in a Larger Context.* The focus of this section is on the meaning and scope of the Eleventh Amendment, but as the previous Paragraphs have indicated, those issues cannot be isolated from the larger questions of the appropriate extent to which issues of federalism can and should be resolved by the recognition of *judicially* enforceable limits on federal power. Thus Seminole may fairly be seen as part of a trend in the last decade to expand the authority of the Supreme Court to impose limits on congressional power, either directly under the Constitution, as in New York v. United States, 505 U.S. 144 (1992)(Fourth Edition pp. 287, 477), and United States v. Lopez, 514 U.S. 549 (1995)(Fourth Edition p. 989), or through the application of rigorous rules of clear statement, as in Gregory v. Ashcroft (Paragraph (2)(b), *supra*; Fourth Edition p. 477). Compare Meltzer, note 1, *supra,* at 65 (viewing Seminole not as one of a "mounting series of blows" to national power but instead as a "gesture in the direction of a diffuse conception of state sovereignty that in the end will not be generally enforced by the Court").

(6) *Additional Bibliography.* Especially noteworthy among other scholarly comments in the wake of Seminole are Monaghan, *The Supreme Court, 1995 Term—Comment: The Sovereign Immunity "Exception",* 110 Harv.L.Rev. 102 (1996)(criticizing the notion of state sovereign immunity, arguing that Seminole could more appropriately have been decided on other grounds, and suggesting that Seminole will have little more than rhetorical effect in view of the continued viability of the rule of state accountability under Ex Parte Young); Vázquez, *What is Eleventh Amendment Immunity?* 106 Yale L.J. 1683 (1997)(disagreeing with those who view the Eleventh Amendment as plainly nothing more than a "forum allocation" clause; contending that a significant line of authority, culminating in Seminole, supports an alternative "immunity from liability" theory protecting state entities from damage liability in *any*

court; and concluding (at p. 1806) that rule-of-law values do not require rejecting Seminole and the immunity theory but can be as effectively maintained by pursuing an "officer-liability regime" supported by "indemnity or insurance arrangements"); Hovenkamp, *Judicial Restraint and Constitutional Federalism: The Supreme Court's Lopez and Seminole Tribe Decisions,* 96 Colum.L.Rev. 2213 (1996)(criticizing both decisions as instances in which "activist Justices have struck down federal legislation on historically inaccurate constitutional grounds in an area, state-federal relations, where the political process has shown itself to be quite up to the task of allocating decisionmaking power" (p. 2213)); Jackson, *Seminole Tribe, The Eleventh Amendment, and the Potential Evisceration of Ex Parte Young,* 72 N.Y.U.L.Rev. 495 (1997)(contending, *inter alia,* that the Seminole Court failed to establish that the injunctive relief sought would have been broader than the statutory remedy, and that the holding threatens the future availability of relief under the doctrine of Ex parte Young); Pfander, *History and State Suability: An "Explanatory" Account of the Eleventh Amendment,* 83 Cornell L.Rev. 1269 (1998)(discussed at p. 60, *supra*) (concluding that his thesis "strongly supports the revisionist challenges to the sweeping immunity of Hans and Seminole Tribe" (p. 1281)).

For a delightful, tongue-in-cheek appraisal of Seminole in terms of economic costs and benefits, see Farber, *The Coase Theorem and the Eleventh Amendment,* 13 Const.Comm. 141 (1996)(arguing that the Seminole decision is sound whether or not it is consistent with the history or text of the Eleventh Amendment because, under a transaction cost analysis, Congress as the "best briber" should have the burden of negotiating out of the prevailing rule).

B. Consent to Suit in Federal Court

(1) *Introduction.* The majority opinion in Seminole focuses on the question whether Congress may "unilaterally" abrogate a state's immunity from federal court suit—recognizing the long established rule that a state, like any sovereign entity, may waive its immunity and consent to suit. See, *e.g.,* Petty v. Tennessee–Missouri Bridge Comm'n, 359 U.S. 275 (1959); Clark v. Barnard, 108 U.S. 436, 447 (1883). Is this an anomaly (however well-established) in light of the ordinary rule that the parties lack power to confer jurisdiction on the federal courts? Or, despite the constitutional text, is the question of Eleventh Amendment immunity not a true question of "jurisdiction" at all—at least not in the sense of "subject matter" jurisdiction?

The Court has taken a range of positions on this issue, indicating, for example, in Edelman v. Jordan, 415 U.S. 651 (1974)(Fourth Edition p. 1066), that the matter is jurisdictional, but stating in Patsy v. Board of Regents, 457 U.S. 496, 515–16 n. 19 (1982), that an Eleventh Amendment question is not jurisdictional "in the sense that it must be raised and decided by this Court on its own motion", and most recently, in Wisconsin Dep't of Corrections v. Schacht, Paragraph A(4)(a), *supra,* observing that the issue had yet to be resolved.

(2) *Consent to Suit Confined to State Tribunals.* Smith v. Reeves, 178 U.S. 436, 441 (1900), held that a state may waive sovereign immunity as to suits for tax refunds in its own courts, while retaining its Eleventh Amendment immunity from such lawsuits in federal court. Earlier cases looked the other way, see, *e.g.,* Reagan v. Farmers' Loan & Trust Co., 154 U.S. 362, 391 (1894), but Smith reasoned that a limitation upon tax refund actions could not be seen as "hostile to the General Government, or as touching upon any right granted or

secured by the Constitution of the United States" (p. 445). Subsequent cases have permitted selective waiver by the state without regard to Smith's qualifications. See, *e.g.,* Edelman v. Jordan, *supra.* Should they have, especially when other efforts by states to restrict lawsuits to the state courts have been held unlawful? See, *e.g.,* Chicago & N.W. Ry. Co. v. Whitton's Adm'r, 80 U.S. (13 Wall.) 270 (1871), Fourth Edition p. 731, holding that a state statute purporting to permit enforcement of a state wrongful death action only in state court could not prevent the exercise of federal diversity jurisdiction. See also Shapiro, *Wrong Turns: The Eleventh Amendment and the Pennhurst Case,* 98 Harv. L.Rev. 61, 76–78 (1984). Or is the purpose of the Eleventh Amendment not to exempt the state from suit altogether, but rather to give it a forum choice? Compare Vázquez, Paragraph A(6), *supra.*

(3) *"Constructive" Consent.*

(a) *On the Basis of Non–Litigation Activity.* In Parden v. Terminal Ry., 377 U.S. 184 (1964), the Supreme Court (per Brennan, J.) held, 5–4, that Alabama had constructively consented to a federal court negligence action under the Federal Employers' Liability Act (FELA) brought by an employee of a state-owned railway. In the Court's view, the case presented two questions (p. 187): "(1) Did Congress in enacting the FELA intend to subject a State to suit in these circumstances? (2) Did it have power to do so, as against the State's claim of immunity?" After answering the first question in the affirmative, the Court answered the second in the affirmative as well, but in doing so, appeared to combine an abrogation theory ("imposition of the FELA right of action upon interstate railroads * * * cannot be precluded by sovereign immunity" (p. 192)), with a theory of state consent ("Alabama, when it began operation of an interstate railroad * * * [after enactment of the FELA] necessarily consented to such suit as was authorized by that Act")(*id.*).

Nine years later, in Employees of Dep't of Public Health & Welfare v. Department of Public Health & Welfare, 411 U.S. 279 (1973), the Court held that simply by running state hospitals, Missouri had not consented to federal court suit for overtime compensation under the Fair Labor Standards Act; Parden was distinguished as involving a "for profit" operation of the kind normally run by private parties (p. 284). The Court contended that its ruling would not leave plaintiffs unprotected; the Act provided other remedies against state employers, including suits by the Secretary of Labor for unpaid compensation or injunctive relief.[9]

Then in Welch v. Texas Dep't of Highways & Public Transp., 483 U.S. 468 (1987), the Court overruled the aspect of Parden that rested on a theory of congressional abrogation. In a damages action under the Jones Act[10] brought in federal court by a seaman against a state agency that operated a ferry, the plurality assumed (contrary to its later holding in Seminole) that Congress' power to subject unconsenting states to federal court suit was not confined to section 5 of the Fourteenth Amendment. The plurality concluded that "Congress has not expressed in unmistakable statutory language its intention to allow States to be sued in federal court under the Jones Act" (p. 475). The

9. Is it clear that a suit by the Secretary as parens patriae would be deemed a suit by the United States, as to which the Eleventh Amendment does not apply? *Cf.* New Hampshire v. Louisiana, 108 U.S. 76 (1883), Fourth Edition p. 1064 n. 1.

10. The Jones Act authorizes such damages actions in accordance with the provisions of the FELA.

decision in Parden, the plurality said (p. 477), failed to recognize that "the constitutional role of the States sets them apart from other employers".[11]

The question of waiver or consent to suit was not reached in Welch on the ground that it had not been presented for review. Had the question been properly presented, do you think the Court would have overruled that aspect of Parden as well? (Note that in a number of instances the Court has insisted that if a claim of waiver or consent is based on a state statute, the language of the statute must leave no doubt as to its purpose.[12])

Closely related to the problem of "constructive consent" in a case like Welch is the question of the ability of Congress to condition the state's receipt of funds on the state's consent to suit in a federal court. Subject to limits that have yet to be fully developed, Congress may condition the grant of funds to a state on the state's agreement to do something that Congress has no power to require the state to do directly. See, *e.g.*, South Dakota v. Dole, 483 U.S. 203 (1987). Nor does the Seminole decision purport to limit congressional authority to make a grant of funds conditioned on a waiver of immunity. See Kinports, *Implied Waiver After Seminole Tribe*, 82 Minn.L.Rev. 793 (1998). If that authority does exist, would a state's acceptance of a conditional grant be sufficient to constitute a waiver, or would the waiver have to be explicit (through legislation or some other form of pronouncement)?

To return again to the Welch case, if Congress has the authority to require a waiver as a condition of receiving a financial grant, may it also condition a state's ability to engage in activity that Congress has the power to preempt on the state's waiver of immunity? What of a state's ability to operate a railroad in or affecting interstate commerce?

(b) *On the Basis of the State's Conduct in Litigation.* Whatever the fate of the notion of constructive waiver in other contexts, can a state's conduct in the course of litigation be construed as a waiver of an Eleventh Amendment defense? For instance, by suing an individual in federal court, does a state waive its immunity from recoupment and setoff (and possibly some affirmative counterclaims)? In considering this question, is it relevant that Congress has explicitly provided—as in the bankruptcy law, 11 U.S.C. § 106(b)—that the state's filing of a claim is "deemed" to be a waiver of the state's immunity with respect to certain counterclaims? What if Congress instead had explicitly conditioned the state's ability to file a claim in bankruptcy on such a waiver? If

---

11. Justice Scalia, concurring in part and concurring in the judgment, agreed that Parden should be overruled, but on a different ground: that, in light of the general acceptance of Hans v. Louisiana when the FELA and the Jones Act were enacted, those statutes should not be interpreted as providing a cause of action against a state employer.

Justice Scalia's approach was rejected in Hilton v. South Carolina Pub. Rys. Comm'n, 502 U.S. 197 (1991), in which the Court allowed an injured worker to bring a *state court* FELA action against a state-owned railway. The Court in Hilton noted, *inter alia*, that in a state court action, a claim of Eleventh Amendment immunity is not available.

The state court in Hilton, however, had not relied on state sovereign immunity as a ground for dismissing the action. (On the availability of a sovereign immunity defense in such a state court suit, see Paragraph A(4)(a), *supra*.)

12. But *cf.* Port Auth. Trans–Hudson Corp. v. Feeney, 495 U.S. 299 (1990)(holding that there was a valid waiver even though the "consent to suit" provision in the relevant state statutes creating a bi-state entity did not explicitly consent to suit in federal court; the Court relied both on the expansive language of the consent provision and on the language of the venue provision in those statutes).

Congress has explicitly provided that certain action in litigation will constitute a waiver?

The potential significance of waiver in the context of litigation was brought to the fore in Wisconsin Dep't of Corrections v. Schacht, Paragraph A(4)(a), *supra*. As noted above, the Court, in reaching its conclusion with respect to removal jurisdiction, relied in significant part on its earlier holding that an Eleventh Amendment defense need not be recognized by the court *sua sponte* if the state chooses not to raise it. And the significance of waiver was further underscored by Justice Kennedy's strong suggestion, in his concurring opinion, that a state's decision to remove a state court action to federal court might itself constitute a waiver of any Eleventh Amendment defense. Noting the "hybrid nature of the jurisdictional bar erected by the Eleventh Amendment" (i.e., that, like the defense of personal jurisdiction, it can be waived), as well as the Court's holding in Clark v. Barnard (Paragraph B(1), *supra*) that a state's voluntary intervention in a federal court action waived any claim of immunity with respect to the controversy at issue, Justice Kennedy suggested that voluntary removal might similarly be held to waive any such claim.

In answer to the argument that, under precedents in other contexts, a waiver must be explicitly authorized by state law in order to be binding, Justice Kennedy observed that "the absence of specific authorization * * * is not an insuperable obstacle * * * where the State, through its attorneys, consents to removal * * *. If the States know or have reason to expect that removal will constitute a waiver, then it is easy enough to presume that an attorney authorized to represent the State can bind it to the jurisdiction of the federal court (for Eleventh Amendment purposes) by the consent to the removal" (pp. 2056–57). Distinguishing Edelman v. Jordan, Paragraph B(1), *supra,* Justice Kennedy contended that the act of removal is "far less equivocal" than the conduct at issue in that case (and others like it) (p. 2057).

end →

SUBSECTION C: FEDERAL STATUTORY PROTECTION AGAINST STATE OFFICIAL ACTION: HEREIN OF 42 U.S.C. § 1983

Page 1122. Add to footnote 6:

For more recent data on § 1983 litigation, including data on the correlation between the number of state prisoners and the number of suits, the types of issues raised, and the average disposition time of such suits, see Hanson & Daley, U.S. Dep't of Justice, Challenging the Conditions of Prisons and Jails: A Report on Section 1983 Litigation (1995); Kreimer, *Exploring the Dark Matter of Judicial Review: A Constitutional Census of the 1990s*, 5 Wm. & Mary Bill Rts.J. 427, 485–90 (1997)(reporting that (a) from 1984 to 1994, prisoner civil rights cases and habeas petitions increased from 1/10 to almost 1/5 of the federal civil docket (an increase "largely attributable to the growth in the American prison population") and (b) between four and seven of every thousand prisoners have their claims to obtain relief "seriously considered" by the federal courts).

Page 1125. Add a new footnote a at the end of Paragraph (1):

a. Jeffries, *In Praise of the Eleventh Amendment and Section 1983*, 84 Va.L.Rev. 47 (1998), argues that the availability of suits against state officers under § 1983 renders state immunity from suit under the Eleventh Amendment "largely irrelevant". He contends that, in part because states typically defend and indemnify defendants in § 1983 suits, such suits often serve as the functional equivalents of suits against the states.

Consider Professor Jeffries' thesis in the light of several factors addressed by Professor Jeffries in his discussion—in particular, the broad reach of official immunity doctrines referred to in text (and more fully developed in Section 3 of this chapter), as well as such other limitations on suits against individual officers as that articulated in Edelman v. Jordan, Fourth Edition p. 1066. Consider also (a) whether there is a difference between a policy of indemnification of judgments paid by another, on the one hand, and direct responsibility for a judgment, on the other, and (b) whether juries, in determining the amount of damages, are likely to take into account the identity and resources of the named defendant.

Pages 1125–26. Add to footnote 2:

The Court's decision in Pulliam v. Allen was recently overruled by Congress. See p. 104, *infra.*

Page 1130. Add to Paragraph (6)(c):

State law is significant not only in determining who is a policymaking official (as in the Praprotnik case) but also in determining the entity that the official represents when exercising a policymaking function. In McMillian v. Monroe County, Alabama, 117 S.Ct. 1734 (1997), a § 1983 action against an Alabama county (and others) alleging that the county sheriff had suppressed exculpatory evidence in a criminal case, the Court held, 5–4, that under Alabama law, county sheriffs acting in their law enforcement capacity represent the state and not their counties. Thus there could be no local government liability under the Monell rule.

Justice Ginsburg, joined in dissent by Justices Stevens, Souter, and Breyer, contended that the sheriff was acting for the county under Alabama law. In a clear effort to confine the impact of the decision, Justice Ginsburg noted that even in Alabama, county sheriffs may be county policymakers for some purposes, stressed that the decision did not call into question the many lower court rulings that such officials were county policymakers in other states, and said that the Court's recognition of "the historic reasons why Alabama listed sheriffs as members of the State's 'executive department,' should discourage endeavors to insulate counties and municipalities from Monell liability by change-the-label devices" (p. 1746).

Page 1131. Add a new Paragraph (6)(e):

(e) In Board of County Comm'rs v. Brown, 117 S.Ct. 1382 (1997), the Court continued to draw fine distinctions for purposes of determining municipal liability, but in this instance the dissenters urged that the time had come to reexamine the Monell rule itself.

In Brown, the plaintiff brought a § 1983 damages action against the county, alleging that a deputy had arrested her with excessive force and that the county was liable for her injuries because the sheriff—a policymaking official—had hired the deputy without adequate review of his background (which included a conviction for assault and battery). The Court, per Justice O'Connor, reversed a judgment for the plaintiff, noting that unlike the Pembaur case (Fourth Edition p. 1129), the present case did not involve a claim that action by a policymaking official itself violated federal law or directed or authorized the deprivation of federal rights. In the absence of such a claim, the plaintiff must establish deliberate indifference, on the part of the policymaking representative of the municipality, not merely to the risk of *any* constitutional

to particular injury

injury but to the *particular injury suffered by the plaintiff*. To cross that threshold on the basis of a single instance of inadequate screening might not be possible, and in any event, is far more difficult than the showing required by the Court in City of Canton (Fourth Edition p. 1130) to establish municipal liability on the basis of a failure to train. On the present record, Justice O'Connor concluded that the requisite deliberate indifference had not been shown. *not shown here*

too high? Justice Souter, joined by Justices Stevens and Breyer, dissented. He contended that in cases involving a single act that neither violates nor directs a violation of federal law, the Court had raised the requirements for establishing deliberate indifference far too high. He then examined the record in detail to support his conclusion that deliberate indifference had been shown, and concluded that the Court's "enhanced fault standard" demonstrated the instability of the Monell rule, and thus lent support to the "powerful call [offered in Justice Breyer's separate dissent] to reexamine § 1983 municipal liability afresh" (p. 1400). *Monell instable?*

Justice Breyer's dissent, joined by Justices Stevens and Ginsburg, suggested that since the Monell rule was "leading us to spin ever finer distinctions * * * we should reexamine the soundness of [Monell's] basic distinction itself" (p. 1401). Justice Breyer contended that all the prerequisites for such a reexamination were present: the doubtfulness of the original principle, the complex body of interpretive law that the principle had generated, developments that had divorced the Monell rule from its apparent original purposes, and the lack of significant reliance on the rule itself. To aid the Court in its reconsideration, Justice Breyer would have asked the parties for further argument that would "focus upon the continued viability of Monell's distinction between vicarious municipal liability and municipal liability based upon policy and custom" (p. 1404). *?*

Page 1136. Add to Paragraph (3)(a):

Recall that in the Seminole decision, p. 62, *supra,* the Supreme Court held that an action against state officers under the doctrine of Ex parte Young was unavailable because such an action could not be reconciled with the statutory scheme. What significance, if any, should be attached to the Court's silence with respect to the § 1983 remedy as a basis for the requested relief? Was that silence perhaps due to the plaintiff's understandable failure to invoke § 1983 in light of the remedy afforded in IGRA itself—a remedy that turned out to be constitutionally barred? See Meltzer, *The Seminole Decision and State Sovereign Immunity*, 1996 Sup.Ct.Rev. 1, 40 n. 165 (Seminole Tribe's failure to rely on § 1983 "does not justify the Court's failure to consider that provision's implications").

Page 1136. Add to footnote 6:

The latest in the series of decisions struggling with the question whether and to what extent a federal statute creates private rights enforceable under § 1983 is Blessing v. Freestone, 117 S.Ct. 1353 (1997). In this case, plaintiffs brought an action under § 1983 to compel the director of a state agency to achieve substantial compliance with Title IV–D of the Social Security Act (dealing with child support services). The Supreme Court, reversing a lower court decision, held that Title IV–D does not create an across-the-board private right to enforce substantial state compliance with its provisions in all respects, and remanded for consideration of the question whether Title IV–D gave rise to "some individually enforceable rights" (p. 1362). The Court went on, however, to reject the contention that Title IV–D's remedial scheme was sufficiently comprehensive to establish the legislature's intention to preclude a private action under § 1983.

Some observers thought that the Court might use the occasion of the Blessing case to roll back, or even to overrule, the holding of Maine v. Thiboutot, Fourth Edition p. 1133. Instead, the majority's opinion appears to reaffirm the Thiboutot baseline. (In a narrower concurring opinion, Justice Scalia, joined by Justice Kennedy, confined himself to the suggestion that a § 1983 action might not be available to beneficiaries of a federal-state funding and spending agreement.)

Page 1150. Add to footnote 1:

In County of Sacramento v. Lewis, 118 S.Ct. 1708 (1998), the Court considered the significance of Daniels v. Williams and related cases in the context of a § 1983 claim for damages for an accidental death occurring in the context of a high speed chase by law enforcement officials. The majority held that in order to state a claim of violation of substantive due process in these circumstances, it was not necessary to prove intentional harm, but it was necessary to show an abuse of power that is "shocking to the conscience" (p. 1712).

SECTION 3.   OFFICIAL IMMUNITY

Page 1166. Add a new footnote a at the end of Paragraph (2)(a):

a. A 1994 study of Maryland law concluded that in some circumstances, a suit against a state official brought under that state's law may be more advantageous to the plaintiff than a suit under § 1983 because "Maryland does not seem to recognize qualified immunity for state officials" and "does not recognize a distinction between suits against officials in their individual versus their official capacities". S. Shapiro, *Suits Against State Officials for Violations of Constitutional Rights: Comparing Maryland and Federal Law*, 23 U.Balt.L.Rev. 423, 427 (1994).

Page 1170. Add a new footnote 6a at the end of Paragraph (4):

6a. See also Kalina v. Fletcher, 118 S.Ct. 502 (1997)(holding that a prosecutor who allegedly filed a false "Certification of Determination of Probable Cause" in support of an application for an arrest warrant was not entitled to absolute immunity from suit because, in filing the certification, the prosecutor was acting as a complaining witness, not as a lawyer).

Page 1171. Add a new footnote 9a at the end of Paragraph (5):

9a. In Bogan v. Scott–Harris, 118 S.Ct. 966 (1998), the Court held that local legislators are entitled to the same absolute immunity from § 1983 civil liability as are state and regional legislators. The Court then determined that a mayor's preparation of a budget eliminating the plaintiff's position and his signing of the ordinance so providing, as well as the city council vice president's vote on the measure, were legislative actions entitled to absolute immunity. In its opinion, the Court stated that the determination whether a particular activity should be classified as legislative hinges on the nature of the activity, not the subjective intent of the actor.

Page 1171.   Add to footnote 11:

In Clinton v. Jones, 117 S.Ct. 1636 (1997), the Supreme Court unanimously affirmed the decision of the Eighth Circuit cited in this footnote. The case involved sexual harassment claims (under federal and state law) that were made against President Clinton and that arose out of alleged conduct occurring prior to his Presidency, when he was governor of Arkansas. While not deciding whether a *state* court could entertain a private action in such a case, or whether the trial court in the case at hand could compel the President's appearance at any specific time or place, the Supreme Court denied the President's broad claim of "temporary immunity" from civil damages actions relating to events outside the scope of his Presidential duties. The Court disagreed, however, with the Eighth Circuit's conclusion that the district court's stay of trial proceedings was the functional equivalent of a grant of temporary immunity. Rather it held that the trial judge had broad discretion to control its own docket and that the respect owed the Presidency should inform the exercise of that discretion, but that any determination of the need for a stay of the trial was, at this point, premature.

Justice Breyer, concurring in the judgment, argued at length that "ordinary case-management principles" must be "supplemented with a constitutionally based requirement that district courts schedule proceedings so as to avoid significant interference" with the President's conduct of his office (p. 1659).

Page 1172.   Add a new footnote b at the end of Paragraph (8):

b.   For an extensive analysis of the absolute/qualified immunity distinction based on the view that absolute immunity is "rule-like" while qualified immunity is a "paradigmatic standard" (calling for application on a case-by-case basis), see Chen, *The Ultimate Standard: Qualified Immunity in the Age of Constitutional Balancing Tests*, 81 Iowa L.Rev. 261, 262–63 (1995). After discussing the strengths and weaknesses of the two approaches, Chen advocates "unqualifying immunity"—articulating all immunity doctrine as a set of rules rather than standards. Without attempting a comprehensive outline of such rules, Chen gives as examples rules that would flatly confer or deny immunity for certain kinds of conduct, *e.g.*, conferring immunity for officials acting pursuant to formal authorization, and denying immunity for warrantless searches not permitted under the Fourth Amendment.

Page 1173:   Add to footnote 13:

Wyatt v. Cole, discussed in this footnote, was used as a point of departure by the Court in holding (5–4) that prison guards employed by a private firm are not entitled to qualified immunity from suit. Richardson v. McKnight, 117 S.Ct. 2100 (1997). Richardson involved a § 1983 action for physical injuries brought by an inmate at a Tennessee correctional center whose management had been privatized. Acknowledging that Wyatt did not control, the Court (per Justice Breyer) said that the case "does tell us * * * to look both to history and to the purposes that underlie government employee immunity in order to find the answer" (p. 2104).

Although the Court had held (in Procunier v. Navarette, Fourth Edition p. 1173) that government-employed prison guards enjoyed an immunity defense arising out of their common-law status as public employees, the Court found "no [corresponding] evidence that the [common] law gave purely private companies or their employees any special immunity from such suits" (p. 2104). Turning to the purposes of immunity, the Court noted the difficulties with any "functional" analysis of the immunity question but went on to assert that when prison management is privatized, "marketplace pressures provide the private firm with strong incentives to avoid overly timid * * * job performance" (pp. 2106–07), and that the government's requirement of liability insurance "reduces the employment-discouraging fear of unwarranted liability" (p. 2107).

Finally, the Court noted that the question of the defendants' liability under § 1983 remained unresolved, that its decision depended on the particular facts (including limited government supervision), and that the defendants might still be able to assert a "special 'good faith' defense" (p. 2108). (How would such a defense differ from a defense of qualified immunity?)

Dissenting for himself, the Chief Justice, and Justices Kennedy and Thomas, Justice Scalia took issue with the majority's discussion of historical materials. Although protesting that "history and not judicially analyzed policy governs this matter" (p. 2110), he went on to disagree at length with the majority's "market" analysis. If a private contractor must keep costs down in order to remain competitive, he contended, it has an incentive to "down-play" discipline and thus to reduce the costs of litigation. Since prison guards who are public employees and those who are employed by private contractors are "indistinguishable" in terms of the source of their authority, their powers, and their duties to prisoners, he concluded, the majority's decision will "artificially raise the cost of privatizing prisons" (pp. 2111–13).

Note the analogy to Justice Scalia's reasoning on the question of cost in Boyle v. United Technologies Corp. Fourth Edition pp. 770, 774, recognizing, as a matter of federal common law, a government contractor defense in a private action for injuries caused by an allegedly defective product.

Page 1174. Insert a new footnote 14a at the end of the second paragraph of Paragraph (10)(a):

14a. In United States v. Lanier, 117 S.Ct. 1219 (1997), a criminal case brought under 18 U.S.C. § 242, the Court stated that it was possible for a right to be "clearly established" even in the absence of a Supreme Court decision so holding, but that disparate decisions in the lower courts might well preclude such a determination.

Page 1175. Insert at the end of footnote 16:

For a thorough discussion of the difficulties of reconciling the doctrine of qualified immunity and the concepts normally applicable to motions for summary judgment, see Chen, *The Burdens of Qualified Immunity: Summary Judgment and the Role of Facts in Constitutional Tort Law*, 47 Am.U.L.Rev. (1997).

Page 1176. Add at the end of Paragraph (10)(c):

Crawford–El v. Britton, 118 S.Ct. 1584 (1998), presented a question of the burden on the plaintiff to establish liability in a case in which the defendant's motive is relevant to the plaintiff's claim of violation of constitutional right. (The plaintiff, a prison inmate, alleged that a prison officer had temporarily deprived him of his property in retaliation for the exercise of his First Amendment rights.) In such a case, the Court held, the plaintiff need not meet a heightened "clear and convincing evidence" standard in order to prevail. (In an extensive discussion, the Court concluded that the holding and rationale of Harlow v. Fitzgerald (Fourth Edition p. 1155), which dealt with the affirmative defense of qualified immunity, was not controlling.) In responding to concerns about the burdens of litigating frivolous claims, the Court noted the procedural tools available to district court judges to prevent the prosecution of such claims.[a]

Chief Justice Rehnquist, joined by Justice O'Connor, dissented, arguing that the defendant should be entitled to immunity if he offers a legitimate reason for his action and the plaintiff is unable to establish, by "objective evidence", that the reason is a pretext.

a. In the course of its decision, the Court appeared to endorse and even extend, with very little discussion, the Fifth Circuit's rule (see Fourth Edition pp. 1175–76, Paragraph (10)(c)) that before discovery occurs, a plaintiff may be required under Fed.R.Civ.P. 7(a) to file a reply to a defendant's or a third party's answer.

In a separate dissent, Justice Scalia, joined by Justice Thomas, invoked Justice Frankfurter's criticism of the Court's interpretation of § 1983 in Monroe v. Pape, (Fourth Edition p. 1111), and contended that a defendant's motive should be irrelevant in any § 1983 action if the conduct complained of is "objectively valid".

Page 1176. Add a new Paragraph (10)(d):

(d) *Should a Difficult Constitutional Question Be Avoided if It Is Clear That a Qualified Immunity Defense Is Available?* In County of Sacramento v. Lewis, 118 S.Ct. 1708 (1998), the Court, over an objection by Justice Stevens (endorsed by Justice Breyer), rejected the view that the policy of avoidance of difficult constitutional issues favored ruling on a claim of qualified immunity when there was (at the time of the action complained of) no clearly defined rule of constitutional conduct. Such a policy, the Court stated, would tend to leave standards of official conduct "uncertain, to the detriment both of officials and individuals. * * * [T]herefore the better approach is to determine the right before determining whether it was previously established with clarity" (p. 1714 n.5). The Court went on to hold that in the context of a death occurring accidentally in the course of a high speed chase, only official conduct that is "shocking to the conscience" can constitute a violation of substantive due process rights.

Is the policy of avoidance advocated by Justice Stevens less compelling here than when avoidance can be achieved either through interpretation of a statute or through abstention to permit a narrowing construction by a state court? Is one difference that avoidance in this context might tend to forestall indefinitely the articulation of the constitutional norm?[b]

Pages 1179–80. Add to Section B:

The Court's decision in Pulliam v. Allen was overruled by The Federal Courts Improvement Act of 1996, Pub.L.No. 104–317, § 309(b)-(c), 110 Stat. 3847. That act amended § 1988 to bar the collection of any costs, including attorney's fees, from judicial officers in suits against them arising from actions taken in their judicial capacity, and also amended § 1983 to bar suits against judicial officers for injunctive relief, except when declaratory relief was unavailable or the officer was acting in violation of a prior declaratory decree.

b. Is Justice Stevens' position in this case consistent with the argument in his concurrence in Teague v. Lane (Fourth Edition pp. 1392, 1400) that before determining whether a habeas petitioner is unable to obtain relief on the ground that a "new rule" of constitutional law should not be retroactively applied, the Court should first determine what the precise content of the rule is? Is the majority's position in this case consistent with Justice O'Connor's approach in the plurality opinion in Teague?

CHAPTER X

JUDICIAL FEDERALISM: LIMITATIONS ON DISTRICT COURT JURISDICTION OR ITS EXERCISE

SECTION 1. STATUTORY LIMITATIONS ON FEDERAL COURT JURISDICTION

SUBSECTION B: OTHER STATUTORY RESTRICTIONS ON FEDERAL COURT JURISDICTION

Page 1213. Add to Paragraph (2):

See generally Solimine, *The Three–Judge District Court in Voting Rights Litigation*, 30 U.Mich.J.L.Ref. 79 (1996).

A 1996 statute includes a provision (codified at 18 U.S.C. § 3626(a)(3)(B)) that an order, in a civil action, requiring the release of prisoners or limiting prison population may be entered only by a three-judge court convened in accordance with 28 U.S.C. § 2284.

Page 1217. Add to Paragraph (1):

In De Buono v. NYSA–ILA Medical and Clinical Services Fund, 117 S.Ct. 1747 (1997), the Court rejected on the merits a claim that ERISA preempts a state tax; the Court presumed that the court of appeals had found that the state remedy was not "plain" and hence that § 1341 did not bar relief, without itself deciding that question. Justice Scalia's dissent (joined by Justice Thomas) protested that the reasons given by the Court for not resolving the applicability of § 1341—that the question turned on state law issues as to which the Court's settled practice was to defer to the court of appeals, and that the state had abandoned its objection under the Act—did not justify the failure to determine the existence of federal court jurisdiction.

Page 1221. Add to Paragraph (5):

In Arkansas v. Farm Credit Services of Central Arkansas, 117 S.Ct. 1776 (1997), the Court unanimously ruled that a Production Credit Association (PCA) chartered under a federal statute for the purpose of making loans to farmers is, unlike the United States itself, subject to the Tax Injunction Act. The Court did not say that all federal instrumentalities are subject to the Act,

105

and indeed referred to the exemption of the National Labor Relations Board from the Anti–Injunction Act, see NLRB v. Nash–Finch Co., Fourth Edition p. 1202. But Justice Kennedy's opinion stressed that PCAs lack governmental regulatory power, are privately owned, and serve commercial interests little different from, and no more coterminous with governmental concerns than, most other commercial interests.

The opinion is notable for the general assertion that "[t]he federal balance is well served when the several States define and elaborate their own laws through their own courts and administrative processes and without undue interference from the federal judiciary"; the further statement that this policy is of "particular moment" in tax cases; and the admonition that "federal courts must guard against interpretations * * * which might defeat [the Act's] purpose and text" (p. 1780).

SECTION 2.   DOCTRINES OF EQUITY, COMITY, AND FEDERALISM

SUBSECTION A: EXHAUSTION OF STATE NONJUDICIAL REMEDIES

Page 1228.   Substitute the following for Paragraph (5)(b):

(b) *Actions by prisoners.* The Prison Litigation Reform Act of 1995, 110 Stat. 1321 (1996), requires the exhaustion of "such administrative remedies as are available" prior to the filing of federal suits by prisoners challenging prison conditions under § 1983 "or any other Federal law". 42 U.S.C. § 1997e(a). The court may, however, dismiss the underlying claim without requiring exhaustion "[i]n the event that a claim, on its face, is frivolous or malicious, fails to state a claim on which relief can be granted, or seeks monetary relief from a defendant who is immune from such relief". *Id.* § 1997e(c)(2).

SUBSECTION B: ABSTENTION: PULLMAN AND RELATED DOCTRINES

Page 1236.   Add to Paragraph (3)(b):

In Quackenbush v. Allstate Ins. Co., 517 U.S. 706 (1996), the Court affirmed a court of appeals decision holding an abstention-based remand order inappropriate in a suit for damages and ruled that "federal courts have the power to dismiss or remand cases based on abstention principles only where the relief being sought is equitable or otherwise discretionary" (p. 731). Petitioner Quackenbush, California's Insurance Commissioner, was appointed trustee of an insurance company ordered into liquidation by a California court. On behalf of that company, Quackenbush filed a common law damages suit against Allstate in state court, alleging breach of reinsurance agreements. Allstate removed to federal court on diversity grounds and filed a motion to compel arbitration under the Federal Arbitration Act. Quackenbush then sought to remand the suit to state court, arguing that federal abstention was appropriate under the doctrine of Burford v. Sun Oil Co., Fourth Edition p. 1247, because federal adjudication might interfere with California's resolution of the underlying insolvency and because the viability of Allstate's set-off claims depended on a disputed question of state law pending before the California courts in another case arising out of the same insolvency. The district court concluded that abstention was appropriate and ordered the case remanded, but the court of appeals reversed, and the Supreme Court affirmed, 9–0.

Writing for the Court, Justice O'Connor viewed prior decisions as establishing that "the authority of a federal court to abstain from exercising its jurisdiction extends to all cases in which the court has discretion to grant or deny relief" (p. 718), but concluded that "we have not previously addressed whether the principles underlying our abstention cases would support the remand or dismissal of a common-law action for damages." Prior decisions cited to support the propriety of abstention in damages actions—including Clay, United Gas Pipe Line, and Fornaris (Fourth Edition p. 1236)—were distinguished as involving a "stay" or "postponement", rather than the dismissal or remand, of the federal action.[a] The Court acknowledged that "federal courts have discretion to dismiss damage actions * * * under the common-law doctrine of forum non conveniens", but concluded that the abstention doctrine was "of a distinct historical pedigree" and that it more narrowly circumscribed judicial discretion to dismiss or remand a case (pp. 722–23). Although abstention principles "might support a federal court's decision to postpone adjudication of a damages action" under the Burford abstention doctrine, see Fourth Edition pp. 1247–51, dismissal or remand was inappropriate.

Justice Kennedy, concurring, noted that he would "not rule out * * * the possibility that a federal court might dismiss a suit for damages in a case where a serious affront to the interests of federalism could be averted in no other way" (517 U.S. at 733). In response, Justice Scalia, also concurring, said that he "would not have joined [the Court's] opinion if [he] believed it left such discretionary dismissal available" (id. at 731–32).

Do persuasive reasons support the distinction between a stay or postponement of a federal damages action, which Quackenbush treats as permissible under abstention principles, and a dismissal or remand, which Quackenbush holds impermissible?[b] Suppose a plaintiff files a damages action in federal court and the federal defendant files a parallel state court action presenting the same

---

a. The Court distinguished Fair Assessment in Real Estate Ass'n, Inc. v. McNary, Fourth Edition p. 1219, which held that a federal court should not entertain a § 1983 action for damages arising from a state tax scheme, on the ground that it had been construed by the subsequent decision in National Private Truck Council, Inc., Fourth Edition pp. 1221, 1228, as "a case about the scope of the § 1983 cause of action, not the abstention doctrines" (517 U.S. at 719).

b. Compare the similar distinction drawn by Frankfurter, J., in Louisiana Power & Light Co. v. City of Thibodaux, Fourth Edition pp. 1253–54 n. 8.

issues. If the federal action is stayed pending resolution of the state action, won't the state court's determination be dispositive of the federal action under doctrines of claim and issue preclusion? If so, isn't the practical effect of a stay identical to that of an order dismissing the federal action? See Moses H. Cone Memorial Hosp. v. Mercury Constr. Corp., discussed at Fourth Edition pp. 1317–19.[c] Consider next a case, such as Quackenbush, in which a plaintiff files suit in state court and a defendant removes to federal court on diversity grounds. How useful is a stay or postponement likely to be under this scenario?

Is the notion that a federal court may not dismiss or remand a case that does not involve discretionary remedies consistent with judicial practice declining to exercise jurisdiction in other cases? Compare Shapiro, *Jurisdiction and Discretion,* 60 N.Y.U.L.Rev. 543, 555–61 (1985)(discussing exercises of discretion to decline jurisdiction including, *inter alia,* the forum non conveniens doctrine and the Supreme Court's assumption of discretion to decline jurisdiction of cases—including suits for damages—within its original jurisdiction). Is the Court's basis for distinguishing forum non conveniens cases—that they have a "distinct historical pedigree" that justifies a broader ambit of judicial discretion—more than an ipse dixit? Is there any reason of principle why the considerations of convenience and judicial administration that underlie forum non conveniens doctrine should be treated as more important than the considerations of comity and federalism that support abstention doctrines?

The Court, in Quackenbush, did not consider the circumstances under which a stay of a suit for damages in federal court might be appropriate under abstention principles.

Page 1237.   Add a new Paragraph (3)(f):

(f) *Displacement by Certification Procedures?* Since the decision in Pullman, nearly all states have implemented "certification" procedures, pursuant to which federal courts can "certify" difficult state law issues for decision by the state supreme court. (For a discussion of certification procedures, see Fourth Edition pp. 1245–47, and p. 109, *infra.*) Because certification permits state courts to decide state law issues, and because the resulting decisions may either narrow federal constitutional questions or permit their avoidance altogether, "[c]ertification today covers territory once dominated by * * * 'Pullman abstention' ". Arizonans for Official English v. Arizona, 117 S.Ct. 1055, 1073 (1997). Yet "[c]ertification procedure, in contrast [with Pullman abstention], allows a federal court faced with a novel state-law question to put the question directly to the State's highest court, reducing the delay, cutting the cost, and increasing the assurance of gaining an authoritative response" (*id.*). Citing these advantages, a unanimous Court (per Justice Ginsburg), in Arizonans for Official English, suggested that federal courts should sometimes certify "[n]ovel, unsettled questions of state law" that might simplify a federal adjudication,

c.   In an earlier part of its opinion in Quackenbush, which held that the district court's remand order was appealable under the collateral order doctrine, see p. 151, *infra,* the Court relied on the holding of Moses H. Cone that a stay order was immediately appealable because it " 'amount[ed] to a refusal to adjudicate' the case in federal court" that would not be effectively reviewable on appeal from a final judgment in the federal action, "because the district court would be bound, as a matter of res judicata, to honor the state court's judgment" (517 U.S. at 713). The stay in Moses H. Cone, the Court said, was "functionally indistinguishable" from the remand order in Quackenbush. If a stay and a remand order are "functionally indistinguishable" for purposes of collateral order doctrine, why aren't they equally so for purposes of abstention?

even if the standards for the more burdensome procedures of Pullman absten- *even if not up to Pullman?* tion were not met (p. 1074). Where available, is certification likely to subsume or displace Pullman abstention? Should it?

Page 1245. Substitute the following for the second sentence of Paragraph (6):

As of 1995, 45 jurisdictions (including the District of Columbia and Puerto Rico) provided for certification. See Schneider, *"But Answer Came There None": The Michigan Supreme Court and the Certified Question of State Law*, 41 Wayne L.Rev. 273, 275 & n. 1 (1995).

Page 1245. Add to Paragraph (6)(a):

See also Clark, *Ascertaining the Laws of the Several States: Positivism and Judicial Federalism After Erie*, 145 U.Pa.L.Rev. 1259 (1997)(arguing that the federal courts should employ a presumption in favor of certifying unsettled questions of state law to state courts in order to avoid inequitable administration of state law and encroachment on states' lawmaking powers, on the one hand, and separation-of-powers objections to abstention, on the other hand).

Page 1245. Add the following after the first sentence of Paragraph (6)(b):

In Arizonans for Official English v. Arizona, 117 S.Ct. 1055, 1075 (1997), a unanimous Court, per Justice Ginsburg, held that a federal court should not have ruled on the constitutionality of an Arizona constitutional amendment prescribing that the State "shall act in English and in no other language" without first certifying the question of the amendment's meaning to the Arizona Supreme Court. The Court quoted Justice O'Connor's concurring opinion in Brockett v. Spokane Arcades, Inc., 472 U.S. 491, 510 (1985): " 'Speculation by a federal court about the meaning of a state statute in the absence of prior state adjudication is particularly gratuitous when * * * the state courts stand willing to address questions of state law on certification from a federal court' "(p. 1074, omission in original). The Court also emphasized the importance of the policy of avoiding or narrowing unsettled questions of federal constitutional law and the absence under certification procedures of "the delays, expense, and procedural complexity that generally attend abstention decisions" (p. 1075). Under the circumstances, the Court ruled, the court of appeals erred in suggesting that "unique circumstances" were necessary to justify certification. "Novel, unsettled questions of state law" sufficed (p. 1074).

Page 1245. Add to footnote 6:

For further examples of cases in which state courts have "take[n] an inordinately long time to answer questions, or * * * issue[d] terse refusals to answer," see Selya, *Certified Madness: Ask a Silly Question . . .*, 29 Suff. U.L.Rev. 677, 681 & nn. 18–19 (1995). See also Schneider, *"But Answer Came There None": The Michigan Supreme Court and the Certified Question of State Law*, 41 Wayne L.Rev. 273, 316–22 (1995)(reporting the number of occasions on which state supreme courts have declined to answer questions certified to them by the Sixth Circuit: Michigan, eight of fourteen; Ohio, three of seven; Kentucky, one of five; and Tennessee, zero of six). According to Judge Selya, *supra*, "certification has been plagued by theoretical and practical difficulties since its inception. Federal courts evince no clear understanding of when, how, or even why to certify questions, and state courts remain anxiously ambivalent about how, or even whether, to respond" (p. 691). Concluding that "certification often does not provide a means of achieving its anticipated goals, and frequently adds time and expense to litigation that is already overlong and overly expensive" (*id.*), Judge Selya suggests that the process does not "make sense * * *, either in theory or experience" (p. 678). By contrast, Schneider, *supra,* generally supports certification, based partly on the favorable response of a sample of federal and state judges within the Sixth Circuit to a survey questionnaire (pp. 302–04).

Page 1246. Add to footnote 7:

A few states have procedures permitting the certification of questions by the courts of other states. See Selya, *Certified Madness: Ask a Silly Question . . . ,* 29 Suff.U.L.Rev. 677, 683 & n. 21 (1995). Does the failure of more states to permit certification by state courts "severely undermine the claim that certification is required to protect the sovereignty and integrity of state law" (p. 682)?

Page 1250. Add to Paragraph (2)(b):

The Court again assumed the continuing validity of the Burford doctrine, albeit without applying it, in Quackenbush v. Allstate Ins. Co., 517 U.S. 706 (1996), also discussed p. 106, *supra,* and pp. 112, 113, 151, *infra.* Quackenbush, the California Insurance Commissioner, acting in his capacity as trustee of a California insurance company that was in state liquidation proceedings, brought a damages action against Allstate in state court. Allstate removed the case to federal court on diversity grounds and filed a motion to compel arbitration under the Federal Arbitration Act, but the district court ordered the case remanded under the Burford doctrine without ruling on the arbitration motion. According to the district court, federal adjudication could interfere with the state's " 'overriding interest in regulating insurance insolvencies and litigations in a uniform and orderly manner' " (p. 709) and, in particular, risked erroneous federal decision of the important and unresolved state law issue whether Allstate was entitled to set off its own contract claims against any recovery by the commissioner. The court of appeals reversed on the ground that federal courts can abstain under the Burford doctrine only in cases in which equitable relief is sought.

The Supreme Court affirmed, 9–0, on a somewhat narrower basis: although Burford abstention principles might permit a federal court, in exceptional cases, to stay or postpone its action in a suit for damages pending resolution of relevant state court proceedings, the dismissal or remand of an action in federal court, though "not strictly limited" to "equitable" cases, is permissible only when "a federal court is asked to provide some form of discretionary relief" (pp. 730–31). In its review of Burford abstention principles, the Court observed that the balance of state and federal interests contemplated by the doctrine "only rarely favors abstention" (p. 728). But, having held remand improper, it declined to consider whether "this case presents the sort of 'exceptional circumstance' in which Burford abstention * * * [in the form of a stay of the federal action] might be appropriate" (p. 731).

Page 1255. Add to Paragraph (3)(c):

See also Quackenbush v. Allstate Ins. Co., 517 U.S. 706 (1996), discussed on p. 106, *supra,* asserting that the distinction between Thibodaux and Mashuda rested "in large measure" on the ground that Thibodaux involved a permissible "stay" of the federal suit pending state court action, whereas

Mashuda involved an outright dismissal of the federal suit.[a] Is that a meaningful distinction, given that resolution of the state court action in Thibodaux would effectively determine the outcome of the federal suit under normal principles of claim and issue preclusion? See pp. 106–08, *supra.*

Page 1305.   Add to footnote 9:

In Spencer v. Kemna, 118 S.Ct. 978 (1998), discussed at p. 142, *infra,* five Justices appear to have adopted Justice Souter's position in Heck v. Humphrey, Fourth Edition p. 1504: although a prospective plaintiff must exhaust available habeas remedies before bringing a § 1983 action that challenges the basis for a criminal conviction, a demonstration that the earlier conviction has been invalidated is not a substantive prerequisite of the § 1983 cause of action.

Page 1307.   Add at the end of Paragraph 4(c):

Cf. Chicago v. International College of Surgeons, 118 S.Ct. 523, 534 (1997)(holding that a suit presenting constitutional challenges to the decision of a municipal agency, as well as state law claims for on-the-record review of the agency's decision that lie within federal supplemental jurisdiction, may be removed to federal court, but noting that "there may be situations in which a district court should abstain from reviewing local administrative determinations even if the jurisdictional prerequisites are otherwise satisfied").

———

SUBSECTION D: PARALLEL PROCEEDINGS

———

Page 1319.   Add to Paragraph (3):

Although Wilton held only that the district court's *refusal* to entertain a declaratory judgment action was not an abuse of discretion, several subsequent decisions by panels of the Ninth Circuit overturned, as an abuse of discretion, a district court's *acceptance* of declaratory judgment jurisdiction to decide state law issues in diversity actions. These appellate decisions rested primarily on the failure of the district court to acknowledge that declaratory judgment jurisdiction is discretionary and to explain why it should be exercised.

However, when one of these cases was reheard en banc, the court of appeals held that a district court with subject matter jurisdiction over a declaratory judgment action may decide it without sua sponte raising the question whether its discretion to entertain the action should be exercised. Government Employees Ins. Co. v. Dizol, 133 F.3d 1220 (9th Cir.1998)(7–4). Moreover, on review of such a decision, the court of appeals need not decide sua sponte whether the district court abused its discretion in exercising jurisdiction. (As the dissenters noted, the majority did not state that the court of appeals was prohibited from making such a sua sponte determination.) If, however, the district court is asked by a party to decline jurisdiction, then it must explain on

---

a. The page of the Mashuda opinion cited to establish the centrality of this distinction, 360 U.S. at 190, provides somewhat less than straightforward support. Justice Stewart's concurring opinion in Thibodaux can be read as resting squarely on this ground, see 360 U.S. at 31, but it was not joined by any other member of the Court.

the record the basis for its decision to exercise jurisdiction—a course that the Ninth Circuit stated was preferred in any event.

As to how discretion should be exercised, the en banc court stated that district courts should avoid needless determinations of state law issues and duplicative litigation, and that where parallel state proceedings involving the same parties and state law issues are pending at the time the federal declaratory action is filed, there is a presumption that the entire case should be heard in state court.[a]

The Ninth Circuit has also held, here following other decisions, that the standards governing the exercise of discretion under the federal Declaratory Judgment Act apply equally when actions filed in state court, under state declaratory judgment acts, are removed. See, *e.g.*, Polido v. State Farm Mutual Auto. Ins. Co., 110 F.3d 1418, 1421 (9th Cir.1997), *overruled on other grounds by Dizol, supra.* Is that conclusion correct? Suppose a state declaratory judgment act limits discretion to decline jurisdiction more narrowly than does the federal act. Congress presumably has power to enact "arguably procedural" legislation that would govern an action brought under a state declaratory judgment but filed in or removed to federal court. But should 28 U.S.C. § 2201 be interpreted as having exercised that power? *Cf.* Fourth Edition p. 713.

Page 1319. Add a new Paragraph (3a):

(3a) *The Quackenbush Decision.* The Court's decision in Quackenbush v. Allstate Ins. Co., 517 U.S. 706 (1996), discussed more fully at pp. 106, 110, *supra*, drew a sharp distinction between a federal court's staying an action and its dismissing or remanding the action. Dismissal or remand, the Court ruled, is justified only in cases (like those seeking an equitable remedy or a declaratory judgment) in which a federal court has discretion whether to grant relief. Thus, the Court found that the district court had erred by remanding to state court a common law action for damages.

The case itself involved application of the Burford abstention doctrine. The Court's opinion appears, however, to have more general applicability, as it discussed a broad range of related doctrines, and cited, *inter alia*, the Colorado River, Moses H. Cone, and Wilton decisions.

Thus, the decision seems to reject the view of the Moses H. Cone decision— noted at the top of p. 1319 of the Fourth Edition—that stays and dismissals of federal actions are functionally indistinguishable. See generally pp. 107-08, *supra*. However, the Court did not reach the question of what substantive standards govern issuance of a stay in a common law damages action. The ruling therefore does not appear to change the circumstances in which a federal court should defer to state proceedings, but only addresses the form (stay versus dismissal or remand) that such deference should take.

Page 1321. Add a new footnote 16 at the end of Paragraph (5)(b)(i):

16.   The Court's decision in Quackenbush v. Allstate Ins. Co., 517 U.S. 706 (1996), discussed at p. 106, *supra,* implicitly endorsed broader discretion to dismiss or remand in

---

a.   See also Aetna Cas. & Sur. Co. v. Ind–Com Elec. Co., 139 F.3d 419 (4th Cir. 1998)(per curiam)(affirming the district court's refusal to entertain an insurer's diversity complaint for a declaration as to its liability on certain performance and payment bonds; the fact that no state court action was pending is a significant but not dispositive factor).

service of judicial administration than in service of comity and federalism. The opinion distinguished forum non conveniens decisions (in which, the Court ruled, a federal court may dismiss or remand an action seeking non-discretionary relief) from abstention decisions (in which dismissal or remand of such a case was held to be unwarranted). Abstention doctrines, which rest on deference to the paramount interest of another sovereign, "differ markedly" from the forum non conveniens doctrine, which historically reflects "a far broader range of considerations" (p. 723). The Court did not discuss in what circumstances federalism concerns justify a stay (rather than dismissal or remand) of an action seeking non-discretionary relief, however, and thus in the end the difference between abstention based on judicial administration and abstention rooted in federalism concerns may be largely one of form. See generally pp. 107–08, *supra.*

SUBSECTION E: MATTERS OF DOMESTIC RELATIONS AND PROBATE

Page 1333. Add to Paragraph (5):

Note, however, that the decision in Quackenbush v. Allstate Ins. Co., 517 U.S. 706 (1996), more fully discussed at p. 106, *supra,* suggests that where the suit is not one for a discretionary remedy like an injunction or declaratory judgment, a federal court may not refuse to exercise jurisdiction altogether; at most it can stay the action pending the resolution of state court proceedings.

Page 1333. Add a new Paragraph (7):

(7) *The Violence Against Women Act of 1994.* Title IV of the Violent Crime Control and Law Enforcement Act of 1994, 108 Stat. 1796, the Violence Against Women Act of 1994, not only makes criminal certain gender-motivated violence, but also creates a private civil right of action (codified at 42 U.S.C. § 13981(c)) for damages, injunctive, or other relief against any person who commits a crime of violence motivated by gender.

The Act expressly grants concurrent federal jurisdiction over the civil cause of action, but two provisions could be viewed as reflecting some unease about that grant. The first (codified at 28 U.S.C. § 1445(d)) makes state court actions under the Act non-removable. The second (codified at 42 U.S.C. § 13981(e)(4)) reinforces Ankenbrandt by limiting the reach, in suits under the Act, of supplemental jurisdiction over domestic relations matters.[a]

The latter provision appears to be the first statutory recognition of some kind of domestic relations exception to federal jurisdiction. Does that recognition imply congressional ratification of Ankenbrandt's holding? What if anything does it imply about whether federal courts should adjudicate domestic relations matters that fall under the *federal question* jurisdiction?

Page 1336. Add to Paragraph (6):

Regarding abstention, consider the implications of the decision in Quackenbush v. Allstate Ins. Co., 517 U.S. 706 (1996), pp. 106, 110, *supra.*

---

a. See 42 U.S.C. § 13981(e)(4)(neither the new private right of action nor the supplemental jurisdiction statute, 28 U.S.C. § 1367, "shall be construed, by reason of a claim arising under such subsection, to confer on the courts of the United States jurisdiction over any State law claim seeking the establishment of a divorce, alimony, equitable distribution of marital property, or child custody decree").

CHAPTER XI

FEDERAL HABEAS CORPUS

SECTION 1. INTRODUCTION

Pages 1338–39. Add to the Introductory Note:

Much attention has been given to the use of habeas corpus as a means of testing the legality of detention in immigration matters in the wake of the Illegal Immigration and Immigrant Responsibility Act, Pub. L. No. 104–208, 110 Stat. 3009 (1996), some provisions of which might be read to preclude all judicial review (including review via habeas corpus) of certain executive decisions that result in detention. For further discussion, see p. 27, *supra*.

Page 1341. Add a new Paragraph (6), to follow the first full paragraph on the page:

(6) *The 1996 Amendments.* The Antiterrorism and Effective Death Penalty Act of 1996, 110 Stat. 1214, contains numerous amendments to the habeas jurisdiction, which are designed to restrict the availability of the writ in post-conviction cases. See generally Yackle, *A Primer on the New Habeas Corpus Statute,* 44 Buff.L.Rev. 381 (1996).

The Act's most important section, codified in 28 U.S.C. § 2254(d), provides that habeas relief cannot be awarded to a state prisoner solely because a state court misapplied established constitutional principles to the facts in a particular case; rather, relief is available only when the state court determination was "contrary to, or involved an unreasonable application of, clearly established Federal law, as determined by the Supreme Court of the United States". See pp. 122, 126–29, *infra*.

In addition, the Act provides, for the first time, a statute of limitations (of one-year) governing collateral attacks by both state and federal prisoners. 28 U.S.C. §§ 2244(d), 2255; see pp. 117, 136, *infra*. And it includes a set of provisions designed to speed adjudication under § 2254 in capital cases, but which apply only when the state prisoner was afforded competent counsel in state post-conviction proceedings. 28 U.S.C. §§ 2261–66; see pp. 120–22, *infra*.

These and other provisions added by the Act are discussed in more detail below. Except for the special rules applicable to capital cases, the 1996 amendments generally do not govern petitions already pending when the Act was passed. Lindh v. Murphy, 117 S.Ct. 2059 (1997).

Page 1345. Add to Paragraph (5):

For a recent decision discussing the availability of the original writ, while denying the petition, see Felker v. Turpin, 116 S.Ct. 2333 (1996), p. 133, *infra*.

SECTION 2. COLLATERAL ATTACK ON STATE JUDGMENTS OF CONVICTION

Page 1345. Substitute, for the "Introductory Note on the Operation of Federal Habeas Corpus Jurisdiction for State Prisoners" on pp. 1345–49, the following revised version:

INTRODUCTORY NOTE ON THE OPERATION OF FEDERAL HABEAS CORPUS JURISDICTION FOR STATE PRISONERS

Federal habeas corpus jurisdiction provides a method for prisoners convicted in state court to obtain federal court review of federal constitutional questions that were decided adversely to them by the state courts. (Post-conviction relief for *federal* prisoners is governed by 28 U.S.C. § 2255, discussed in Section 3 of this Chapter.) Habeas corpus is not an appeal from, but rather a collateral attack upon, the state criminal conviction. Unlike most collateral attacks, however, habeas proceedings are not governed by the ordinary rules of res judicata, thus permitting the federal court to relitigate federal issues that were fully and fairly litigated in state court.

Between 1867 and 1996, Congress amended the habeas statute infrequently, without purporting to make fundamental changes in the jurisdiction. Decisional law wove an intricate web of doctrinal rules, which have changed significantly over time. The Warren Court generally defined the habeas jurisdiction broadly and imposed relatively few procedural restrictions on its exercise. The Burger and Rehnquist Courts in turn narrowed the jurisdiction and tightened procedural requirements.

On April 24, 1996, the President signed the Antiterrorism and Effective Death Penalty Act of 1996 (the "1996 Act"), 110 Stat. 1214, which contains the first significant legislative re-shaping of the writ—one designed to restrict its availability.

Both the judge-made doctrines that pre-date the 1996 Act and the new statutory provisions are enormously intricate. The following general, and necessarily simplified, overview of how the habeas jurisdiction operates in actions commenced by state prisoners may therefore be useful.

A. Cognizable Issues

(1) *The Statutory Grant.* For all practical purposes, federal habeas corpus relief is limited to claims that the state court proceedings leading to the defendant's detention were infected with federal constitutional error. See Fourth Edition pp. 1360–61. Studies have found that although most state prisoners are convicted by guilty plea, roughly 70–80% of habeas petitioners were convicted after a trial.[1]

---

1. Flango, Habeas Corpus in State and Federal Courts 36 (1994); Robinson, An Empirical Study of Federal Habeas Corpus Review of State Court Judgments 7 (1979); Faust, Rubenstein & Yackle, *The Great Writ in Action: Empirical Light on the Federal*

During the Warren Court era, a habeas court could review all constitutional issues that the Supreme Court could have considered on direct review of a state criminal conviction. The Burger and Rehnquist Courts created exceptions to that general rule, two of which deserve special note.

First, a habeas court lacks power to award relief when the prisoner alleges only that the state court erred in denying a motion to suppress evidence under the Fourth Amendment. See Fourth Edition pp. 1376–85.

Second, subject only to extremely narrow exceptions, a habeas court lacks power to award relief when the prisoner's constitutional claim is based on "new law"—*i.e.*, a constitutional rule that was not dictated by precedent at the time that the prisoner's conviction became final on direct review. See Fourth Edition pp. 1392–1413.

The 1996 Act has narrowed the scope of habeas review still further. Most fundamentally, the Act provides that habeas relief cannot be awarded solely because a state court misapplied established constitutional principles to the facts in a particular case; rather, the federal habeas court must also find that the erroneous state court determination was "contrary to, or involved an unreasonable application of, clearly established Federal law". See pp. 122, 126–29, *infra*.

B. Prerequisites to Review

A state prisoner seeking to obtain federal habeas relief must satisfy two pre-conditions.

(1) *Custody*. By its nature, habeas corpus extends only to a person in custody at the time a petition is filed. See 28 U.S.C. § 2241(c)(3); Fourth Edition pp. 1450–54. "Custody" includes not only physical detention but also subjection to parole or probation conditions. But a convict who has served the entire sentence (including parole or probation terms) before filing a habeas petition, or whose only penalty was a monetary fine, is not in custody and may not seek relief.

(2) *Exhaustion of State Remedies*. A prisoner may not obtain habeas relief without having first exhausted state remedies. See 28 U.S.C. § 2254(b-c); Fourth Edition pp. 1443–50. Exhaustion refers only to remedies still available at the time the habeas corpus petition is filed, not to remedies no longer available.

Typically, the exhaustion requirement obliges a prisoner to pursue direct appellate review in the state courts. There is no need, however, to seek Supreme Court review of the state court conviction. Nor, ordinarily, is there any need to pursue state post-conviction remedies as to issues decided on direct review. But a prisoner must exhaust state post-conviction remedies as to issues not previously presented to the state courts (as might be true, for example, of claims of ineffective assistance of counsel or of non-disclosure of exculpatory evidence). Studies suggest that 30–50% of petitions are dismissed for failure to exhaust.[2]

Note the important interaction of the custody and exhaustion requirements: in cases involving short sentences, a prisoner may no longer be in custody by the time state remedies have been exhausted.

Habeas Corpus Debate, 18 N.Y.U.Rev.L. & Soc. Change 637, 678 (1991).

2. See Fourth Edition p. 1449.

C. Initiation and Nature of the Proceedings

(1) *Filing a Petition.* A state prisoner in custody, having exhausted state remedies, may file a petition (sometimes also called an "application") for a writ of habeas corpus in federal district court, seeking relief on the ground that federal constitutional error infected the state court proceedings that resulted in the petitioner's detention. The state officer having custody of the petitioner— ordinarily the prison warden or the director of the state correctional system—is named as respondent. (The convention is to refer to habeas decisions by the prisoner's name. For example, the Supreme Court's decision in Wainwright v. Sykes, Fourth Edition p. 1418, is usually called "Sykes", after the prisoner, rather than "Wainwright", who was a state official.)

(2) *Civil Nature of Proceedings and Applicable Rules.* Habeas corpus actions are *civil* proceedings. Since 1977, they have been subject to the special "Rules Governing Section 2254 Cases in the United States District Courts" (the "§ 2254 Rules"), Rule 11 of which states: "The Federal Rules of Civil Procedure, to the extent that they are not inconsistent with these rules, may be applied, when appropriate, to petitions filed under these rules."

(3) *Time Limits.* Until 1996, there was no statute of limitations for habeas proceedings. The only provision dealing with delay was Rule 9(a) of the § 2254 rules, which states that a petition may be dismissed if the state "has been prejudiced in its ability to respond to the petition by delay in filing unless the petitioner shows that it is based on grounds of which he could not have had knowledge by the exercise of reasonable diligence before the circumstances prejudicial to the state occurred."[3] In Vasquez v. Hillery, 474 U.S. 254, 265 (1986), the Court ruled that difficulties in retrying the defendant (as distinguished from difficulties in responding to the petition) are not "prejudice" within the meaning of Rule 9(a).

The 1996 Act created a one-year statute of limitations. See 28 U.S.C. § 2244(d). The time begins to run from the latest of four specified dates; ordinarily, the operative date will be "the date on which the judgment became final by the conclusion of direct review or the expiration of the time for seeking such review."[4] The statute is tolled while a properly filed state post-conviction proceeding is pending.

Is this a sensible reform? Or is it unrealistic to expect prisoners, most of whom are poorly educated and lack legal representation, to appreciate the possible availability of a legal claim and to prepare a petition within the limitations period?

(4) *Availability of Counsel.* The great majority of habeas petitioners are indigent, and studies have found that about 80–90% lack counsel.[5] The Supreme Court has held that petitioners generally have no *constitutional* right to counsel in state or federal collateral attacks on their convictions.[6] Thus, any federal right to counsel derives from statutes or court rules.

---

3. See generally Clinton, *Rule 9 of the Federal Habeas Corpus Rules: A Case Study on the Need for Reform of the Rules Enabling Acts,* 63 Iowa L.Rev. 15 (1977).

4. The other three dates are those of (a) removal of an impediment to filing that was created by state action in violation of the Constitution or federal law; (b) initial recognition by the Supreme Court of a new consti-

tutional right, retroactively applicable to cases on collateral review, see p. 128, *infra;* and (c) discovery of the factual predicate of the claim.

5. See Flango, note 1, *supra,* at 37; Robinson, note 1, *supra,* at 9.

6. *E.g.,* Pennsylvania v. Finley, 481 U.S. 551, 554–55 (1987); Johnson v. Avery,

(a) *Capital Cases*. A statutory provision enacted in 1988 confers a right to appointed counsel upon indigents who are attacking a capital sentence or conviction in federal habeas cases. 102 Stat. 4393, codified at 21 U.S.C. § 848(q)(4)(B). In McFarland v. Scott, 512 U.S. 849 (1994), the Supreme Court ruled that this provision permits the appointment of counsel even before a habeas petition has been filed, in order to provide assistance in preparing the petition.

(b) *Non-Capital Cases*. Appointment of counsel in non-capital cases is governed by Rules 6(b) and 8(c) of the § 2254 Rules. The court *must* appoint counsel for an indigent petitioner if an evidentiary hearing is required (Rule 8(c)) or when necessary for effective utilization of discovery authorized by the court (Rule 6(b)); both circumstances are rare. Otherwise, counsel may be appointed at any stage "if the interest of justice so requires" (Rule 8(c)).

D. Processing of Cases

(1) *Petition and Response*. Many habeas petitions are summarily dismissed. When the judge orders the warden to respond, often the response (sometimes accompanied by excerpts from the record or by affidavits) establishes a basis for dismissal without further proceedings. Discovery proceeds only insofar as leave is granted by "the judge in the exercise of his discretion and for good cause shown," § 2254 Rules, Rule 6(a); see Bracy v. Gramley, 117 S.Ct. 1793 (1997), and in practice is extremely limited. Evidentiary hearings to develop the facts are rarely conducted.[7]

In the twelve month period ending September 30, 1997, of the 14,440 petitions on which court action was taken, 14,348 were terminated "Before Pretrial", 81 "During or After Pretrial", and only 31 (or 0.2%) "During or

---

393 U.S. 483, 488 (1969). See also Fourth Edition p. 1433 note 5; p. 129, *infra*.

Though there is no general right to counsel, in Bounds v. Smith, 430 U.S. 817, 828 (1977), the Court recognized "the fundamental constitutional right of access to the courts". The Court thus upheld an order requiring that prisoners be provided adequate law libraries or assistance from law-trained persons to permit preparation of meaningful legal papers.

Subsequent decisions have not defined the right of access expansively. In Murray v. Giarratano, 492 U.S. 1 (1989)(5–4), the Court rejected the argument that prisoners on death row—who labor under special time constraints and emotional burdens, and whose cases often are unusually complex— have a right to counsel on request. Four Justices ruled that Pennsylvania v. Finley governed capital as well as non-capital cases. The fifth vote came from Justice Kennedy, who acknowledged the distinctiveness of capital cases. But noting that Bounds can be satisfied in many ways and that judges have limited capacity to design a comprehensive system of representation, he was not pre-

pared to find the state's existing efforts (providing legal advisers in penal institutions and appointing counsel after a petition was filed) inadequate under Bounds. And in Lewis v. Casey, 518 U.S. 343 (1996), a class action against Arizona officials, the Supreme Court vacated an order requiring system-wide changes in prison law libraries and legal assistance programs. Justice Scalia's majority opinion emphasized that the standing doctrine requires plaintiffs to show actual injury meriting relief, and that as only two instances of such injury had been established, the sweeping relief ordered was unjustified. The Court's opinion added that a prisoner's right of access encompasses only the capacity to file nonfrivolous legal claims, and repudiated suggestions in Bounds that the right extends to assistance in discovering grievances or in litigating effectively once in court. To credit those suggestions, the Court said, would be tantamount to demanding that prisoners be permanently provided with counsel, which the Constitution does not require.

7. See Weisselberg, *Evidentiary Hearings in Federal Habeas Corpus Cases*, 1990 B.Y.U.L.Rev. 131, 165–68.

After Trial". Annual Report of the Director of the Administrative Office of the United States Courts, Table C–4 (1997).

(2) *The Role of Magistrate Judges.* In many districts, federal magistrate judges have the primary responsibility for processing habeas petitions. If a party objects to the magistrate judge's proposed findings and recommendations, the district judge must make a "de novo determination" with respect to any such contested matter.[8] 28 U.S.C. § 636(b)(1).

(3) *Deference to State Court Determinations.* Although *res judicata* does not apply in habeas proceedings, a statutory provision added in 1966, and tightened by the 1996 Act, requires the federal court to presume that state court findings of fact are correct; that presumption may be rebutted only by clear and convincing evidence. 28 U.S.C. § 2254(e)(formerly § 2254(d)); see Fourth Edition pp. 1371–76; p. 124, *infra.*

Traditionally, a habeas court was not bound to defer to a state court's decision on a question of law or on the application of law to the facts. But § 2254(d), added by the 1996 Act, now requires deference, by precluding habeas relief unless the state court's determination was "contrary to, or involved an unreasonable application of, clearly established Federal law, as determined by the Supreme Court of the United States". See generally pp. 126–29, *infra.*

E. Procedural Default

(1) *Forfeiture of Federal Claims.* Sometimes a habeas petitioner failed to present the state courts with the federal constitutional claim raised in the habeas petition—or failed to present it in accordance with state procedural rules (*e.g.*, by not raising it in a timely manner). And as a result of that procedural default, the state courts may not have reached the merits of that federal constitutional claim. When that is so, subject to only the narrowest exceptions, the federal habeas court will not consider the defaulted claim. See Fourth Edition pp. 1413–40.

Note that a procedural default typically involves a failure to pursue opportunities to litigate in state court that once were but no longer are available. A failure to exhaust state remedies, by contrast, involves opportunities to litigate in state court that remain available at present.

F. Remedy, Appeals, and Successive Petitions

(1) *Relief.* The only remedy awarded is release from custody, but as is true when a conviction is reversed on appeal, the remedy is tailored to the nature of the constitutional violation. Thus, if a petitioner had been convicted for conduct that was constitutionally protected (for example, burning the American flag), the remedy would be unconditional release from custody. If instead a constitutional error occurred in the state proceedings (for example, admission of a confession in violation of the Miranda rules), the remedy would be conditional, requiring release from custody only if a retrial and re-conviction do not occur within a specified period.

---

8. That obligation was narrowly construed, however, in United States v. Raddatz, 447 U.S. 667 (1980), Fourth Edition p. 439. There, the Supreme Court ruled that after a magistrate had heard a motion to suppress evidence in a federal criminal prosecution, the district judge was not obliged to rehear the evidence even with respect to critical issues of credibility.

(2) *Appeals.* The custodian may appeal a district court's grant of relief. A prisoner seeking to appeal a denial of relief must first obtain a "certificate of appealability," which may be issued only upon a showing that the applicant "has made a substantial showing of the denial of a constitutional right," 28 U.S.C. § 2253(c)(2),[9] and which must indicate the specific issue(s) that satisfy that standard, § 2253(c)(3). Before 1996, a prisoner could seek a certificate from either the district court or court of appeals (and could try both); the courts of appeals have uniformly interpreted the 1996 Act as not altering that arrangement, despite some language seeming to restrict the power of issuance to the courts of appeals.[10]

(3) *Successive Petitions.* A prisoner is permitted to file more than one habeas petition only in exceedingly narrow circumstances. See Fourth Edition pp. 1440–43; pp. 132–34, *infra.*

G. Procedures in Capital Cases

The Court has encountered special problems in habeas proceedings brought by prisoners on death row. On the one hand, the finality of execution had led to calls for special solicitude, and past studies have found that capital petitioners obtained relief in over 40% of cases (compared to a 1–3% success rate overall). See Fourth Edition p. 1364. On the other hand, some observers contend that death row inmates and their lawyers, in seeking to forestall executions, have abused the writ by filing multiple petitions and/or petitions at the eleventh hour, and then seeking a stay of execution to permit adjudication of the claims raised.

Recent decisions have come close to laying down a rule that a petitioner under death sentence is entitled to a stay of execution in connection with a first habeas petition,[11] while suggesting that a stay in connection with a successive

---

9. The House Report accompanying the 1996 Act indicates that this language was meant to codify the previous judge-made standard that a certificate of probable cause (as it was called before 1996) should issue if the appeal presents a question of substance that is " 'debatable among jurists of reason' " or is not "squarely foreclosed by statute, rule or authoritative court decision", Barefoot v. Estelle, 463 U.S. 880, 893 n. 4, 894 (1983)(quoting Gordon v. Willis, 516 F.Supp. 911, 913 (N.D.Ga.1980)). See H. Rpt. 104–23 at 9 (1995).

10. See Tiedeman v. Benson, 122 F.3d 518, 522 & cases cited (8th Cir.1997). The question arose because § 2253, as amended in 1996, authorizes issuance of a certificate only by the court of appeals, but the 1996 Act also amended Fed.R.App.Proc. 22(b), and the amended Rule states that an appeal may not proceed "unless a *district* or a circuit judge issues a certificate of appealability pursuant to section 2253(c)" (emphasis added).

11. See, *e.g.,* Lonchar v. Thomas, 517 U.S. 314 (1996), where the prisoner did not file his first petition until the day of his scheduled execution—more than six years af-

ter his conviction and death sentence had become final on direct review. (The case predated the enactment of a statute of limitations. See Paragraph C(3), *supra.*) Before that time, saying that he wanted to die, he had opposed "next friend" petitions filed by relatives who claimed he was incompetent. He admitted that his last-minute change of heart was a delaying tactic; he hoped that the state would change its method of execution so that he could donate his organs.

The Court (per Breyer, J.) held it was error for the court of appeals to have vacated the stay of execution if the petition was properly filed. The petition could not be dismissed under Rule 9(a)(see Paragraph C(3), *supra*), which governs a petitioner's delay, for that rule "requires, as a condition of dismissal, a finding of 'prejudice' ", which was not made (p. 326). Nor could the petition be dismissed for "ad hoc 'equitable' reasons not encompassed within the framework of Rule 9" (p. 322)—especially here, as "[d]ismissal of a *first* federal habeas petition is a particularly serious matter" (p. 324). Four Justices concurred only in the judgment.

petition will be far more difficult to obtain.[12]

The 1996 Act "incorporates reforms * * * to address the acute problems of unnecessary delay and abuse in capital cases." See H. Conf. Rpt. 104–518, at 111 (1996). The provisions in question, 28 U.S.C. §§ 2261–66, apply only if the state has established a mechanism for the provision of counsel in *state* post-conviction proceedings brought by indigent prisoners under sentence of death. § 2261(b). That mechanism "must provide standards of competency for the appointment of such counsel", though § 2261 establishes no standards itself, except to provide that counsel shall not have represented the prisoner at trial or on direct review "unless the prisoner and counsel expressly request continued representation". § 2261(d).

Where such a mechanism exists, the following provisions, designed to expedite federal habeas corpus actions filed by prisoners under sentence of death, take effect:[13]

1. A 180–day statute of limitations, similar in operation to the general one-year limitations period in § 2244(d), see Paragraph C(3). § 2263.[14] (Will this deadline exacerbate the difficulties in finding competent lawyers to handle federal petitions?)

2. Special time limits within which federal courts must decide habeas cases—for the district courts, 180 days after filing (with one 30–day extension possible); for the courts of appeals, 120 days after the reply brief is filed. § 2266.

3. A requirement that any stay of execution shall expire if the prisoner (a) fails to file a timely petition, (b) "fails to make a substantial showing of the denial of a Federal right", or (c) "is denied relief in the district court or at any subsequent stage of review". § 2262(b). Once the stay has expired, "no Federal court thereafter shall have the authority to enter a stay of execution in the

The Court has also held that although § 2251, the provision governing stays, authorizes their issuance when "a habeas corpus proceeding is pending", a habeas court may issue a stay as soon as a petitioner has sought appointment of counsel, even before the petition is actually filed. McFarland v. Scott, 512 U.S. 849 (1994), Paragraph (C)(4)(a), *supra*.

12. One week after the decision in Lonchar, note 11, *supra*, a different 5–4 majority, acting the day before a prisoner's scheduled execution, vacated a summary order of the Eighth Circuit that had stayed the execution and had scheduled oral argument on an appeal from the district court's denial of the prisoner's third habeas petition. See Bowersox v. Williams, 517 U.S. 345 (1996)(per curiam). "Entry of a stay on a second or third habeas petition is a drastic measure, and we have held that it is 'particularly egregious' to enter a stay absent substantial grounds for relief. Delo v. Blair, 509 U.S. 823 (1993)(citation omitted)" (p. 346). The Eighth Circuit's order, the Court found,

failed to reveal substantial grounds for relief, and the stay constituted an abuse of discretion in view of the report of the Magistrate Judge, adopted by the District Court, which "meticulously addresses each of Williams' claims and finds each to be abusive, successive, procedurally defaulted, or meritless" (*id.*). The four dissenters noted that "[a] diligent appellate court has granted a certificate of probable cause" and "[a]t the very least, before acting irretrievably, this Court might have invited prompt clarification of the Court of Appeals' order" (p. 347).

13. In addition to the provisions noted in text, a special provision further restricting federal court power to hear claims not raised in state court, see Paragraph E, *supra*, takes effect. § 2264(a); see p. 130, *infra*.

14. The 180–day period is tolled for only the *first* state post-conviction petition filed, whereas the general statute of limitations in § 2244 is tolled during the pendency of any "properly filed" state post-conviction proceeding.

case, unless the court of appeals approves the filing of a second or successive application under section 2244(b)". § 2262(c).[15]

It may be difficult to judge whether a state has established a qualifying mechanism, but resolution of that question determines, *inter alia*, whether a petitioner under death sentence faces a limitations period of 180 days or of one year. In Calderon v. Ashmus, 118 S.Ct. 1694 (1998), a California death row inmate filed a class action in federal court, seeking a declaratory judgment that the state's mechanism did not satisfy the standards of § 2261. The Supreme Court unanimously held the action non-justiciable, reasoning that it presented only a collateral legal issue whose resolution would not conclusively determine the underlying controversy between the parties (namely, whether a particular inmate is entitled to federal habeas corpus relief). See p. 6, *supra*.

Page 1359.   Add a new Paragraph (2a):

(2a) *The Effect of the 1996 Act.* The 1996 Act effects a major change in the scope of habeas review. The Act amends § 2254(d) to provide that habeas relief shall not be granted with respect to a claim "that was adjudicated on the merits in State court proceedings unless the adjudication of the claim—

"(1) resulted in a decision that was contrary to, or involved an unreasonable application of, clearly established Federal law, as determined by the Supreme Court of the United States; or

"(2) resulted in a decision that was based on an unreasonable determination of the facts in light of the evidence presented in the State court proceeding."

The provision clearly bears on the appropriate conception of the nature of habeas review. At least some observers have viewed habeas as an independent inquiry into the constitutionality of detention, rather than as a review of the correctness of a state court determination. See Fourth Edition pp. 1357–59, Paragraph (2). (The differences between these two conceptions may have been greater in theory than practice. See Fourth Edition p. 1358, note 3.) But § 2254(d) now appears to require a federal court to focus on the state court's determination rather than independently on the legality of detention.

More important, § 2254(d)(1) suggests that a federal court is no longer to make a de novo determination of constitutional claims previously litigated in state court. Thus, relief can no longer be based on the conclusion that a state court's constitutional decision was erroneous; the federal court must also find that the state court's determination was "contrary to, or involved an unreasonable application of, clearly established Federal law".

What theory of the purpose of habeas corpus does this provision serve? How likely is a federal court to find that a state court's constitutional decision was not merely wrong but also unreasonable? Insofar as habeas is designed to

---

15. Suppose a district court grants habeas relief to a prisoner whose petition is governed by §§ 2261–66, but the court of appeals reverses, 2–1. Section 2262(c) seems to suggest that even were the Supreme Court to grant certiorari, neither it nor any other federal court could stay an impending execution? Does that restriction raise any constitutional problem? Would the state's Governor have any obligation to postpone the execution in such a situation?

give the state courts an incentive faithfully to apply federal norms, how strong will that incentive be after enactment of § 2254(d)(1)?

For further discussion of § 2254(d)(1), see pp. 126–29, *infra*.

Page 1365. Add after the carryover paragraph at the top of the page:

In Felker v. Turpin, 116 S.Ct. 2333, 2340 (1996), discussed in more detail on p. 133, *infra*, Chief Justice Rehnquist's opinion for a unanimous Court stated that "it was not until well into this century that this Court interpreted [the habeas statute] to allow a final judgment of conviction in a state court to be collaterally attacked on habeas. See, e.g., Waley v. Johnston, 316 U.S. 101 (1942); Brown v. Allen, 344 U.S. 443 (1953)." Nothing in the case turned, however, on the accuracy of that description.

Page 1369. Add to footnote 3:

See also Freedman, *The Suspension Clause in the Ratification Debates*, 44 Buff.L.Rev 451 (1996)(arguing that materials from the Founding period support a broad view of habeas corpus embracing review of both federal and state convictions); *cf.* Neuman, *Habeas Corpus, Executive Detention, and the Removal of Aliens*, 98 Colum.L.Rev. 961, 968–86 (1998) (discussing the Suspension Clause in relation to habeas corpus as a remedy for executive detention rather than for post-conviction custody).

Page 1371. Add a new Paragraph (4):

(4) *Constitutionality of the 1996 Act.* The 1996 Act imposed a number of significant restrictions on the operation of habeas corpus for state prisoners, including (a) a statute of limitations, see p. 117, *supra*; (b) the new § 2254(d), see p. 122, *supra*, which appears generally to restrict the grounds for issuing relief; (c) limitations on the provision of evidentiary hearings, see the material immediately following; and (d) limitations on power to entertain successive petitions, see p. 132, *infra*. Does any of these raise a serious constitutional question under the Suspension Clause?

In Felker v. Turpin, 116 S.Ct. 2333 (1996), the Supreme Court considered the last of these limitations, that on entertaining successive petitions. Chief Justice Rehnquist's opinion for a unanimous Court began by noting that until the Civil War there was no general habeas jurisdiction available for persons in state custody, and that collateral attacks on judgments of conviction were not permitted until well into this century. He continued (p. 2340): "But we assume, for purposes of decision here, that the Suspension Clause of the Constitution refers to the writ as it exists today, rather than as it existed in 1789."

The Court proceeded to find no unconstitutional suspension of the writ. The Chief Justice acknowledged that the Act tightens some of the pre-existing restrictions on successive petitions, "and further restricts the availability of relief to habeas petitioners. But we have long recognized that 'the power to award the writ by any of the courts of the United States, must be given by written law,' Ex parte Bollman, 4 Cranch 75, 94 (1807), and we have likewise recognized that judgments about the proper scope of the writ are 'normally for Congress to make.' Lonchar v. Thomas, 517 U.S. 314, 323. * * * The added restrictions which the Act places on second habeas petitions are well within the compass of this evolutionary process, and we hold that they do not amount to a 'suspension' of the writ contrary to Article I, § 9" (p. 2340).

Page 1374. Add to Paragraph (4):

The 1996 Act adopted the provisions of the Senate Bill noted in Fourth Edition p. 1374 n. 2, which amend the statutory treatment of both (1) federal court deference to state court factfindings and (2) the availability of federal evidentiary hearings.

1. The 1996 Act extends, across the board, the presumption (rebuttable only by clear and convincing evidence) that state court factfindings are correct; no longer does that presumption expressly depend on the quality of state factfinding processes. See § 2254(e)(an amendment and re-designation of former § 2254(d)).[a] Compare Yackle, *Federal Evidentiary Hearings Under the New Habeas Corpus Statute*, 6 B.U.Pub.Int.L.J. 135 (1996)(reading the provision as dispensing with former § 2254(d)'s specific requirements but not with the habeas court's responsibility to ensure the adequacy of the state process that generated factual findings).

2. The 1996 Act also expressly limits, for the first time, the power of a habeas court to hold an evidentiary hearing. Codifying but tightening the approach of Keeney v. Tamayo–Reyes, Fourth Edition p. 1373, § 2254(e)(2) precludes an evidentiary hearing when the prisoner failed in state court to develop the factual basis for a claim,[b] unless:

(A) the claim relies on (i) a new constitutional rule, made retroactive on collateral review by the Supreme Court, or (ii) a factual predicate that could not previously, with due diligence, have been discovered; *and*

(B) the facts underlying the claim would establish, by clear and convincing evidence, that but for the constitutional error, no reasonable factfinder would have found the applicant guilty of the underlying offense.

Note how this formulation differs, in at least three respects, from the procedural default doctrine that Tamayo–Reyes had applied:

(i) Part (A) appears for the most part to track the restrictive standards under which "cause" for a procedural default had been found by the Supreme Court.[c] But formerly, a showing that the prisoner was "actually innocent"

---

a. The new provision also omits former § 2254(d)'s limitation of the presumption of correctness to determinations that were "evidenced by a written finding, written opinion, or other reliable and adequate written indicia".

Section 2254(e)'s treatment of state factfindings would appear, for the most part, to subsume the new provision, found in § 2254(d)(2), p. 122, *supra*, which precludes relief based on a challenge to the correctness of a state court's factual determination unless the determination was "unreasonable". Suppose, however, that a state trial judge made a finding that was reasonable in view of the state court record, but the prisoner presents powerful new evidence to the federal court—not previously available—that rebuts, by clear and convincing evidence, the state court's factual determination. Is federal relief available under § 2254(e)(2)—at least assum-ing that the new evidence establishes that the prisoner was not guilty within the terms of § 2254(e)(2)(B)? Could the state counter that federal relief remains unavailable under § 2254(d)(2) because the state court determination was reasonable when made? Or does § 2254(d)(2) not apply when new evidence may be introduced under § 2254(e)?

b. The President's Signing Statement took the position that § 2254(e)(2) "is not triggered when some factor that is not fairly attributable to the applicant prevented evidence from being developed in State court." Statement of President William J. Clinton On Signing The Antiterrorism and Effective Death Penalty Act of 1996, 32 Wkly. Compilation of Presidential Documents 719 (Apr. 29, 1996).

c. For exploration of possible differences, see Yackle, *supra*, at 142–47.

would suffice by itself to permit federal adjudication; § 2254(e)(2), by contrast, requires that such a showing (under part (B)) be coupled with a showing of "cause" (under part (A)).[d]

(ii) When a prisoner does claim innocence of the underlying offense, the Court had suggested that a state court procedural default would be excused if the prisoner could show that "it is more likely than not that no reasonable juror would have convicted". Schlup v. Delo, Fourth Edition p. 1435. The standard in § 2254(e)(2)(B), by contrast, not only is coupled with the need to show "cause", but also is the more stringent test advocated by the dissent in Schlup—requiring proof by clear and convincing evidence that no reasonable factfinder would have found the applicant guilty.

(iii) The "innocence" standard in part (B) requires a showing that the prisoner was not guilty of the *offense*. Would new evidence, not previously discoverable, that petitioner's conduct was constitutionally protected, or that the death sentence was constitutionally defective, establish that the prisoner did not commit the offense? If not, is a habeas court therefore barred from holding an evidentiary hearing on such a claim?

Page 1388. Add a new footnote 4a at the end of Paragraph (3)(b):

4a. In Kimmelman, the Court clearly opined, albeit in dictum, that the "prejudice" necessary to warrant relief for ineffective assistance of counsel may be established by proof that, had the defense lawyer properly made a meritorious motion under the Fourth Amendment to suppress evidence, there is a reasonable probability that the verdict would have differed. Justice Powell's opinion concurring in the judgment (joined by Chief Justice Burger and Justice Rehnquist) objected to that suggestion as unnecessary to the decision and as mistaken. In Holman v. Page, 95 F.3d 481 (7th Cir.1996), the court followed Justice Powell's lead, ruling that the failure to object, on appeal, to the introduction of reliable evidence cannot constitute the prejudice necessary to establish a denial of the right to counsel. Contra, *e.g.*, Huynh v. King, 95 F.3d 1052 (11th Cir.1996).

Pages 1406–08. Add to Paragraphs (2–4):

In three recent decisions—O'Dell v. Netherland, 117 S.Ct. 1969 (1997), Lambrix v. Singletary, 117 S.Ct. 1517 (1997), and Gray v. Netherland, 518 U.S. 152 (1996)—the Court followed prior decisions that broadly defined new law, in each case holding a prisoner's habeas claim to be barred by Teague. Justices Stevens, Souter, Ginsburg, and Breyer dissented in all three cases.

Page 1410. Add a new Paragraph (5)(c):

(c) Teague was held to be inapplicable in Bousley v. United States, 118 S.Ct. 1604 (1998), where a *federal* prisoner claimed that he had pled guilty based on a misunderstanding of the elements of the offense, and that his plea therefore was not knowing and intelligent. In ruling that Teague did not

d. Clarifying an issue that was unresolved under pre–1996 decisional law, the statute also provides that the facts establishing innocence, so as to permit excuse of a default, must be those underlying a constitutional claim that is cognizable. Thus, under the statute, for example, a petitioner would not be entitled to a federal evidentiary hearing if he alleged (a) that DNA evidence establishes his actual innocence, and (b) that that showing of innocence should excuse his failure to have developed in state court the factual basis for a claim that his Miranda rights were violated—even, apparently, if he was without fault in having failed to generate a fuller state court record (for example, because the state had concealed a videotape of the interrogation). The DNA evidence would not make out a *constitutional* claim, and the facts underlying the Miranda claim would not show his innocence.

preclude collateral relief, the Court suggested that the constitutional claim—that the prisoner's plea was not knowing and intelligent—was hardly new. But Chief Justice Rehnquist's opinion continued more broadly: "And because Teague by its terms applies only to procedural rules, we think it is inapplicable to the situation in which this Court decides the meaning of a criminal statute enacted by Congress.

"This distinction between substance and procedure is an important one in the habeas context. The Teague doctrine is founded on the notion that one of the 'principal functions of habeas corpus [is] "to assure that no man has been incarcerated under a procedure which creates an impermissibly large risk that the innocent will be convicted."' Consequently, unless a new rule of criminal procedure is of such a nature that 'without [it] the likelihood of an accurate conviction is seriously diminished,' there is no reason to apply the rule retroactively on habeas review. By contrast, decisions of this Court holding that a substantive federal criminal statute does not reach certain conduct, like decisions placing conduct ' "beyond the power of the criminal law-making authority to proscribe," ' necessarily carry a significant risk that a defendant stands convicted of 'an act that the law does not make criminal' "(p. 1610; internal citations omitted).

For further discussion of the Bousley decision, see p. 130, *infra*.

Page 1410.   Add a new Paragraph (5a):

(5a) *The Effect of the 1996 Act.* The 1996 Act added a new § 2254(d)(1), which provides that habeas relief shall not be granted with respect to a claim "that was adjudicated on the merits in State court proceedings unless the adjudication of the claim—

"(1) resulted in a decision that was contrary to, or involved an unreasonable application of, clearly established Federal law, as determined by the Supreme Court of the United States".

The lower courts have given this provision a variety of interpretations. One approach views § 2254(d)(1) as requiring federal courts to apply, across-the-board, a deferential rather than a de novo standard when reviewing a state court determination. See, *e.g.*, Perez v. Marshall, 946 F.Supp. 1521, 1532–33 (S.D.Cal.1996), *affirmed without reported opinion*, 121 F.3d 716 (9th Cir.1997). A second approach distinguishes the standard of review of general propositions of law from that for "mixed questions" (*i.e.*, applications of law to fact). See, *e.g.*, Drinkard v. Johnson, 97 F.3d 751, 767–68 (5th Cir.1996) (in reviewing questions of law, relief is permitted when the state decision was "*contrary to* ... clearly established Federal law, as determined by the Supreme Court", while in reviewing mixed questions, relief is permitted when the state decision was "*an unreasonable application of* [] clearly established Federal law, as determined by the Supreme Court"). A third approach views the Act less as mandating deference than as adopting a choice-of-law rule, similar to that of Teague, in which a habeas court evaluates a state court judgment based on the state of the law when that decision was rendered.[a] See O'Brien v. Dubois, ___ F.3d ___, ___ (1st Cir.1998) (adopting a two-step approach, in which a habeas

---

a. Note that the statute does not clearly indicate whether one measures a state court's consistency with clearly established Supreme Court law as of the time the conviction becomes final on direct review—the approach of Teague—or the time that the state court rendered its decision.

court first determines whether a state court decision is contrary to any governing rule prescribed by the Supreme Court, and if not, whether the "state court's use of (or failure to use) existing law in deciding the petitioner's claim involved an 'unreasonable application' of Supreme Court precedent," which is the case only when "the state court decision [was] so offensive to existing precedent, so devoid of record support, or so arbitrary, as to indicate that it is outside the universe of plausible, credible outcomes").[b]

Whichever of these views is taken, several other features of § 2254(d)(1) deserve special note:

1. Unlike the Teague doctrine, this provision recognizes no exceptions. Suppose a state court "reasonably" decides that Jones' primary conduct was not constitutionally protected, and after the conviction becomes final, the Supreme Court decides (in a different case) that the Constitution does protect the conduct in question. Does § 2254(d)(1) preclude a habeas court from granting relief to Jones? Recall that in the nineteenth century, when habeas relief for persons convicted in state court was limited (at least in the view of some) to "jurisdictional" defects, that category embraced challenges to the constitutionality of the statute under which the prisoner had been convicted. See Ex parte Siebold, Fourth Edition p. 1365.

2. Under Teague, a rule of law was "new" if it was not compelled by prior decisions; if the rule was susceptible to debate among reasonable minds, then (absent an exception) habeas relief was barred. Under § 2254(d)(1), habeas relief is barred if the state court's decision did not violate "clearly established Federal law"—perhaps a reference to the official immunity doctrine in constitutional tort actions. See Fourth Edition, Chap. IX, Sec. 3. Are the two standards equivalent?[c]

Note, however, that § 2254(d)(1) speaks of "clearly established Federal law, *as determined by the Supreme Court*" (emphasis added). Under Teague, it is difficult, but not necessarily impossible, to show that a rule of law not specifically endorsed by the Supreme Court was nonetheless compelled by precedent and not subject to debate among reasonable minds. Suppose, for example, that every federal circuit had found a particular practice to deny due process; no state court had disagreed; and the Supreme Court, therefore, had never faced a conflict requiring resolution. If thereafter a state court, in a particularly unpersuasive opinion, upholds the practice, does § 2254(d)(1) preclude habeas relief? The prisoner might argue, of course, that older Supreme Court decisions, not directly on point, clearly established the rule followed by all the circuits; but plainly the more general the principles in the pertinent Supreme Court precedents, the harder the argument that they clearly established the illegality of the practice in question.

3. Unlike Teague, § 2254(d)(1) bars relief only where the federal claim was adjudicated on the merits in state court. Of course, where there is no such adjudication, the prisoner usually has failed properly to have raised the issue in

b. A still different, and minimalist, interpretation views § 2254(d)(1) as directing attention initially to the state court's decision but not otherwise restricting the power of a habeas court to reach its own determination of the constitutional issue. See Yackle, p. 114 *supra*, at 412.

c. In O'Brien v. DuBois, *supra*, the court reasoned that because state judges do not face personal liability for erroneous constitutional decisions, a governing constitutional rule need be less clear or specific to provide the basis for habeas relief than such a rule must be to supply the basis for official liability in a constitutional tort action.

state court, and that state court procedural default ordinarily provides an independent basis for barring habeas relief.

But one instance in which a state court procedural default does not bar habeas review is where the constitutional claim is "novel"—where the defense lawyer in state court could not reasonably have been expected to make a constitutional argument later accepted by the Supreme Court. See Reed v. Ross, Fourth Edition pp. 1430–31. Yet a claim that is "novel" so as to avoid the procedural default problem will virtually always be barred by Teague because it rests on "new law".

Could the 1996 Act give a prisoner a *greater* opportunity to prevail on a novel claim in habeas—by contending that (i) § 2254(d)(1) does not apply so long as the claim was not decided on the merits in state court, and (ii) that section "occupies the field" and thus displaces the Teague doctrine? That possibility was not addressed, and thus may have been rejected, in Breard v. Greene, 118 S.Ct. 1352 (1998) (per curiam). There, a Paraguayan citizen sentenced to death filed a federal habeas corpus petition alleging for the first time that his conviction and sentence should be overturned because the state had failed to notify Paraguay at the time of his arrest, in violation of the Vienna Convention on Consular Relations. After the lower courts had denied relief, the International Court of Justice (ICJ), acting on a complaint by Paraguay, issued an order requesting the United States to take all measures at its disposal to prevent execution pending final decision in the ICJ proceeding. Breard then filed a petition for leave to file a petition for an original writ of habeas corpus, relying on the ICJ order; he had previously filed a petition for certiorari.

On the eve of execution the Supreme Court issued a per curiam opinion denying both petitions on the ground that Breard had forfeited his claim under the Treaty by having failed to raise it in state court; the Court rejected Breard's submission that the procedural default doctrine is inapplicable to treaty obligations. In response to Breard's contention that the claim was "novel" and hence there was cause for the default, the Court relied on Teague as holding that the habeas court should not entertain a claim based on new law.[d]

4. Several provisions of the 1996 Act other than § 2254(d)(1) impose procedural restrictions on the exercise of habeas jurisdiction, but then create exceptions to those restrictions when the prisoner is relying on a new constitutional rule that has been made retroactively applicable to cases on collateral review. See, *e.g.,* § 2244(d)(1)(C)(statute of limitations), p. 117, *supra;* § 2254(e)(2)(A)(i)(availability of federal evidentiary hearings), p. 124, *supra;*

d. The Republic of Paraguay had previously filed a federal court suit against Virginia officials, alleging that their conduct violated the Vienna Convention. After losing in the court of appeals, Paraguay filed a petition for certiorari, and, after the ICJ ruling, a petition for leave to file an original action in the Supreme Court. The Breard opinion rejected both petitions, finding that neither the Vienna Convention nor 42 U.S.C. § 1983 authorized Paraguay's suit.

The Breard decision plainly raises important questions of international law—notably whether the ruling of the ICJ should have received greater deference, whether there is any remedy in American courts for apparently widespread violations of the Vienna Convention, and whether the decision will prejudice the rights under that convention of Americans prosecuted in foreign countries.

§ 2264(a)(2) (procedural default rules conditionally applicable in capital cases), see p. 130, *infra*; § 2244(b)(2)(A)(limits on successive petitions), p. 132, *infra*.

How could the Court today ever recognize a new right *and* make it retroactively applicable on collateral review? In a case on direct review, the Court would have no occasion to consider the retroactivity issue. And in a federal collateral attack, if the claimed right is "new", won't § 2254(d)(1) require dismissal of the claim? Or does the reference to new rules made retroactively applicable suggest that the statute contemplates some collateral review of new constitutional rules (for example, in cases falling within Teague's exceptions)?

For discussion of § 2254(d), see Lee, *Section 2254(d) of the New Habeas Statute: An (Opinionated) User's Manual*, 51 Vand.L.Rev. 103 (1998); Note, 110 Harv.L.Rev. 1868 (1997); Note, 96 Mich.L.Rev. 434 (1997).

Page 1433.   Add to footnote 5:

The question left open in Coleman—whether there is a constitutional right to counsel in a state collateral attack based on a claim of ineffective assistance at trial and on direct appeal—was answered in the negative in Mackall v. Angelone, 131 F.3d 442 (4th Cir.1997)(en banc)(10–2). After Mackall's conviction and death sentence were affirmed, the lawyer who had represented Mackall at trial and on appeal filed a state post-conviction petition that, unsurprisingly, did not contend that his own performance at trial had been constitutionally ineffective. After the petition was denied, Mackall filed a second state post-conviction petition, pro se, claiming that he had received ineffective assistance of counsel at trial. The state court denied the second petition on the ground that the claim there raised had not been presented in the first post-conviction petition.

In his federal habeas corpus action, Mackall alleged that any procedural default in his first state post-conviction petition should be excused on the ground that (i) he had no prior opportunity to challenge the constitutional adequacy of his trial counsel (under state law, that claim could not have been presented on direct review of the conviction), (ii) he had a constitutional right to effective assistance of counsel when raising that claim for the first time, and (iii) such assistance had been denied him in the first post-conviction proceeding. Without disputing the first part of the argument, the court of appeals rejected the second, viewing the precedents as establishing an across-the-board rule that there is no constitutional right to counsel in collateral proceedings. (Compare 28 U.S.C. § 2254(i), a provision added by the 1996 Act though not discussed in Mackall, which states without qualification that the ineffectiveness of counsel during federal or state post-conviction proceedings is not a ground for habeas relief.) The two dissenters stressed that the constitutional right to counsel extends to the first direct appeal, and that a state post-conviction attack was equivalent to a first appeal with respect to an issue that could not have been raised on direct review.

Mackall and similar decisions thus hold that persons who never received competent representation at any stage may be condemned to death and then deprived of any judicial review of the effectiveness of their trial lawyers on the ground that those (incompetent) lawyers failed to raise a claim of ineffective assistance of counsel at trial (by challenging their own conduct) in an earlier post-conviction proceeding. Might judicial concerns about delays in capital cases from repetitive petitions explain this holding? Could such concerns justify it?

Page 1435.   Add a new Paragraph (8):

(8) *The Effect of the 1996 Act*. Although the 1996 Act does not contain any general provision dealing with state court procedural defaults, two sections bear on that problem:

(a) In capital cases arising in states whose system for providing counsel in state post-conviction proceedings satisfies § 2261, see p. 121, *supra*, the habeas court may not consider a claim not raised and decided on the merits in state court unless the default resulted from (i) unconstitutional state action, (ii) the Supreme Court's recognition of a new right made retroactively applicable, or (iii) the prisoner's inability, through the exercise of due diligence, to have discovered the factual predicate for the claim. § 2264(a). No longer would "actual innocence" permit a habeas court to reach the merits of a defaulted claim presented by a death row inmate from a "qualifying" state. What justifies stricter procedural default rules for prisoners under sentence of death?

(b) The second provision, if it is pertinent at all, applies only indirectly. Section 2254(e)(2), p. 124, *supra*, narrows the circumstances in which a federal evidentiary hearing may be provided when a prisoner failed to develop the facts in state court. Previously, the Court had borrowed its doctrine dealing with procedural defaults to govern the availability of evidentiary hearings in such cases. See Keeney v. Tamayo–Reyes, Fourth Edition p. 1373. Can it be argued that in shaping its procedural default doctrine, the Court ought to be guided by the new statutory standards governing provision of evidentiary hearings—an area that the Court had previously deemed to be analogous? Or does Congress' failure to have enacted similar language directly dealing with procedural defaults suggest that pre-existing doctrine remains in place?

Page 1436.   Add to Paragraph (3):

Cf. Stutson v. United States, 516 U.S. 193 (1996)(per curiam), p. 135, *infra*, suggesting that a lawyer's failure to file a timely appeal from a *federal* criminal conviction may sometimes constitute excusable neglect under Fed.R.App.Proc. 4(b). Does the resolution of that question bear on the proper treatment of procedural defaults in state court—to which the federal rules do not apply? See Fourth Edition p. 1464 n. 9.

Page 1437.   Add a new Paragraph (6):

(6) *Procedural Default and Guilty Pleas*. The applicability of procedural default doctrine to collateral attacks on guilty pleas was at issue in Bousley v. United States, 118 S.Ct. 1604, (1998), p. 126, *supra*. Bousley pled guilty to a federal offense and filed no appeal. After the Supreme Court, in a different case, interpreted the offense of which Bousley had been convicted more narrowly than had the district court in which Bousley had pled guilty, he filed a collateral attack, contending that his plea was not knowing and intelligent because he had not understood the elements of the offense. The lower courts denied relief. On review, the Supreme Court first ruled that because the voluntariness and intelligence of Bousley's guilty plea could have been attacked on direct review, his failure to have appealed from his conviction constituted a procedural default, at least where, as here, the appeal could have been decided without further factual development. However, the Court added that Bousley might be able to demonstrate "actual innocence" so as to excuse the default, and remanded to give him that opportunity.

In dissent, Justice Scalia, joined by Justice Thomas, argued that when a prisoner has pled guilty, a procedural default should not be excusable by a showing of actual innocence: no trial transcript exists, and thus the government, many years after the fact, would have to produce witnesses saying that Bousley committed the crime. Noting that nearly 93% of federal convictions are by guilty plea, Justice Scalia warned that the Court's ruling could produce a flood of collateral attacks. He also observed that guilty pleas often are entered in exchange for dismissal of more serious charges. In an effort to respond to these concerns, the majority stressed that the government was free to introduce any admissible evidence of guilt even if that evidence had not been presented during the plea colloquy,[a] and added, "[i]n cases where the Government has forgone more serious charges in the course of plea bargaining, petitioner's showing of actual innocence must also extend to those charges" (p. 1611).[b]

Justice Stevens, concurring in part and dissenting in part, objected to the majority's approach from a different direction. He asserted that the Court had never before held that the failure to take a direct appeal from a constitutionally invalid guilty plea constituted a procedural default. He added that such a holding would be "unwise and would defeat the very purpose of collateral review. A layman who justifiably relied on incorrect advice from the court and counsel in deciding to plead guilty to a crime that he did not commit will ordinarily continue to assume that such advice was accurate during the time for taking an appeal" (p. 1614). Thus, without requiring a showing of actual innocence to excuse a purported default, he would have treated Bousley's petition as meritorious, vacated his conviction, and remanded for Bousley to plead anew.

Note the difference between the approach of the majority and that of Justice Stevens. Suppose that on remand there is factual uncertainty whether Bousley committed the offense as properly defined, that Bousley cannot establish "actual innocence"—i.e., that "it is more likely than not that no reasonable juror would have convicted" him of the offense—but the government cannot establish his guilt beyond a reasonable doubt. Under the majority's approach, his conviction remains in force; under Justice Stevens' approach, his conviction would be vacated and the government would be unable to convict him at a retrial. Which result is more appropriate?

Page 1438.   Add to Paragraph (2)(a):

In Trest v. Cain, 118 S.Ct. 478 (1997), the Supreme Court unanimously ruled that a state court procedural default does not deprive a federal habeas

---

a. A footnote appended to the Court's opinion at this point noted that federal law requires that guilty pleas be accompanied by proffers demonstrating a factual basis for the plea. But proffers are not themselves *admissible* evidence, as the body of the Court's opinion appeared to require.

b. What exactly does this last statement mean? One could understand the view that if a prisoner is permitted to overturn a conviction, the government should be free to re-open charges that had been dismissed as part of a plea bargain. But the Court seems to say more than that—that a prisoner, to establish actual innocence so as to permit him to attack the conviction of the offense as to whose elements he was misinformed, must show his innocence of other charges that were dismissed. Suppose a prisoner had pled guilty to the same offense as had Bousley—a serious drug offense that carries a five-year mandatory sentence—and in exchange the government dropped an unrelated charge of possession of cocaine. Can the majority mean that if the prisoner can establish that he is innocent of the more serious charge as authoritatively interpreted by the Supreme Court, but cannot show his innocence of possession of cocaine on a different occasion, he has not established "actual innocence" so as to excuse his failure to have filed a direct appeal from his conviction?

court of jurisdiction, but is normally a defense that the state must raise. While thus ruling that the court of appeals had erred in holding that it *must* raise a procedural default question sua sponte, the Court declined to decide whether the court of appeals *was permitted* to do so.

But even if not a jurisdictional question, procedural default is a threshold issue that, the Court ruled in Lambrix v. Singletary, 520 U.S. 518 (1997), a habeas court should ordinarily resolve before considering the applicability of Teague v. Lane. Teague's statement that retroactivity is a "threshold" issue means only that it should be addressed before reaching the merits, not that retroactivity is antecedent to procedural default issues. Nonetheless, a habeas court might deviate from that preferred order of decision if, for example, the Teague issue were simple while the procedural default issue raised difficult state law questions. In Lambrix itself, the Court—while expressing puzzlement that the court of appeals had denied relief by relying on Teague, without reaching the question of procedural default—decided the case in the same fashion, expressing reluctance to address the procedural default issue because it depended on questions of state law not addressed by the lower courts.

Page 1443.   Add a new Paragraph (5):

(5) *The Effect of the 1996 Act.*

(a) The 1996 Act amends § 2244(b) to restrict the power of a habeas court to hear a successive petition.

Section 2244(b)(1) requires dismissal (without exception) of a claim that was presented in a prior petition.

Section 2244(b)(2) requires dismissal of claims not previously presented unless:

"(A) * * * the claim relies on a new rule of constitutional law, made retroactive to cases on collateral review by the Supreme Court, that was previously unavailable; or

"(B)(i) the factual predicate for the claim could not have been discovered previously through the exercise of due diligence; and (ii) the facts underlying the claim, if proven and viewed in light of the evidence as a whole, would be sufficient to establish by clear and convincing evidence that, but for constitutional error, no reasonable factfinder would have found the applicant guilty of the underlying offense."

These provisions are more restrictive than the prior judge-made regime established by McCleskey v. Zant, Fourth Edition p. 1442. Under prior law, a successive claim could be entertained if (i) it rested on "new facts" (at least in some circumstances), *or* (ii) the prisoner could establish "actual innocence"; § 2244(b)(2)(B) requires that a successive claim satisfy both conditions.[a] Moreover, that section tightens the "actual innocence" standard. See pp. 124–25, *supra*.[b]

a. The new provision also requires a nexus between the facts underlying the constitutional violation and the facts establishing innocence. See p. 125, n. d, *supra*.

b. The McCleskey decision, which dealt with claims not raised in a previous federal habeas petition, applied the standards developed for state court procedural defaults. Since the 1996 Act does not change the latter standards, "defaults" in a prior habeas proceeding (where a prisoner not under death sentence is unlikely to have had counsel) are now treated more strictly than are defaults in state court.

Section 2244(b)(3) also requires that a prisoner, before filing a successive petition in a district court, first file a motion before a three-judge panel of the court of appeals, seeking authorization; the court of appeals is to act on the motion within 30 days. Only if approval is granted may the prisoner then file the petition in the district court. Why should application of the substantive standards limiting successive petitions be made initially in the courts of appeals rather than in the district courts?[c]

Finally, the 1996 Act provides that the grant or denial of authorization "by a court of appeals * * * shall not be appealable and shall not be the subject of a petition for rehearing or for a writ of certiorari." § 2244(b)(3)(E).

(b) This last provision was at issue in Felker v. Turpin, 116 S.Ct. 2333 (1996). There, following denial of authorization by the court of appeals to file a successive petition, a prisoner filed a "Petition for Writ of Habeas Corpus, for Appellate or Certiorari Review [of the court of appeals' decision], and for Stay of Execution." The Supreme Court ruled unanimously that § 2244(b)(3) did not preclude the prisoner from filing a petition in the Supreme Court seeking an original writ of habeas corpus. Chief Justice Rehnquist's opinion relied heavily on the similar holding in Ex parte Yerger, 75 U.S. (8 Wall.) 85 (1869), Fourth Edition p. 358 n. * * *. The ruling in Felker effectively eliminated any question whether Congress had unconstitutionally restricted the scope of Supreme Court appellate jurisdiction.

The Court added, however, that the provisions of § 2244(b)(1)–(2) restricting consideration of successive petitions—unlike the provisions regulating the procedure for seeking authorization contained in § 2244(b)(3)—contain no reference to filings "in the district court". "Whether or not we are bound by these restrictions, they certainly inform our consideration of original habeas petitions" (p. 2339).

Turning finally to the prisoner's pleading itself, the Court stated that the claims presented "do not materially differ from numerous other claims made by successive habeas petitioners which we have had occasion to review on stay applications to this Court. Neither of [the prisoner's constitutional claims] satisfies the requirements of the relevant provisions of the Act, let alone the requirement [in Sup. Ct. R. 20(a), governing original writs of habeas corpus] that there be 'exceptional circumstances' justifying the issuance of the writ" (p. 2340). Hence, the petition for certiorari was dismissed for want of jurisdiction, and the petition for an original writ of habeas corpus was denied.

After Felker, consider these questions:

(i) Suppose a prisoner contends that the court of appeals erroneously failed to authorize a successive petition. Is it harder to satisfy the "exceptional circumstances" requirement of Sup.Ct.R. 20(a) than it would have been (absent the statutory preclusion in § 2244(b)(3)) to persuade the Court to grant certiorari, see Sup.Ct.R. 10 ("a petition for certiorari will be granted only for compelling reasons")? If not, is there any reason why Congress would have wanted to enact a provision whose only effects were (a) to preclude a petition for rehearing in the court of appeals, and (b) to require that a prisoner's

---

c. If there is a dispute, for example, about the question whether "the factual predicate for the claim could not have been discovered previously through the exercise of due diligence", should the court of appeals hold an evidentiary hearing itself? Appoint a special master?

petition in the Supreme Court be labeled one for an original writ of habeas corpus rather than for a writ of certiorari?

(ii) Would any original action permitted by the Court be limited to the question whether the court of appeals correctly denied authorization to file a successive petition? If so, would there be an objection that because the Court itself could not issue an order of release, the original action would not really be in the nature of habeas corpus? Is it a sufficient answer that the Court, after deciding the authorization issue, has authority (see 28 U.S.C. § 2241(b)) to transfer any proceedings on the merits to a district court?

(iii) How might a warden obtain Supreme Court review of a court of appeals decision authorizing the filing of a successive petition? Concurring opinions in Felker by Justices Stevens and Souter (each joined by the other, and by Justice Breyer) noted that § 2244(b)(3) does not purport to restrict the Court's appellate jurisdiction under 28 U.S.C. § 1254(2) (dealing with certification) or under the All Writs Act, 28 U.S.C. § 1651. See generally Fourth Edition pp. 1672–81.

For discussion of Felker, see Tushnet, *"The King of France with Forty Thousand Men": Felker v. Turpin and the Supreme Court's Deliberative Processes*, 1996 Sup.Ct.Rev. 163.

(c) In Stewart v. Martinez–Villareal, 118 S.Ct. 1618 (1998), the Supreme Court found § 2244(b)'s limits on successive petitions to be inapplicable. There a death row inmate filed a federal habeas petition raising several claims, among them that he was incompetent to be executed. The district court dismissed the incompetency claim as premature. After the court of appeals ruled that he was not entitled to relief on other grounds, the prisoner, fearing that the 1996 Act might foreclose a later petition raising his incompetency claim, unsuccessfully moved to re-open the earlier petition.

Thereafter, a warrant of execution was issued, and the prisoner, after failing to persuade the state courts that he was incompetent to be executed, again moved in federal court to re-open his incompetency claim. In response to the state's argument that that motion constituted a successive petition barred by § 2244(b), the Supreme Court ruled, 7–2, that the prisoner had filed only one petition, that a district court should rule on each claim presented in a petition at the time that that claim becomes ripe, and that the incompetency claim was therefore cognizable. To accept the state's argument would have "seemingly perverse" implications (p. 1621), such as requiring a habeas court, after dismissing a petition for want of exhaustion, to treat a renewed petition following exhaustion as successive—an approach the Court had never taken.

The Court expressly reserved the question whether an incompetency claim could be heard if not included in an initial petition. Is there any reason, however, to insist that a clearly unripe claim be filed prematurely in order to preserve federal power to adjudicate it after it ripens?

Page 1450.   Add a new Paragraph (8a):

(8a) *The Effect of the 1996 Act.* The 1996 Act added two provisions concerning the exhaustion doctrine. One, following the suggestion of Professor Shapiro (see Fourth Edition p. 1449), permits the denial (but not the grant) of a petition notwithstanding the failure to exhaust. § 2254(b)(2).

The second modifies the rule of Granberry v. Greer (see Fourth Edition pp. 1449–50) by providing that only an express waiver of the exhaustion requirement by counsel can bar the state from invoking the doctrine. § 2254(b)(3).

Consider also the interaction of the exhaustion requirement and the new one-year statute of limitations, see p. 117, *supra*. Although the statute is tolled while state post-conviction remedies are pending, time spent shuttling back and forth between federal and state courts does count. Do the complexities posed by the exhaustion requirement—and particularly by the rule of Rose v. Lundy, Fourth Edition p. 1446, which requires dismissal of "mixed" petitions—make the new limitations period excessively harsh for uncounseled prisoners?

Page 1459.   Add to the beginning of Paragraph (9):

On April 24, 1996, Congress enacted the Antiterrorism and Effective Death Penalty Act of 1996, 110 Stat. 1214, which contains all of the "reform" proposals described in Paragraph (9) of the Fourth Edition, except the provision discussed in sub–Paragraph (9)(g)(iv). The Act also contains a few additional provisions not described in Paragraph (9). The Act's specific provisions are described in detail above, in connection with particular topics.

SECTION 3.   COLLATERAL ATTACK ON FEDERAL JUDGMENTS OF CONVICTION

Page 1465.   Add to Paragraph (5)(c):

Compare Stutson v. United States, 516 U.S. 193 (1996)(per curiam), where the notice of appeal from a criminal conviction arrived, by mail, one day late, and at the court of appeals rather than at the district court. The district court ruled the appeal untimely, and the court of appeals summarily dismissed the appeal. The Supreme Court vacated and remanded to give the court of appeals the opportunity to reconsider whether a lawyer's inadvertent failure to file a timely appeal could in some circumstances constitute "excusable neglect" under Fed.R.App.Proc. 4(b). Much of the opinion discussed the appropriateness of granting, vacating, and remanding in view of (i) the summary nature of the decision below, (ii) the conflict between that decision and the decisions of six other circuits, and (iii) the government's having changed its legal position. But the Court added: "it is not insignificant that this is a criminal case. When a litigant is subject to the continuing coercive power of the Government in the form of imprisonment, our legal traditions reflect a certain solicitude for his rights, to which the important public interests in judicial efficiency and finality must occasionally be accommodated" (p. 196).

Page 1466.   Add to Paragraph (6):

Bousley v. United States, 118 S.Ct. 1604 (1998), like Davis v. United States (Fourth Edition pp. 1464 n. 7, 1466), involved a § 2255 petition premised on an intervening decision that had narrowed the scope of the criminal offense of which the prisoner had been convicted. Unlike Davis, however, Bousley had been convicted by guilty plea. The Court (per Rehnquist, C.J.) held the claim—which it treated as based not on a change in statutory law alone but on the constitutional principle that a defendant must know the elements of the offense to which he enters a guilty plea—to be cognizable and not limited by Teague v. Lane. See p. 125, *supra*.

Page 1467.   Add a new Paragraph (9):

(9) *The Effect of the 1996 Act.* The Antiterrorism and Effective Death Penalty Act of 1996, 110 Stat. 1214, added several important provisions that affect the operation of § 2255:

1.   A one-year statute of limitations (in § 2255 itself), whose substance parallels § 2244(d)'s limitations period for state prisoners, see p. 117, *supra*.

2.   Time limits within which federal courts must decide § 2255 motions filed by prisoners under sentence of death—for the district courts, 180 days after filing (with one 30–day extension possible); for the courts of appeals, 120 days after the reply brief is filed. See 28 U.S.C. § 2266.

3.   An extension to federal prisoners of the rule, previously applicable only to state prisoners, that an appeal from a district court's denial of relief cannot be filed without having first obtained a certificate of appealability. See 28 U.S.C. § 2253 and Fed.R.App.Proc. 22, discussed at p. 120, *supra*.

4.   Strict conditions (in § 2255 itself) limiting the consideration of second or successive motions—conditions that generally parallel those contained in § 2244(b)(2) for state prisoners[a]—and a requirement that a prisoner seeking to file a successive petition first obtain a ruling from a panel of the court of appeals that the conditions have been satisfied. Compare pp. 132–33, *supra*.[b]

Section 2255, however, extends to a broader range of claims than does § 2254, notably in embracing some non-constitutional claims. Thus, Congress' apparently unthinking borrowing of language from § 2254 may have untoward consequences in dealing with successive § 2255 motions. For example:

(a) Section § 2255 extends to a claim that the federal criminal statute under which a prisoner was convicted has since been authoritatively interpreted more narrowly. See generally Davis v. United States, Fourth Edition pp. 1464 n. 7, 1466. The 1996 Act does not restrict jurisdiction to entertain such claims in an initial § 2255 motion. Suppose, however, that after a district court rejects an initial § 2255 motion raising, for example, a Miranda claim, the Supreme Court in a different case interprets the criminal offense of which the prisoner was convicted more narrowly than did the convicting court. Is the prisoner foreclosed from filing a second § 2255 motion relying on the intervening Supreme Court decision, because the second motion does not rest on either "newly discovered evidence" or "a new rule of *constitutional* law, made retroactive by the Supreme Court, that was previously unavailable"?

Could the prisoner contend that the second motion does rest on a new rule of *constitutional* law—that due process precludes conviction of a crime when

---

a.   In two respects, § 2255 is less strict than the parallel provisions in § 2244(b) restricting multiple filings by state prisoners. First, § 2255 contains no provision, like that in § 2244(b)(1), that unqualifiedly requires the dismissal of a claim in a second or successive petition that was presented in a prior application. Second, § 2255 permits a successive petition based on newly discovered evidence of innocence, without the further requirement found in § 2244(b)(2)(B)(i) that "the factual predicate for the claim could not have been discovered previously through the exercise of due diligence".

b.   Section 2255 contains no provision, parallel to that in § 2244(b)(3)(E), precluding appeal from the court of appeals' determination. Compare p. 133, *supra*.

the jury (or the judge accepting a guilty plea) misunderstood the law and hence did not find that the elements of the offense were present? The fact that this claim incorporates a statutory element does not rob it of constitutional status, a prisoner might argue; and the application of a general principle of due process to the particulars of the Supreme Court's statutory ruling is "new" within the meaning of Teague. Would acceptance of that argument read the word "constitutional" out of the statute? The courts that have considered the question to date appear to think so, as they have uniformly refused to entertain such claims in successive § 2255 motions. See, *e.g.*, Triestman v. United States, 124 F.3d 361, 369–70 & cases cited (2d Cir.1997). See also Bousley v. United States, 118 S.Ct. 1604, 1607 (1998), p. 125, *supra,* not a successive petition case, but one in which the Court said that "there is nothing new" about a prisoner's claim that his plea was not knowing and intelligent because he was misinformed of the elements of the offense.

(b) A prisoner may file a § 2255 motion that presents newly-discovered evidence as the basis for challenging a sentence. But Hope v. United States, 108 F.3d 119 (7th Cir.1997), interpreted the 1996 Act as foreclosing such a claim in a successive petition.

(c) Could either of the kinds of claims just discussed, if foreclosed under § 2255 by the limits on successive petitions, instead be raised in a habeas corpus petition? Recall that § 2255, rather than repealing federal habeas corpus jurisdiction for federal prisoners, instead contains a safety valve, precluding habeas corpus unless "the remedy by motion [under § 2255] is inadequate or ineffective to test the legality of [the prisoner's] detention." Do the restrictions on successive petitions make § 2255 "inadequate or ineffective" when a prisoner has already filed a § 2255 motion? Or do they instead not only expressly limit the availability of § 2255, but also impliedly preclude resort to habeas corpus—even in situations in which a prisoner could not reasonably have been expected to raise the claim in an initial § 2255 motion?

Several circuits have authorized habeas relief in the situation described in sub-Paragraph (a), above. See, *e.g.*, Triestman v. United States, *supra* (holding that a serious constitutional question would be raised under the Eighth Amendment and Due Process Clause were all collateral relief unavailable to one convicted under a broad understanding of a criminal offense that the Supreme Court has since repudiated, and in turn finding that because such a question cannot be raised in a successive petition under § 2255, habeas relief is available under the safety valve provision); In re Dorsainvil, 119 F.3d 245 (3d Cir.1997) (permitting habeas relief in similar circumstances on the ground that preclusion of relief would be a "complete miscarriage of justice" and in this unusual circumstance relief under § 2555 is "inadequate or ineffective").

CHAPTER XII

ADVANCED PROBLEMS IN JUDICIAL FEDERALISM

SECTION 1. PROBLEMS OF RES JUDICATA

Page 1473.   Add a new footnote 8a at the end of Paragraph (4):

8a.   For discussion of the res judicata effects of certain adjudications in bankruptcy—a question that has generated conflicting circuit court decisions—see Martinez, *The Res Judicata Effect of Bankruptcy Court Judgments: The Procedural and Constitutional Concerns,* 62 Missouri L.Rev. 9 (1997).

Page 1474.   Add to footnote 10:

In a comprehensive and thoughtful study, Professor Erichson—noting the many ways in which the behavior of parties in litigation is affected by the preclusion rules applicable to that litigation—argues forcefully that courts should almost always apply the preclusion doctrines of the court (whether federal or state) that rendered the judgment at issue. Erichson, *Interjurisdictional Preclusion,* 96 Mich.L.Rev. 945 (1998). In the empirical portion of the study, however, Erichson reports that state courts frequently apply their own preclusion law in interjurisdictional cases.

Page 1484.   Add a new Paragraph (3a):

(3a) *Mendoza and the Supreme Court's Original Jurisdiction.* If the initial decision adverse to the United States is handed down by the Supreme Court in the exercise of its original jurisdiction, do the policy considerations articulated in Mendoza apply, or do they lose their force when the action is itself commenced in the Supreme Court? In United States v. Alaska, 117 S.Ct. 1888 (1997), the Court said that the question need not be resolved in the case before it because the particular issue had not been necessary to the prior judgment. (Note that the question may not be of great consequence in view of the stare decisis effect of Supreme Court decisions.)

Page 1484.   Add to Paragraph (4):

The foregoing discussion in this Paragraph assumes that the Mendoza rationale applies also to the use of nonmutual issue preclusion against a *state* or *local* government. But are the problems sufficiently different that, even if Mendoza itself is sound, a different approach should apply to state and local governmental entities? See Note, 109 Harv.L.Rev. 792 (1996)(arguing that nonmutual issue preclusion should be presumptively unavailable against states unless a multi-factor balancing test suggests otherwise).

Page 1492. Add a footnote a at the end of the title of the Note beginning on this page:

a. A topic that is not the focus of this chapter, but that is a major subject of study with respect to the Full Faith and Credit Clause and its implementation, is the effect to be given in the courts of one state to judicial proceedings in the courts of another state. See generally Restatement (Second) of Conflict of Laws §§ 93, 103–121 (1971). Some of the issues raised in that context are the same as, or similar to, those discussed in this Note, which addresses the effects of a state judgment in a subsequent *federal* proceeding.

Page 1500. Add to Paragraph (7) at the top of the page:

The Supreme Court reversed the Ninth Circuit judgment in the Matsushita case and held the federal class action precluded as a result of the state court settlement. Matsushita Elec. Indus. Co. v. Epstein, 516 U.S. 367 (1996). In this case, shareholders in an acquired corporation brought a state court class action, on behalf of all the acquired corporation's shareholders, based purely on state-law grounds, while another group of shareholders in the same company brought a federal court class action complaining of violation of the Securities Exchange Act of 1934 with respect to the same underlying transaction.[10] (The federal action fell within the exclusive jurisdiction of the federal courts.) While the federal action was pending, the state court entered a judgment approving a settlement that provided, *inter alia,* for release by all class members (who did not opt out of the class) of *all* claims arising out of the events in question, "including but not limited to claims arising under the federal securities laws".

The question presented to the Supreme Court was whether, under § 1738, the settlement had preclusive effect with respect to those who had not opted out of the state court class, so that prosecution of the federal securities claim by such persons was barred. Although the Justices disagreed on what questions should be open to the Ninth Circuit on remand, the Court unanimously agreed that so long as the demands of due process are met and federal law does not provide otherwise, § 1738 requires reference to state law in order to determine whether such a settlement has preclusive effect—even with respect to a federal claim over which the state court had no jurisdiction.[11] The Court also agreed that nothing in the 1934 Exchange Act constituted a repeal, in whole or in part, of § 1738.

If the claim under the 1934 Exchange Act had been litigated in the state court class action, isn't it clear that, given the state court's lack of subject-matter jurisdiction over that claim, any judgment with respect to it would have had no res judicata effect—either as a matter of generally accepted preclusion law or as a matter of federal law in light of the exclusive jurisdiction provisions of the 1934 Act? (*Cf.* the discussion of Marrese v. American Academy of Orthopaedic Surgeons, Fourth Edition pp. 1496–98.) If so, then how can a

10. Matsushita, the acquiring company, was a defendant in both actions.

11. The majority analyzed the state cases and concluded that under state law, such a "global settlement" does operate to preclude litigation of any federal claims within the scope of the settlement. The majority also stated that any due process issue relating to the adequacy of representation in the state proceeding fell outside the scope of the question presented to the Supreme Court.

Justice Ginsburg, joined by Justice Stevens, contended that the question of the effect of the judgment under state law should have been left to the court of appeals on remand. And Justice Ginsburg, joined by Justice Souter as well as Justice Stevens, also contended that the court of appeals should be free on remand to consider issues relating to the adequacy of representation of the class in the state proceeding.

settlement of a claim over which the state court had no subject-matter jurisdiction be given broader preclusive effect?

One possible answer is that, unlike an adjudication, a settlement is a contract that acquires the force of a binding judgment when approved by a court.[12] Surely, that result would cause no difficulty if a judgment had been entered based on a consent agreement between two individuals or entities both of whom were parties to the litigation. Does the problem become more difficult when the question is the effect of a class-wide settlement on class members who did not themselves participate in the settlement negotiations or in the judicial proceeding leading to its approval? Even if it does, is the question in any way different from any other question of the binding effect of a class action judgment, *i.e.,* one that turns on such due process issues as the adequacy of notice and opportunity to opt out, and the adequacy of representation of the class in the proceedings leading up to the settlement and its final approval?

Is there any basis other than a contract theory on which the Court's decision could be persuasively defended?

For a particularly interesting analysis of the Matsushita case, see Kahan & Silberman, *Matsushita and Beyond: The Role of State Courts in Class Actions Involving Exclusively Federal Claims,* 1996 Sup.Ct.Rev. 219. The authors contend that special problems are presented by state court class action settlements encompassing exclusive federal claims, that state courts should therefore take more than the usual precautions in determining whether to approve such settlements, but that if such precautions are taken, collateral attack (even on the question of the adequacy of representation of absent class members) should be barred.

Perhaps the most controversial aspect of this thesis is the view that an absent class member's claim of inadequate representation may be waived if the class member had an adequate opportunity to raise the objection in the initial action. Such cases as Hansberry v. Lee, 311 U.S. 32 (1940), and Phillips Petroleum v. Shutts, 472 U.S. 797 (1985), at least suggest that adequacy of representation is an essential basis for establishing the court's jurisdiction to render a binding judgment against absent class members.

SECTION 2.   OTHER ASPECTS OF CONCURRENT OR SUCCESSIVE JURISDICTION

Page 1503. Add a new Paragraph (2)(d):

(d) The lower courts have had difficulty interpreting and applying the Rooker–Feldman doctrine, and to date, the Supreme Court has done virtually

---

12. The majority purported not to consider this theory. The opinion stated (p. 379 n. 6) that the issue whether the settlement could bar the federal suit "as a matter of contract law, as distinguished from § 1738 law, is outside the scope of the question on which we granted certiorari. We note, however, that if a State chooses to approach the preclusive effect of a judgment embodying the terms of a settlement agreement as a question of pure contract law, a federal court must adhere to that approach under § 1738 [citing the Kremer case, Fourth Edition pp. 1493–94]."

nothing to give them guidance. Compare, *e.g.,* Robinson v. Ariyoshi, 753 F.2d 1468 (9th Cir.1985)(viewing Rooker–Feldman as essentially an application of the doctrine of res judicata), *vacated on other grounds,* 477 U.S. 902 (1986), with, *e.g.,* Garry v. Geils, 82 F.3d 1362, 1365 (7th Cir.1996)(holding that the two doctrines "are not coextensive").

In Kamilewicz v. Bank of Boston Corp., 92 F.3d 506 (7th Cir.), *rehearing denied,* 100 F.3d 1348 (7–5)(1996), a nationwide class action had been brought in an Alabama state court and, under the terms of the settlement approved by the state court, some members of the class discovered that their share of the lawyers' fee paid to plaintiffs' attorneys in the case exceeded the amount of their recovery. When a class action was later brought in a federal court on behalf of absent class members (a) against the original defendants and (b) against the class' lawyers for malpractice in the Alabama proceeding, the Seventh Circuit ruled that under Rooker–Feldman, the federal action was barred *even if* the Alabama judgment was entered without personal jurisdiction over the absent class members, in violation of their due process rights.

Page 1513.   Add a new footnote a at the end of the first paragraph of Paragraph (2):

a.   For a concise summary of Heck and its implications, see S. Steinglass, *The Impact of Heck v. Humphrey on Section 1983 Litigation*, 554 PLI/Lit 765 (1996).

Page 1514.   Substitute the following text for Paragraph (2)(d) and footnote 2:

(d) Heck v. Humphrey clearly bars a § 1983 damages action for a confession obtained by torture if a conviction that was based on that confession has not been invalidated on direct or collateral attack. But as noted in Paragraph (2)(a) of this Note, it does not bar a damages action for a constitutional violation that would not invalidate a conviction under the harmless error doctrine. A "harmless" constitutional error is likely (though not certain) to have been less egregious than one that is presumed or found to have affected the outcome. Is there a sound basis for a rule that may, as an empirical matter, be more permissive with respect to damages actions under § 1983 for *less serious* constitutional violations? (Note, however, that individual liability in damages for marginal violations may be precluded on the basis of qualified immunity.)

Prior to 1996, the Supreme Court had imposed a number of limitations on the availability of federal habeas corpus to a prisoner in state custody. (As to persons not in custody, see Paragraph (2)(e) of this Note.) Legislation enacted in 1996, which is described and analyzed at pp. 114-37, *supra,* limited the availability of federal habeas corpus even further. In a case in which federal habeas corpus does not lie but in which the conviction was subject to reversal on direct appeal, is the prisoner who has failed to obtain such a reversal (because of a procedural forfeiture, the denial of certiorari, or any other reason) left without any remedy whatever unless the state chooses to afford one either by allowing collateral attack or by permitting a damages action? What policy is served by denying the availability of a § 1983 damages action in such a case? (Compare the availability of injunctive relief against future prosecutions in a case like Wooley v. Maynard, Fourth Edition pp. 1288, 1290–91. Heck does not affect the status of that decision, does it?)

Page 1515.   Add at the end of Paragraph (2)(e):

In Spencer v. Kemna, 118 S.Ct. 978 (1998), Spencer was released on parole before his sentence expired, but was returned to prison after his parole was revoked. He then filed a federal habeas petition challenging the parole revocation. Because Spencer's prison term ended before the district court could rule on the habeas petition, the district court dismissed the petition as moot, and the Eighth Circuit affirmed. One of Spencer's arguments on certiorari was that his habeas petition could not be considered moot given the holding in Heck v. Humphrey that an inmate can initiate a § 1983 action based on the invalidity of his conviction only after that conviction has been declared invalid. The Court rejected this argument as a "great non sequitur", pointing out the erroneous assumption implicit in Spencer's argument that § 1983 relief must always be available. The Court did not rule on whether Heck barred a § 1983 action initiated by Spencer (p. 988).

In a concurring opinion, Justice Souter, joined by three other Justices (O'Connor, Ginsburg, and Breyer) contended that Spencer's argument against mootness based on Heck failed only because Heck did not bar a § 1983 action in the case of a released inmate. In his dissenting opinion, Justice Stevens agreed with Justice Souter on this point. Thus Justice Souter's position in Heck now appears to command a majority.

Page 1515.   Add a new Paragraph (2)(f):

(f) In Edwards v. Balisok, 117 S.Ct. 1584 (1997), the Supreme Court unanimously extended the Heck rationale to § 1983 actions involving prison disciplinary proceedings. There, a state prisoner had been found guilty of violating certain prison rules, and among the sanctions imposed was the loss of 30 days of good time credit that he had previously earned. Alleging various procedural due process violations, the prisoner brought a § 1983 action for damages and declaratory and injunctive relief, preserving the right to seek restoration of the good time credit in an appropriate action. The Court held that the action was barred by the Heck doctrine (and that there was no basis for staying the proceedings pending the disposition of an appropriate action to restore the good time credit) because at least certain allegations, if proved, would necessarily imply the invalidity of the deprivation of the good time credit. (With respect to the limited request for injunctive relief, the Court remanded for further consideration, saying that the ground asserted for such relief—the failure to date-stamp certain witness statements—would not necessarily invalidate the deprivation of good time credit but that other issues, including standing, remained for resolution.)

In concurring in the Court's opinion, Justice Ginsburg (joined by Justices Souter and Breyer) stressed that only one aspect of the prisoner's allegations—the claim of deceit and bias on the part of the decisionmaker—would necessarily imply the invalidity of the deprivation of good time credit.

Note that the Court in Edwards made no explicit effort (as it had in Heck) to analogize the prisoner's action to a common law claim for malicious prosecution or indeed to any other common law action. Note also that the Edwards decision appears to enable a prison authority to avoid a § 1983 action by attaching a very small sentencing sanction to a substantial non-custodial penalty. For example, a prisoner might be penalized by the loss of a whole range of privileges, including mail, visitation rights, vocational training, etc., and also deprived of one day of earned good time credit. If the rationale of

Edwards applies in such a case, does that bear on the soundness of the Court's decision?

Page 1515.   Add a new footnote 5 at the end of Paragraph (3):

5. Several recent developments relating to federal habeas corpus are relevant to the question—discussed in this Paragraph—of the availability of a stay of execution in connection with the filing of a habeas corpus petition. These developments—which include the Supreme Court's decisions in Lonchar v. Thomas, 517 U.S. 314 (1996), and Bowersox v. Williams, 517 U.S. 345 (1996), as well as the enactment in 1996 of 28 U.S.C. § 2262 as part of a new set of provisions relating to federal habeas corpus in capital cases—are discussed at pp. 120-122, *supra*.

Page 1515.   Add a new footnote 6 at the end of Paragraph (4):

6. In Calderon v. Ashmus, 118 S.Ct. 1694 (1998), the Court dealt with the relationship between the writ of habeas corpus and the federal declaratory judgment remedy. In this case, Ashmus brought a federal class action (on behalf of certain death row prisoners in California) for a declaration that the state had not met the conditions necessary in order to invoke the special provisions of Chapter 154 of the Antiterrorism and Effective Death Penalty Act of 1996 (see pp. 120–22, *supra*). The Court held that the controversy was not justiciable under Article III (see p. 98, *supra*), and noted in passing that "[t]he disruptive effects of an action such as this are peculiarly great when the underlying claim must be addressed in a federal habeas proceeding. For we have held that any claim by a prisoner attacking the validity or duration of his confinement must be brought under the habeas sections of Title 28 [citing Preiser] * * *. But if respondent Ashmus is allowed to maintain the present action, he would obtain a declaration as to the applicable statute without ever having shown that he has exhausted state remedies" (p. 1699).

CHAPTER XIII

THE DIVERSITY JURISDICTION OF THE FEDERAL DISTRICT COURTS

SECTION 1. INTRODUCTION

Page 1522. Add to Note on Statutory Development:

The Federal Courts Improvement Act of 1996, Pub.L.No. 104–317, § 205, 110 Stat. 3847, amended § 1332 to raise the jurisdictional threshold for diversity suits to $75,000.

SECTION 2. ELEMENTS OF DIVERSITY JURISDICTION

Page 1526. Add to the second paragraph of footnote 3:

(With the Singh decision, compare Saadeh v. Farouki, 107 F.3d 52 (D.C.Cir.1997), holding that despite the language of the 1988 amendment to § 1332, the legislative history demonstrating that the purpose of the amendment was to *contract* diversity jurisdiction mandated the denial of jurisdiction in a suit between an alien on one side, and an alien and a corporation with its principal place of business in the United States on the other, regardless of the residences of the aliens.)

Page 1526. Add at the end of footnote 3:

For a generally critical discussion of the 1988 amendment—as part of a larger analysis and evaluation of the alienage jurisdiction—see Johnson, *Why Alienage Jurisdiction? Historical Foundations and Modern Justifications for Federal Jurisdiction Over Disputes Involving Noncitizens*, 21 Yale J.Int'l L. 1 (1996)(suggesting that alienage jurisdiction and diversity jurisdiction are conceptually distinct and proposing the addition of a separate alienage statute).

SECTION 3. JURISDICTIONAL AMOUNT

Page 1542. Add to Paragraph (1):

The jurisdictional threshold was recently raised to $75,000.

Page 1545. Insert a new footnote a at the end of Paragraph (1):

a. A recent study reports that the lower courts are uncertain about how to deal with a removed case in which the amount in controversy is unclear on the face of the plaintiff's complaint. The author proposes, *inter alia,* a statutory provision allowing a plaintiff in a removed case to secure remand by entering a binding stipulation that the amount in controversy will not exceed the jurisdictional minimum. See Noble–Allgire, *Removal of Diversity Actions When the Amount in Controversy Cannot be Determined from the Face of Plaintiff's Complaint: The Need for Judicial and Statutory Reform to Preserve Defendant's Equal Access to Federal Courts*, 63 Mo.L.Rev. 681 (1997).

Page 1557. Add a new Paragraph (6a):

(6a) *Punitive Damages.* Although multiple plaintiffs cannot ordinarily add together separate claims to meet the amount-in-controversy requirement, should claims for punitive damages, which serve exclusively deterrent (and not compensatory) goals be treated differently—at least in cases involving a single transaction or occurrence (or a closely related series)—on the theory that such claims constitute the pursuit of a "common or undivided interest"? See Allen v. R & H Oil & Gas Co., 63 F.3d 1326 (5th Cir.1995)(2–1 holding, in a diversity case, that in light of controlling state substantive law on the nature of punitive damages claims, such claims by separate plaintiffs may be aggregated).

SECTION 4. SUPPLEMENTAL (ANCILLARY) JURISDICTION

Page 1565. Add to Paragraph (2)(c):

Can the omission of Rule 20 plaintiffs from the exceptions in subsection (b)—an omission acknowledged by some of the drafters of the new statute—be justified on functional grounds? For a valiant effort to find such a justification, see Stromberg Metal Works, Inc. v. Press Mechanical, Inc., 77 F.3d 928 (7th Cir.1996).

Page 1565. Add to footnote 2:

In City of Chicago v. International College of Surgeons, 118 S.Ct. 523 (1997), the Supreme Court held that § 1367 does apply to removed cases.

Page 1566. Add to first paragraph of footnote 4:

The Seventh Circuit recently followed the Fifth Circuit in holding that the clear language of § 1367 trumps the legislative history and overrules Zahn. See Stromberg Metal Works, Inc. v. Press Mechanical, Inc., 77 F.3d 928 (7th Cir.1996).

Page 1566. Add a new Paragraph (3):

(3) *Proposed ALI Revision of § 1367.* For discussion of a proposed revision of the supplemental jurisdiction statute—a proposal approved by the American Law Institute at its 1998 Annual meeting—see p. 55, *supra.*

Pages 1566–67. Add to footnote 5:

In Peacock v. Thomas, 516 U.S. 349 (1996), the Supreme Court reversed the judgment of the Fourth Circuit. The Court held, 8–1, that federal courts do not possess ancillary jurisdiction over a new action in which a federal judgment creditor sues to impose liability on a person who has not previously been held liable for a monetary judgment against another defendant. The Court noted, in passing, that "Congress codified much of the common-law doctrine of ancillary jurisdiction" in § 1367 (p. 354 n. 5), but then went on to reject any common-law basis of ancillary jurisdiction on the facts presented.

Page 1574.   Add to footnote 5:

The study by Clermont & Eisenberg (*Xenophilia in American Courts*), referred to in this footnote, has been published. See 109 Harv.L.Rev. 1120, 1143 (1996).

CHAPTER XIV

ADDITIONAL PROBLEMS OF DISTRICT COURT JURISDICTION

SECTION 1. CHALLENGES TO JURISDICTION

Page 1580. Insert at the end of Paragraph (2):

The Avrech and Philbrook cases (Fourth Edition p. 1580 n. 1), as well as several other decisions, were distinguished in Steel Co. v. Citizens for a Better Environment, 118 S.Ct. 1003 (1998). In an opinion by Justice Scalia, the Court held that the plaintiffs lacked Article III standing. But first, in an extensive discussion, the Court rejected the doctrine of what it described as "hypothetical jurisdiction"—a view adopted by several courts of appeals that a case may be decided on the merits without reaching a jurisdictional issue when the merits question is more easily resolved, and is resolved in favor of the party that would have prevailed if jurisdiction did not exist. The Court observed that such an approach would offend "fundamental principles of separation of powers" (p. 1012). While admitting that some earlier decisions had "diluted the absolute purity of the rule that Article III jurisdiction is always an antecedent question" (p. 1016), the Court denied that there was any instance in which it had decided whether the plaintiff had a statutory cause of action before resolving a dispute concerning the existence of an Article III case or controversy. Thus, for example, Avrech was distinguished both on the ground that the question reserved was "technically" not one of jurisdiction and on the basis of the unique factual circumstances—that the Court had decided the issue on the merits in another case while the parties in the case at hand were preparing briefs on the question of jurisdiction.

Justice O'Connor, joined by Justice Kennedy, concurred in order to caution against reading the Court's opinion as "cataloging an exhaustive list" of when a jurisdictional issue may be reserved (p. 1020). Justice Breyer, concurring only in part and in the judgment, rejected the notion that courts were always obliged to address jurisdictional questions first. Justice Stevens, concurring in the judgment and joined in relevant part by Justice Souter, argued that the statutory question whether the plaintiff had a cause of action was as much "jurisdictional" as the Article III standing question, but that in any event in the particular context, "the Court clearly has the power to address the statutory question first" (p. 1025). He then expressed skepticism about the Court's discussion of "hypothetical jurisdiction", but argued that the question was in fact "irrelevant" to the case at hand (pp. 1026–27 & n. 15). Justice

Ginsburg, in her opinion concurring in the judgment, did not address the "hypothetical jurisdiction" question at all.

Granting that jurisdictional issues should ordinarily be addressed at the outset, do you think that there is a constitutional or other structural basis for a rule precluding consideration of any other question until subject matter jurisdiction is established? If the question of subject matter jurisdiction goes to the power of the court under Article III?

SECTION 2.   PROCESS AND VENUE IN ORIGINAL ACTIONS

Page 1591.   Add to Paragraph (4):

In 1995, Congress brought § 1391(a)(dealing with venue in diversity cases) into closer conformity with § 1391(b) by changing the "fallback" provision of § 1391(a)(3) to authorize venue in a judicial district in which *"any defendant* is subject to personal jurisdiction at the time the action is commenced, if there is no district in which the action may otherwise be brought" (emphasis added). Thus, it is now clear that this provision, like the analogous provision in subsection (b), is not limited to cases in which there are multiple defendants who are subject to personal jurisdiction in the same district.

Page 1594.   Revise the first sentence of Paragraph (12) as follows:

28 U.S.C. § 1392 provides that any civil action "of a local nature" involving property located in different districts of the same state may be brought in any of such districts. [A 1996 amendment eliminated subsection (a) of this section, so that former subsection (b) now constitutes the sole provision of the section.]

Page 1610.   Add to footnote 7:

For a judicial statement that transfer under § 1631 is available to cure a lack of personal jurisdiction, see Mellon Bank (East) PSFS, N.A. v. DiVeronica Bros., Inc., 983 F.2d 551, 558 n. 3 (3d Cir.1993). However, the legislative history of § 1631 suggests that it was intended to reach only defects in subject matter jurisdiction. See S.Rep.No. 97–180, at 30 (1982).

Page 1613.   Add to footnote 10:

For a later article by Norwood extending her criticism of the present venue options available to plaintiffs and proposing additional restrictions, see Norwood, *Shopping for a Venue: The Need for More Limits on Choice,* 50 U. Miami L.Rev. 267 (1996).

Page 1614.   Delete the last sentence of Paragraph 10(a) and substitute the following:

Rejecting the view of every court of appeals that had ruled on the matter, the Supreme Court, in Lexecon Inc. v. Milberg Weiss Bershad Hynes & Lerach, 118 S.Ct. 956 (1998), unanimously held that a district court to which proceedings have been transferred under § 1407 for conduct of pretrial matters may not (on the basis of the transfer provisions of § 1404, or otherwise) transfer all or part of the proceedings to itself for trial. In reaching its conclusion, the Court relied heavily on the provision of § 1407(a) that any action transferred under its authority (and not previously terminated) "shall" be remanded at or before the conclusion of pretrial proceedings to the district from which it came.

SECTION 3. REMOVAL JURISDICTION AND PROCEDURE

Page 1627. Add a new footnote 2a at the end of the first paragraph of Paragraph (2)(a):

2a. See also Note, 75 Tex.L.Rev. 659 (1997), arguing forcefully that § 1441(c), as revised, should be interpreted to allow removal by parties other than the original defendants, *e.g.*, a person against whom a counterclaim or third-party claim has been made.

Page 1628. Add to Paragraph (2)(a), at end of first full paragraph on the page:

(For a recent decision agreeing with Hartnett that under § 1441(c), a federal court may remand either the nonremovable cause of action or, in appropriate circumstances, the entire case, see Eastus v. Blue Bell Creameries, L.P., 97 F.3d 100 (5th Cir.1996).)

Page 1630. Add a new footnote a to Paragraph (1)(c):

a. The Court had an opportunity to interpret § 1447(c) in another context in Wisconsin Dep't of Corrections v. Schacht, 118 S.Ct. 2047 (1998), discussed in detail at p. 92, *supra*. In that decision, the Court held unanimously that this provision's requirement that a removed case be remanded if "it appears that the district court lacks subject matter jurisdiction" does not require remand of an entire case because of lack of jurisdiction over one or more claims if there are remaining claims over which the district court *does* have subject matter jurisdiction.

Page 1630. Add a new Paragraph (1)(f):

(f) The rationale of the cases discussed in this Paragraph was, somewhat surprisingly, extended by a unanimous Court to a case in which a timely objection to the lack of subject matter jurisdiction had been made. In Caterpillar Inc. v. Lewis, 117 S.Ct. 467 (1996), the plaintiff had moved to remand a removed case on the ground that complete diversity was lacking, and the district court erroneously denied the motion. Before trial, the non-diverse party was dismissed (as a result of settlement), the case was tried, and judgment on the merits was entered for the defendant. The court of appeals vacated the judgment for lack of jurisdiction, but the Supreme Court reversed.

The Court acknowledged that the plaintiff's failure to seek interlocutory review of the trial court's denial of the motion to remand did not constitute a forfeiture of the objection to jurisdiction (see Fourth Edition p. 1654). But after noting that complete diversity was present at the time of trial and judgment, the Court looked to pragmatic considerations usually ignored when the question is one of subject matter jurisdiction, concluding that "[o]nce a diversity case has been tried in federal court * * *, considerations of finality, efficiency, and economy become overwhelming" (p. 476). The Court found support for its decision in Newman–Green, Inc. v. Alfonzo–Larrain, 490 U.S. 826 (1989)(Fourth Edition p. 1532), although that case too was distinguishable because there the court of appeals—whose dismissal of the non-diverse party had been held sufficient to permit judgment against the remaining parties to stand—had been the first to notice the lack of complete diversity.

CHAPTER XV

APPELLATE REVIEW OF FEDERAL DECISIONS AND THE CERTIORARI POLICY

SECTION 2. JURISDICTION OF THE COURTS OF APPEALS

Page 1649. Add to Paragraph (3)(b):

In Johnson v. Fankell, 117 S.Ct. 1800 (1997)(also discussed at pp. 30–31, *supra*), the Court held unanimously that in a § 1983 action brought in a state court, federal law does not require the state courts to allow an interlocutory appeal from a denial of a motion to dismiss based on a claim of qualified immunity. The Court reasoned that the "right" to an interlocutory appeal in such a case was essentially procedural, that its "locus" was in the appeal provisions of § 1291 rather than in § 1983, and that respect for state interests militated strongly against federal preemption of the state's decision about the structure of its system of appeals (p. 1806).

Does the decision cast doubt on the force of the statement in Mitchell v. Forsyth, Fourth Edition p. 1648, that "qualified immunity is in fact an entitlement not to stand trial under certain circumstances"? Or is the question of appealability before final judgment essentially one of the choice of remedy for the violation of that "entitlement"?

Page 1649. Add after the first paragraph of footnote 7:

The Supreme Court reversed the judgment of the Ninth Circuit in the Behrens case. The Court held (7–2) that a defendant who has previously lost an immediate appeal from an unfavorable qualified immunity ruling on a motion to dismiss may take a second appeal—also based on qualified immunity—immediately after an unfavorable ruling on a motion for summary judgment. Behrens v. Pelletier, 516 U.S. 299 (1996). The opinion noted that a motion to dismiss turns only on the allegations of the complaint, while a motion for summary judgment turns on the question whether judgment is warranted on the basis of the uncontested evidence. Johnson v. Jones, Fourth Edition p. 1648 n. 6—which held that a denial of summary judgment on the basis of a qualified immunity defense was not immediately appealable—was distinguished on the ground that it dealt only with a case in which the issue was the sufficiency of the evidence to support a factual finding that certain conduct occurred, not with a case in which the issue was whether particular conduct constituted a violation of clearly established law.

Page 1650. Add at the end of Paragraph (3)(c):

On April 24, 1998, using the power delegated by Congress in 1990 in § 2072(c)(see Fourth Edition p. 1655), the Supreme Court transmitted to Congress a proposed new Federal Rule of Civil Procedure 23(f), which would substantially modify the effect of the decision in Coopers & Lybrand. The new rule would allow the courts of appeals discretion to permit an appeal from a district court's grant or denial of class certification. The district court proceedings would be stayed while such an appeal is pending only if the circuit court or district judge so orders.

The rule will go into effect December 1, 1998, unless Congress decides otherwise.

Page 1651. Add to footnote 11:

In Quackenbush v. Allstate Ins. Co., 517 U.S. 706 (1996)(also discussed at pp. 106–08, and 110–12, *supra*, and also below), the Court relied on Moses H. Cone in holding that when a district court remands a removed case to state court for reasons based on an abstention doctrine, the order is immediately appealable as a "final" judgment under § 1291. While recognizing that the remand order in question did not meet "the traditional definition of finality" (p. 715), the Court said that the order was indistinguishable in all relevant respects from the stay order held appealable in Cone under the collateral order doctrine.

Page 1653. Add to Paragraph (6):

For a recent decision holding the Cohen doctrine applicable to a trial court discovery order that was objected to on grounds of lawyer-client and work-product privilege, see In re Ford Motor Co., 110 F.3d 954 (3d Cir.1997).

Page 1655. Substitute the following for footnote 19:

19. In 1998, the Supreme Court proposed a rule that would give the appellate courts discretion to allow appeals from decisions granting or denying certification of a class action. The rule will go into effect in December 1998 unless Congress decides otherwise. See *supra*.

Page 1661. Add a new Paragraph (2)(e):

(e) Is the appellate court on a § 1292(b) appeal limited by the particular question of law framed by the district court? In Yamaha Motor Corp., U.S.A. v. Calhoun, 516 U.S. 199 (1996), the district court, in its order certifying a matter for interlocutory appeal, reported its conclusion that the plaintiffs' complaint was governed solely by federal maritime law and then formulated certain questions relating to the content of that law. The court of appeals decided, however, that the district court had erred in concluding that federal maritime law had displaced state remedies, and the Supreme Court unanimously affirmed. While recognizing that on an appeal under § 1292(b), the appellate court may not "reach beyond the certified order to address other orders made in the case", the Supreme Court concluded that since the statute provided for interlocutory appeal not of a "question" but of the district court's "order", appellate jurisdiction extends to "any issue fairly included within * * * [that] order" (p. 623).

Page 1667. Add a new footnote 2a at the end of the first sentence of Paragraph (2):

2a. In Quackenbush v. Allstate Ins. Co., 517 U.S. 706, 715 (1996)(also discussed at pp. 106-08, 110-12, *supra*), the Court "disavow[ed]" the ruling in Thermtron that appellate review of a remand order, when not barred by § 1447(d), is available only on mandamus because such an order is not "final" for purposes of an appeal. The Court in Quackenbush stated that the question whether any class of remand order might be immediately appealable as a final decision under the collateral order doctrine had not been addressed in Thermtron, and appealability on that basis—at least with respect to an abstention-based order of remand—was effectively established by the intervening decision in Moses H. Cone, Fourth Edition pp. 1650–51.

Page 1668. Add to Paragraph (2):

After the Thermtron decision, § 1447(c) was amended to embrace motions to remand on the basis not only of lack of subject matter jurisdiction but also of "any defect in removal procedure", and this amendment caused difficulty for the lower courts in determining whether a remand order not dealing with subject matter jurisdiction is reviewable under the Thermtron rationale. See, e.g., Pierpoint v. Barnes, 94 F.3d 813 (2d Cir.1996)(holding, 2–1, that a remand on the ground that actions under the Death on the High Seas Act are not removable was probably not based on a lack of jurisdiction but was nevertheless unreviewable because it was based on a "defect in removal procedure"). The Pierpoint majority determined—in what appeared to be a strained reading of the amendment—that the statutory phrase should be read broadly to include "all removals that are not authorized by law" (p. 820). Quackenbush, *supra*, was distinguished as a case involving a remand based not on the district court's view of what the law required but rather on an attempted exercise of the court's discretion.

Shortly after the Pierpoint decision, Congress amended § 1447(c) again, changing "any defect in removal procedure" to "any defect other than subject matter jurisdiction" (and placing a 30–day time limit on the filing of any motion to remand on such a ground). Does this further amendment lend retroactive support to the result in Pierpoint?

SECTION 3. REVIEW OF FEDERAL DECISIONS BY THE SUPREME COURT

Page 1671. Add to Paragraph (1):

One of a small number of recent statutes providing direct appeals to the Supreme Court is 28 U.S.C. § 3904, which authorizes direct appeal of a judgment, decree, or order of a court "upon the constitutionality of any provision of chapter 5 of title 3" (a chapter relating to the office of the President).

Page 1680. Add to Paragraph (1):

In Hohn v. United States, 118 S.Ct. 1969 (1998), the Court (5–4) overruled House v. Mayo, a case discussed and criticized in this Paragraph of the Fourth Edition.

Hohn had filed a motion to vacate his conviction under 28 U.S.C. § 2255, the district court denied the motion, and a three-judge panel of the court of appeals, ruling that Hohn did not satisfy the conditions for a certificate of appealability (COA) laid down by § 2253(c),[a] refused to issue the certificate.

---

a. This provision states that an appeal may not be taken from a final order in a proceeding under § 2255 unless a COA is issued by a "circuit justice or judge" and that

Petitioner then sought Supreme Court review of the denial of a COA, and the Court held that such review was available under the statutory certiorari provisions of § 1254(1). This holding mooted the question whether the Court should issue a common-law writ of certiorari under the All Writs Act.

In his opinion for the majority, Justice Kennedy reasoned that Hohn's application for a COA had all the requisite attributes of a "case": "[i]t is a proceeding seeking relief for an immediate and redressable injury" and "there is adversity" (p. 1972). Furthermore, the case was "in" the court of appeals within the meaning of § 1254 notwithstanding that § 2253 speaks of actions by individual judges. Action by a single judge is in effect "action of the court of appeals to which the judge is appointed" (p. 1973), and indeed by accepted practice and court rule, the court of appeals itself may review a judge's decision. As for the stare decisis effect of the holding of House v. Mayo that statutory certiorari did not lie under similar circumstances, that case had been inadequately briefed and argued, dealt with a procedural matter that did not affect primary conduct, and had frequently been disregarded by the Court in analogous and even identical circumstances.[b]

Writing for four dissenters, Justice Scalia argued that the matter was never "in" the court of appeals because § 2253(c) provides for action by an *individual* judge, and because "the notion that a request pertaining to a case [i.e., a request for a COA] constitutes its own case * * * is a jaw-dropper" (p. 1979). Moreover, the Court, in his view, should not have overruled House v. Mayo, especially in light of Congress' probable reliance on it in framing the provisions of § 2253(c). Finally, he contended, Hohn had failed to establish the extraordinary circumstances necessary to warrant the issuance of a common-law writ under the All Writs Act.

SECTION 4. THE CERTIORARI POLICY

Page 1692. Add to text of Paragraph (1):

For a provocative analysis of the recent decline in cases given plenary consideration by the Court, see Hellman, *The Shrunken Docket of the Rehnquist Court,* 1996 Sup.Ct.Rev. 403. After testing against the data the reasons frequently given for this decline (*e.g.,* the virtual elimination of the Court's mandatory appellate jurisdiction, the retirement of three "liberal" Justices, a decline in intercircuit conflicts, the growing conservatism of the lower courts), Hellman concludes that these factors do not fully account for the decline, and suggests that the Court has become "less concerned about rectifying isolated errors in the lower courts (except when a state-court decision threatens the supremacy of federal law), and [takes the position] that a relatively small

such a certificate may issue "only if the applicant has made a substantial showing of the denial of a constitutional right."

b. Among the cases cited by the Court was Nixon v. Fitzgerald, 457 U.S. 731 (1982),

also cited in the Fourth Edition p. 1680 as inconsistent with the holding in the House case.

number of nationally binding precedents is sufficient to provide doctrinal guidance for the resolution of recurring issues" (pp. 430–31).

After criticizing what he describes as the Court's "Olympian" "if not imperial" view (p. 433), Hellman notes that a slight increase in cases accepted for plenary review in the 1996 Term may signal an awareness that "the Court cannot entirely escape its common law roots, and that a docket devoted solely to making law may not make law in the most effective way" (p. 438).

Page 1697. Add to footnote 5:

Justice Ginsburg, joined by Justice Souter, recently followed Justice Stevens' practice of writing a memorandum "respecting the denial" of certiorari. In Texas v. Hopwood, a highly publicized case involving the affirmative action admissions program of the University of Texas Law School, Justice Ginsburg, in an opinion accompanying the denial of certiorari (518 U.S. 1033)(1996), stated that since the program at issue had long since been discontinued and would not be reinstated, there was no "final judgment on a program genuinely in controversy". (But the appeals court *had* rendered a judgment, to which the state objected, requiring the law school to exclude race altogether as a factor in its admissions policy.)

Page 1706. Add to Paragraph (2):

For a complete description of the Court's difficulties and disagreements in death penalty cases on issues dealing with the operation of the rule of four, the granting of stays, and decisions to "hold" a case pending the disposition of another case also before the Court, see Tushnet, *"The King of France with Forty Thousand Men": Felker v. Turpin and the Supreme Court's Deliberative Processes,* 1996 Sup.Ct.Rev. 163, 166–81. Tushnet's description, which benefitted from access to many internal Court memoranda, notes that the difficulties abated with the retirement of Justices Brennan and Marshall, who vigorously asserted the unconstitutionality of the death penalty in all cases. Tushnet also notes that after Justice Brennan retired, the Justices voted to change the practice of allowing a case to be held on the basis of three votes to a requirement of four votes for a case to be held (p. 181).

Page 1708. Add to Paragraph (5), at top of page:

In a case in which one or more Justices are recused, an argument can sometimes be made that the rule of four hurts the very party that recusal is designed to protect by making it more difficult for that party to obtain certiorari. See Lubet, *Disqualification of Supreme Court Justices: The Certiorari Conundrum,* 80 Minn.L.Rev. 657 (1996)(discussing, *inter alia,* the advantages and disadvantages of a rule of three in such cases).

Page 1709. Add a new footnote a after the carryover sentence and citation at the top of the page:

a. But see Leavitt v. Jane L., 518 U.S. 137 (1996), a per curiam opinion in which the Court granted certiorari and summarily reversed a decision of the court of appeals on a question of severability under state law. (The lower court had determined that a state statutory provision regulating abortions was not severable from another provision of the same statute that the court had held unconstitutional.) Justice Stevens, writing for four dissenting Justices, noted that a grant of certiorari to review a lower federal court's decision on a question of state law had become "virtually unheard-of" (p. 2073). He also contended that the Court's 1980 revision of its rule on considerations governing review on certiorari (a revision that deleted the prior reference to a conflict between a court of appeals decision and applicable state substantive law) further demonstrated the impropriety of the Court's action.

Was the Court's grant of certiorari justified on the ground that the severability of a state statutory provision, though a question of state law, is a recurring issue in constitutional adjudication, and that the appropriate scope of constitutional invalidation is a critical aspect of federal judicial review?

Page 1713.   Add to footnote 13:

For recent cases in which dissenting Justices objected to summary action vacating the decision below and remanding for further consideration, see, *e.g.*, Department of the Interior v. South Dakota, 117 S.Ct. 286, 287 (1996)(Justice Scalia, joined by Justices O'Connor, and Thomas)(majority's decision—to grant, vacate, and remand in light of the government's changed position *i.e.*, its desire to "try out" a new legal theory after losing below—"is both unprecedented and inexplicable"); Thomas v. American Home Products, Inc., 117 S.Ct. 282, 285 (1996)(Chief Justice Rehnquist, joined by Justice Breyer)(the decision to grant, vacate, and remand on the basis of a state law decision handed down after the judgment below is "just as incorrect as would be our deciding the merits of a question of state law in some other diversity case which is of no general importance beyond the interest of the parties").

See also Mazurek v. Armstrong, 117 S.Ct. 1865 (1997), a case involving a challenge to a state law restricting the performance of abortions. Justice Stevens (joined by Justices Ginsburg and Breyer), in dissenting from the summary reversal and remand of a decision by the court of appeals that the plaintiffs had met the threshold requirements for preliminary injunctive relief, stated: "Surely, the Court of Appeals' determination that a further inquiry into the facts is appropriate before making a final decision on the motion for a preliminary injunction does not provide a proper basis for summary action in this Court" (p. 1871).